Register for Free Membership to

s o l u t i o n s @ s y n g r e s s . c o m

Over the last few years, Syngress has published many best-selling and critically acclaimed books, including Tom Shinder's *Configuring ISA Server 2000*, Brian Caswell and Jay Beale's *Snort 2.0 Intrusion Detection*, and Angela Orebaugh and Gilbert Ramirez's *Ethereal Packet Sniffing*. One of the reasons for the success of these books has been our unique **solutions@syngress.com** program. Through this site, we've been able to provide readers a real time extension to the printed book.

As a registered owner of this book, you will qualify for free access to our members-only solutions@syngress.com program. Once you have registered,

- the book.
  be PDF
  om other
  erage that

- f the key
  ge, pro-
  ou need to

- rs of this
  or addi-
  ed by

Just visit u   the simple
registratio
you regist

Thank you
sure to let
job easier.

SYNGRESS®

Hacking the Code

ASP.NET Web Application Security

Mark Burnett
James C. Foster   Technical Editor

KEY	SERIAL NUMBER
001	HJIR64HGGH
002	PO9FGYG678
003	829KM82NQL
004	HRTCC45189
005	CVQ23THBHN
006	VBP95LPRQQ
007	HJ3ELK7R4F
008	2987MK224G
009	629DJTKLK8
010	IMWT6T774V

PUBLISHED BY
Syngress Publishing, Inc.
800 Hingham Street
Rockland, MA 02370

Hacking the Code: ASP.NET Web Application Security

Printed in the United States of America
1 2 3 4 5 6 7 8 9 0

ISBN: 1-932266-65-8

Technical Editor: James C. Foster   Page Layout and Art: Patricia Lupien
Cover Designer: Michael Kavish   Copy Editors: Darlene Bordwell and Joel Rosenthal
                                           Indexer: Julie Kawabata

Distributed by O'Reilly & Associates in the United States and Canada.

Acknowledgments

We would like to acknowledge the following people for their kindness and support in making this book possible.

Syngress books are now distributed in the United States by O'Reilly & Associates, Inc. The enthusiasm and work ethic at ORA is incredible and we would like to thank everyone there for their time and efforts to bring Syngress books to market: Tim O'Reilly, Laura Baldwin, Mark Brokering, Mike Leonard, Donna Selenko, Bonnie Sheehan, Cindy Davis, Grant Kikkert, Opol Matsutaro, Lynn Schwartz, Steve Hazelwood, Mark Wilson, Rick Brown, Leslie Becker, Jill Lothrop, Tim Hinton, Kyle Hart, Sara Winge, C. J. Rayhill, Peter Pardo, Leslie Crandell, Valerie Dow, Regina Aggio, Pascal Honscher, Preston Paull, Susan Thompson, Bruce Stewart, Laura Schmier, Sue Willing, Mark Jacobsen, Betsy Waliszewski, Dawn Mann, Kathryn Barrett, and Rob Bullington. A special thanks to John Chodacki for all his help with Safari.

The incredibly hard working team at Elsevier Science, including Jonathan Bunkell, Ian Seager, Duncan Enright, David Burton, Rosanna Ramacciotti, Robert Fairbrother, Miguel Sanchez, Klaus Beran, Emma Wyatt, Rosie Moss, Chris Hossack, and Krista Leppiko, for making certain that our vision remains worldwide in scope.

David Buckland, Daniel Loh, Marie Chieng, Lucy Chong, Leslie Lim, Audrey Gan, Pang Ai Hua, and Joseph Chan of STP Distributors for the enthusiasm with which they receive our books.

Kwon Sung June at Acorn Publishing for his support.

David Scott, Tricia Wilden, Marilla Burgess, Annette Scott, Geoff Ebbs, Hedley Partis, Bec Lowe, and Mark Langley of Woodslane for distributing our books throughout Australia, New Zealand, Papua New Guinea, Fiji Tonga, Solomon Islands, and the Cook Islands.

Winston Lim of Global Publishing for his help and support with distribution of Syngress books in the Philippines.

Author

Mark Burnett (Microsoft MVP) is an independent security consultant, freelance writer, and a specialist in securing Windows-based IIS Web servers. Mark is co-author of *Maximum Windows Security* and is a contributor to *Stealing the Network: How to Own the Box* (Syngress Publishing, 1-9311836-87-6) and *Dr. Tom Shinder's ISA Server and Beyond: Real World Security Solutions for Microsoft Enterprise Networks* (Syngress Publishing, ISBN: 1-931836-66-3). He is a contributor and technical editor for Syngress Publishing's *Special Ops: Host and Network Security for Microsoft, UNIX, and Oracle* (ISBN: 1-931836-69-8). Mark speaks at various security conferences and has published articles in *Windows & .NET, Information Security, Windows Web Solutions, Security Administrator,* and is a regular contributor at SecurityFocus.com. Mark also publishes articles on his own Web site, IISSecurity.info.

Contributor

Joshua Skillings is the lead Software Engineer for Trade West Systems, LLC, a consulting company specializing in creating applications for the financial industry. Joshua graduated from Brigham Young University with a BS in Computer Science. He was the BYU ACM club president. He has been using .NET since Beta 2 and has written all manner of games, pocket pc applications, web sites, and security tools using the .NET framework. He lives with his wife and two children in Sandy, Utah.

Technical Editor

James C. Foster, is the Deputy Director, Global Security Development for Computer Sciences Corporation where he is leading the task of developing and delivering managed, educational, informational, consulting, and outsourcing security services. Prior to joining CSC, Foster was the Director of Research and Development for Foundstone Inc. and was responsible for all aspects of product and corporate R&D including corporate strategy and international market expansion. Preceding Foundstone, Foster was a Senior Advisor and Research Scientist with Guardent Inc. (acquired by Verisign in 2004 for $135 Million) and an adjunct author at Information Security Magazine (acquired for an undisclosed amount by TechTarget in 2003.) He is commonly asked to comment on pertinent security issues and has been sited in USAToday, Information Security Magazine, Baseline, Computer World, Secure Computing, and the MIT Technologist. James has co-authored or contributed to *Snort 2.0 Intrusion Detection* (Syngress, ISBN: 1931836744), and *Special Ops Host and Network Security for Microsoft, Unix, and Oracle* (Syngress, ISBN: 1931836698) as well as *Hacking Exposed, Fourth Edition, Advanced Intrusion Detection, Anti-Hacker Toolkit Second Edition,* and *Anti-Spam Toolkit.* James has attended Yale, Harvard, and the University of Maryland and has an AS, BS, MBA and is currently a Fellow at the University of Pennsylvania's Wharton School of Business.

Contents

Chapter 7 Developing Secure ASP.NET Applications   309

Chapter 1

Managing Users

Solutions in this Chapter:

- **Establishing User Credentials**
- **Managing Passwords**
- **Resetting Lost or Stolen Passwords**
- **Empowering Users**

☑ **Coding Standards Fast Track**

☑ **Code Audit Fast Track**

☑ **Frequently Asked Questions**

Introduction

Users are generally a large component of Web applications and a focus point for a Web application's security. In fact, much of a Web application's security is intended to protect users and their private information.

Every Web application has different levels of risk and sensitivity. You must assess this risk in your organization to determine how much emphasis you put on user security. How you build your Web application will greatly affect how your users participate in security. Your users may or may not take security as seriously as you want them to, but as a security professional, it is your job to ensure that the data is properly protected.

Consider a magazine's online article archive that is available to authenticated subscribers. The owners want to protect their copyrighted content, so they require users to authenticate to gain access to certain articles. However, readers will not store personal information on the site, and they might not be careful with security, perhaps even sharing their login information with friends to allow them to gain access to protected articles.

Perhaps more often, users are more concerned about security than are the Web site operators. Too many companies do not put a great emphasis on security until after it is too late. In March 2001, the Federal Bureau of Investigation (FBI) National Infrastructure Protection Center (NIPC) issued an advisory that hackers were targeting e-commerce and e-banking Web sites, stealing credit card information, and attempting to extort money from the site owners. The hackers exploited well-known Windows vulnerabilities, all of which were moot if the site operators had kept up to date with security patches. The NIPC advisory stated that hackers have stolen more than a million credit card numbers from 40 companies. Obviously, these companies recklessly handled sensitive user information by not taking security seriously. Their lack of diligence put private user information at risk.

Whether the weakness lies with Web site operators or users, a Web site's security begins with the basic fundamentals of managing users.

Understanding the Threats

The primary threats covered in this chapter are:

- **Brute-force attacks** These attacks involve the process of discovering user credentials by trying every possible character combination. Brute-force attacks can be optimized by first trying dictionary words, common passwords, or predictable character combinations.

- **Account hijacking** This threat involves taking over the account of a legitimate user, sometimes denying the rightful user access to his or her account.

- **Social engineering** This is the process of using soft skills (rather than software or hardware techniques) to obtain sensitive information (i.e. passwords) that can be used to compromise a system.

- **Spamming** We're all familiar with this one—it involves the process of sending large quantities of unwanted e-mail to a user or Web site, thus jamming Internet lines and sometimes causing servers to crash.

Establishing User Credentials

User security begins with the selection of a username and password. You demonstrate to users the importance of security in the way you select or let users select usernames and passwords. In this section, you will learn about:

- Enforcing strong passwords

- Avoiding credentials that can be guessed easily

- Preventing credential harvesting

- Returning safe error messages

- Limiting idle accounts

TIP

You should always require both a username and a password. Occasionally, we run across Web applications that require only a passcode to log in to the system. But consider the scenario in which a user changes his or her password and finds that the preferred code is already in use: This user now has now obtained another user's credentials. You should always require a public credential (the username) to identify a user and a private credential (the password) to authenticate the user.

Enforcing Strong Passwords

Summary: Use technical measures and policies to ensure strong user passwords

Threats: Brute-force attacks, account hijacking

If passwords are the central mechanism of your application's security, you must ensure that users have strong passwords. Establish a policy to ensure that passwords are complex enough to prevent someone guessing them easily. You can create a robust password policy by:

- Enforcing a minimum password length of at least 8 characters

- Not limiting the maximum password length

- Requiring multiple character sets including lowercase letters, uppercase letters, numbers, and punctuation symbols

- Allowing users to use any keyboard character in their passwords, including spaces

- Not allowing dictionary words

- Not allowing the username in any part of the password

TIP
_____

Users are sometimes frustrated when they cannot come up with a password that meets complexity requirements. To avoid this problem, you might want to consider both length and number of character sets in the password as factors of complexity. Passwords that are longer but all lowercase are just as effective as shorter passwords that use multiple character sets. In general, adding two to four characters to the password's length is just as effective as adding a number or punctuation symbol. A six-character password with upper- and lowercase letters and punctuation is roughly equivalent in complexity to an eight-character password that is all lowercase.
_____

Many popular Web sites do not enforce minimum passwords lengths, or they enforce a minimum length that is much too small to be secure. Figure 1.1 shows a Web site that allows passwords of only three characters and limits the maximum length to 25 characters. The minimum length is much too short, and although 25 characters is a long password, why impose any limit at all?

Figure 1.1 Example of a Weak Password Policy

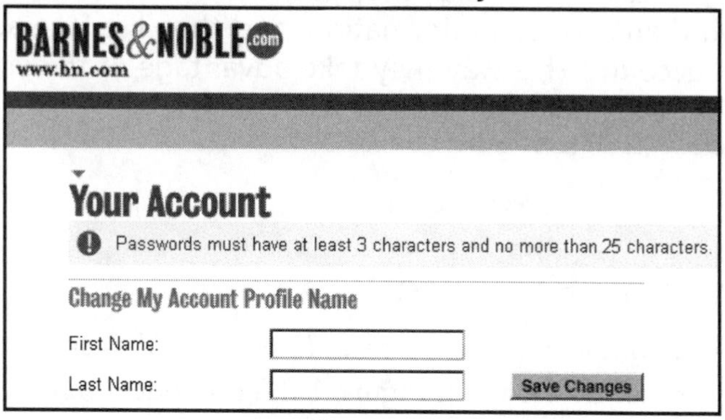

TIP

Another benefit of requiring long passwords is that it reduces the number of dictionary words available to users for use as their passwords. Passwords found in a dictionary are easily cracked and should be avoided. Setting a minimum password length of eight characters eliminates all three- to seven-letter words, of which there are about 50,000 words in an English dictionary. That is 50,000 fewer easily cracked passwords.

Many users will select predictable, easily guessable passwords if you do not enforce complexity requirements. Weak passwords are vulnerable to password-guessing brute-force attacks. If passwords are not long enough and do not contain multiple character sets, the number of guesses required to brute-force the password is greatly reduced. If an attacker is able to guess a user's password, he or she could use those user credentials to access restricted content, obtain sensitive user data, impersonate the user for a variety of purposes, delete or modify sensitive data, or even cancel the user's account.

WARNING

Attackers often try to guess passwords of eBay users by viewing the user's About Me page and gathering information about names of children, pets, friends, automobiles, or other interests. If an attacker can successfully guess a password, they authenticate to the account, change the password and contact information, and then list fake auctions under that user's account. This way they take advantage of the victim's reputation and feedback to defraud other users.

Ensuring Strong Passwords

To check password complexity, use a *RegularExpressionValidator* control or a *CustomValidator* control, as shown in Figure 1.2. This code assigns a *CustomValidator* to *txtPassword*. When validating form input, the control calls the *PasswordCheck* function. This is illustrated using C# in Figure 1.2 and VB.NET in Figure 1.3.

Figure 1.2 Validating Passwords Using a *CustomValidator* Control: C#

```
<HTML>
 <HEAD>
  <TITLE>Password Checker</TITLE>
  <SCRIPT language="C#" Runat="Server">
  public void Button_Click(object sender, EventArgs e)
  {
   if (Page.IsValid)
   {
    Response.Write("Password passes complexity requirements.");
   }
   else
   {
    Response.Write("Password does not pass complexity requirements.");
   }
  }
```

Continued

Figure 1.2 Validating Passwords Using a *CustomValidator* Control: *C#*

```
      public void PasswordCheck(object sender,
    System.Web.UI.WebControls.ServerValidateEventArgs eventArgs)
{
 if (eventArgs.Value.Length < 8)
 {
  eventArgs.IsValid=false;
 }
 else
 {
  // Require any two of the following
  // Change the -2 to adjust complexity requirements
  // The lower the value, the stricter the requirements
  if (0 -
        Convert.ToInt32(Regex.IsMatch(eventArgs.Value,"[a-z]")) -
        Convert.ToInt32(Regex.IsMatch(eventArgs.Value,"[A-Z]")) -
        Convert.ToInt32(Regex.IsMatch(eventArgs.Value,"\\d")) -
        Convert.ToInt32(Regex.IsMatch(eventArgs.Value,".{10,}")) <= -2)
  {

        eventArgs.IsValid = true;
  }
  else
  {
        eventArgs.IsValid = false;
  }
 }
}
</SCRIPT>
</HEAD>
 <BODY>
    <form id="Password" Runat="Server">
      Password:
      <br>
      <asp:TextBox
          id="txtPassword"
          TextMode="Password"
```

Continued

Figure 1.2 Validating Passwords Using a *CustomValidator* Control: C#

```
            Columns="30"
            Runat="Server" />
        <asp:CustomValidator
            runat="server"
            ControlToValidate="txtPassword"
            OnServerValidate="PasswordCheck"
            ErrorMessage="Invalid password."
            id="CustomValidator1" />
        <p>
        <asp:Button Text="Check Password"
            OnClick="Button_Click"
            Runat="server"
            id="Button1" />
        </p>
    </form>
  </BODY>
</HTML>
```

Figure 1.3 Validating Passwords Using a *CustomValidator* Control: VB.NET

```
<HTML>
 <HEAD>
  <TITLE>Password Checker</TITLE>
  <SCRIPT language="C#" Runat="Server">
  Sub Button_Click(s As Object, e As EventArgs )
    If Page.IsValid Then
      Response.Write("Password passes complexity requirements.")
    Else
      Response.Write("Password does not pass complexity requirements.")
    End If
  End Sub

  Sub PasswordCheck(oSource as Object, oArgs as ServerValidateEventArgs)
    If oArgs.Value.Length < 8 Then
      oArgs.IsValid=False
    Else
```

Continued

Figure 1.3 Validating Passwords Using a *CustomValidator* Control: VB.NET

```vb
      'Require any two of the following
      'Change the -2 to adjust complexity requirements
      'The lower the value, the stricter the requirements
      If Regex.IsMatch(oArgs.Value,"[a-z]") + _
        Regex.IsMatch(oArgs.Value,"[A-Z]")+ _
        Regex.IsMatch(oArgs.Value,"\d") + _
        Regex.IsMatch(oArgs.Value,".{108,}") <= -2 Then
        oArgs.IsValid = True
      Else
        oArgs.IsValid = False
      End If
    End If
  End Sub
  </SCRIPT>
</HEAD>
  <BODY>
    <form id="Password" Runat="Server">
      Password:
      <br>
      <asp:TextBox
          id="txtPassword"
          TextMode="Password"
          Columns="30"
          Runat="Server" />
      <asp:CustomValidator
          runat="server"
          ControlToValidate="txtPassword"
          OnServerValidate="PasswordCheck"
          ErrorMessage="Invalid password."
          id="CustomValidator1" />
      <p>
      <asp:Button Text="Check Password"
          OnClick="Button_Click"
          Runat="server"
          id="Button1" />
```

Continued

Figure 1.3 Validating Passwords Using a *CustomValidator* Control: VB.NET

```
      </p>
    </form>
  </BODY>
</HTML>
```

WARNING

The most obvious way to hack weak passwords is to simply use a brute-force attack against the Web application. Any of the tools at http://neworder.box.sk/codebox.links.php?key=wwwcrks are useful for password cracking. If the Web application uses an HTML form for password entry, you might need to use a tool such as Elza (www.securityfocus.com/tools/1127). Of course, you will need some wordlists, which you can find at www.gattinger.org/wordlists/download.html or http://neworder.box.sk/codebox.links.php?key=passdict.

Security Policies

- Ensure that passwords are at least eight characters long. They can be as long as the operating system or application will allow.

- Require at least two character sets, and let users include any keyboard character in the password.

- The password must not be a dictionary word and must not contain the username.

Avoiding Easily Guessed Credentials

Summary: Usernames or passwords that are easy to guess expose accounts to attack

Threats: Brute-force attacks, password guessing, account hijacking

One of the most prevalent security holes in the history of computers is the selection of easily guessed passwords. Despite years of password advice, users and sometimes administrators continue to use passwords such as *password, letmein,* or simply leaving passwords blank. One Web services company had its salespeople assign passwords to new customers. The salespeople made no effort to come up with secure passwords, and customers made no effort to change their default passwords. After two years in business, they had 200 customers, all with the same password: *dragon*.

Several years ago I created an account at a now-defunct online auction site. The registration process never asked for a password, but instead the site owners e-mailed me an automatically generated password, which was my username plus the number 22 at the end. Of course, they recommended that I change my password once I had logged into my account the first time, but they didn't explain how to do that. Curious about how many users actually changed their passwords, I tried logging in as other users, appending the number 22 to the end of the username as each user's password. That didn't work, but I tried 11, 33, 44, and so forth, and was quickly able to guess passwords of nearly any account on the system.

The lesson: If you automatically create passwords for your users, expect that few of them will ever change the default password, unless doing so is enforced on the first logon sequence. Therefore, if you create passwords for users, be sure to use a strong random password algorithm that does not create predictable passwords. One example of a strong password generator is the Pafwert tool, available at www.xato.com/pafwert.

TIP

Your choice of explanatory words can affect how users select passwords. For example, avoid asking for a PIN, which many people associate with an ATM machine, perhaps influencing them to select four-digit numeric passwords. Instead, ask for a passphrase or, as one site puts it, "a very long password."

A common problem with many free or shareware CGI scripts such as Web forums or shopping carts is that they have administrative functions with default passwords. If you provide such an application, simply do not provide default credentials, but do allow users to create the initial password through the installation process.

Just as troublesome as easily guessed passwords are easily guessed usernames. Usernames are not meant to be secret the way passwords are, but you should try to limit other people's ability to guess any username, because they all follow a sequential or predictable pattern. (See the section "Preventing Credential Harvesting" for more detail on credential harvesting.)

It is also important to avoid common default administrative account names such as *administrator, admin, system,* or *operator.* Password lockout policies some-times do not apply to administrative accounts and therefore are attractive targets for brute–force or other attacks.

WARNING

If you allow users to select their own usernames, be sure to block offi-cial-sounding names such as *administrator, support, root, postmaster, abuse, Webmaster, security,* and so forth. A hacker who creates an account with one of these names might be able to social-engineer other users, tricking them into revealing their passwords.

Easily guessed, predictable, or default passwords are vulnerable to password guessing and brute-force attacks, as are easily guessed usernames. Predictable or default passwords may result in the compromise of a large number of accounts. Some common CGI scripts use default passwords, and an attacker could use a search engine to locate vulnerable sites.

Design your system so that users set their passwords the first time they use the account or application. Use randomly generated passwords only if necessary and to allow users to initially log on to their accounts, after which the applica-tion forces them to change their passwords. Avoid designing a system that expects the username or password to follow any specific pattern.

Also avoid any code that automatically generates usernames or passwords, unless you take extra steps to avoid predictable patterns. Allow users to select their own usernames and passwords whenever possible.

Security Policies

- Do not allow customer service personnel to select passwords for customers.

- If randomly generating passwords, do not follow a predictable pattern or base the password on the username.

- Never use default passwords on any system.

- Do not use predictable or sequential user account names.

- Do not use obvious names for administrative accounts.

Preventing Credential Harvesting

Summary: Credential harvesting exposes users to a variety of attacks
Threats: Brute-force attacks, social engineering, spamming

Several years ago I received a phone call. The gentleman on the other end called me by name and said he was from my bank and needed to confirm my account information in their records. I was immediately suspicious, but before I had a chance to respond, he began to read off my full name and street address. But he read my address incorrectly, which happened to be the way it was listed in the phone book, tipping me off to the fact that he simply used information from the publicly available white pages to trick me into revealing other personal information. This person harvested names from the phone book to use as scam targets. Consider these risks in the following examples of credential harvesting.

Scenario: Alice's Checking Account

1. Alice signs up for an account at a banking site, logs in, and notices the following URL:

    ```
    http://bank.example.com/userid=2184&account=checking
    ```

2. Wondering how secure this bank application really is, Alice changes the *userid* parameter to this:

    ```
    http://bank.example.com/userid=2000&account=checking
    ```

3. She now finds she is looking at someone else's checking account ledger. Taking the concept one step further, she tries the following:

    ```
    http://bank.example.com/userid=1&account=checking
    ```

4. She finds this is a test account, so she tries *userid=2,* which turns out to be the account of a member of the bank's board of directors.

In this scenario, Alice finds a flaw in the application and uses the predictably sequential user ID to hop to other accounts.

Scenario: The Spam King

Bob, a well-known spammer, has written a script to crawl through the thousands of Web pages every day at all the popular auction sites. On each page his script extracts the username of every auction user it finds. After collecting several million account names, he takes the lists and combines each username with each of the most common e-mail and Internet service providers: hotmail.com, msn.com, juno.com, aol.com, earthlink.net, yahoo.com, and so forth.

Next Bob sends out an e-mail to every one of these combined addresses and tracks which accounts are valid. When all is done, he has well over a million valid e-mail accounts. Of course, the first spam e-mail he sends out is one offering a million valid e-mail addresses for the low price of $99.

Scenario: Chuck the Hacker

Chuck is a hacker. He steals identities and financial information from unsuspecting e-commerce customers. He knows that one large retailer's Web site allows customers to save their credit card information to make future purchases more convenient. Chuck wants to break into customer accounts and grab this stored credit card information.

For his first attempt, he makes a small list of common usernames and passwords and tries a scripted brute-force attack against the Web site. It doesn't take long for him to realize that this site locks out accounts once a user enters five bad passwords in a row. But there's another way to brute-force passwords: Instead of trying a lot of passwords against one account, he can try one or two common passwords against many different user accounts. Statistically, he knows that if he tries a few common passwords against enough accounts, he will get a match.

Now the only problem is how to collect account names. To do this, he writes a script to sign up for accounts using random but common usernames. The script fills in and submits the signup form and watches for the message, "Sorry, that username is already in use." If he gets that message, the script saved the username. If not, it cancelled the session and started again with the next name.

After several hours, the script gathers several thousand usernames from this busy Web site. He takes that list and feeds it into his brute-force script, which eventually finds three accounts with the password: *asdf*. Three accounts might not be a huge score, but he now has the scripts and runs them every day, changing them slightly each time to turn up more results.

Limiting Credential Exposure

By harvesting usernames, an attacker might be able to collect e-mail addresses for spamming, attempt to trick other users into revealing passwords using social-engineering techniques, attempt brute-force attacks across multiple accounts, or exploit other weaknesses in an application. Stopping credential harvesting is really just a matter of not showing usernames and not using predictable credentials. However, some Web sites are completely based on user credentials, so you must use a variety of measures to limit credential exposure.

Design the system so that the username is not the database primary key. This solution allows users to change their usernames without losing important account information or history. One technique to protect usernames is to allow users to create one or more aliases that are not used to log in to the account. Avoid usernames that are sequential or that follow predictable patterns. If connecting users to external accounts, such as checking accounts, do not use the checking account numbers as user IDs, because these account numbers are often sequential and an attacker could easily discover this information.

WARNING

Allowing users to change their usernames or allowing aliases can, in some instances, facilitate abuse. You should carefully consider the implications of allowing username changes or aliases to determine if doing so is appropriate for your application. One forum Web site, for example, allows you to change your username, but only once a month, to prevent account abuse. However, nothing prevents abusers from simply creating new accounts.

The best way to prevent username harvesting is to simply never show usernames on your site. However, if this is not practical for your Web application, you can try fooling some automated harvester scripts by varying the encoding used to write the usernames.

Another important guideline is to avoid passing the username as a query string parameter to prevent it from showing up in browser histories, proxy logs, and HTTP referer [sic] headers of other sites. Consider the following URLs that may appear in another Web site's Web logs.

Here's a poor example:

`www.example.com/inbox.aspx?userid=mburnett&folder=inbox`

Here's a better example:

`www.example.com/inbox.aspx?session=3FAC-FF2E-8B1C-722A-391D`

In this example, the latter is more secure because the URL contains no identifying information.

Security Policies

- Never use an e-mail address as the username, and avoid otherwise revealing user e-mail addresses.

- Avoid public user directories and white pages.

- Allow users to change their usernames when necessary.

- Allow users to assign one or more public aliases to their accounts.

- Allow for the detection of brute-force or harvesting attacks.

Limiting Idle Accounts

Summary: **Idle accounts make easy targets for hackers**
Threats: **Account hijacking**

If you are a hacker and want to hijack someone's Web site account, what type of account would you go after? You certainly do not want an account that someone uses every day, but you also don't want an account that someone never uses.

Once an attacker gains control of an account, he or she may change the password and completely lock out the legitimate user. Hackers have many motivations for taking over someone else's account. For example, they could use a hijacked auction account to list fake auctions or use a PayPal account to make fraudulent purchases.

Idle accounts are a security risk because:

- The account owner might not be aware of recent activity or changes in account information.

- Passwords could be old.

- Users might not even be aware that they have an online account.

A couple years ago, hackers penetrated a banking Web site and gained access to the bank's entire database. The hackers used their knowledge of electronic funds transfers to move funds to other online financial accounts. Some account holders noticed the problem and reported the transfers to the bank. The bank immediately reviewed all recent electronic transfers and contacted customers to find out if the transactions were legitimate or not. Most customers were surprised by the breach, but many of them were also surprised to find out that they even had online accounts that the bank had automatically created for them.

Users are often the best ones to spot fraud, but not with idle accounts. One travel agent found that she could transfer accrued air miles from one customer to another. She found some seldom-used accounts that had high air-mile balances and transferred small amounts from each to the account of a relative, thinking the customers would not notice the change. However, she was not aware that the airline sent e-mails to the customers confirming any air-mile transfers. Several customers complained, and the company quickly tracked down the agent responsible for the transfers. This company side-stepped the idle account problem by following up with an e-mail to users.

Online accounts are potentially dangerous, especially those that deal with financial transactions. An attacker can potentially steal and abuse the identity of a legitimate account. If users are not aware of the breach, an attacker can sometimes access the account for an extended amount of time without detection.

Design the system to track account activity and aging, and provide a method for placing an idle account on hold without completely closing the account, as shown in Figure 1.4. Clearly define how and when users receive notification of account changes or transactions, and provide a clear method for users to report suspicious or fraudulent transactions.

Centralize the code for account changes and transactions so that you have an integrated location for recording, analyzing, and notifying users of these actions. Develop a process to suspend and eventually purge idle accounts.

Figure 1.4 Expiring Idle Accounts

TIP

Many Web applications have some indications of a user's Web activity. For example, some Web forums will tell you the date of a user's last post and auction, or classified ad sites often show a history of what a user has bought or sold.

Security Policies

- Put an account on hold after it sits idle for an extended period of time, requiring a simple reactivation procedure similar to a password retrieval process.

- Avoid revealing any information to others that indicates that an account is idle.

- Notify users via e-mail, letter, or other means after changing any account information or after performing significant transactions in case the action was not initiated by the users.

- Use antifraud techniques such as monitoring account activity for anomalies.

- Do not automatically activate online account access for all your customers with offline accounts.

Managing Passwords

Once a user has established a username and password, there are certain steps you must take to protect that password. In this section, you will learn about:

- Storing passwords

- Password aging and histories

- Changing passwords

Storing Passwords

Summary: Passwords stored in databases are a risk to your application as well as others
Threats: Account hijacking, potential liability

In February 2001, RealNames, a company that substituted complex Web addresses with simple keywords, announced that hackers had accessed its customer database, revealing credit card information and passwords of all its customers. A month later, Web hosting company ADDR.com announced that a hacker stole personal information and passwords of some 46,000 customers. Month after month since then, we have heard similar stories of hacked servers and stolen passwords.

The risk of these types of attacks can be greatly reduced with one simple strategy: Don't store passwords in your database.

There are three ways to store passwords for later use in authenticating users:

- You can store the password itself in plaintext.

- You can encrypt the password and store the ciphertext.

- You can create a one-way hash of the password and store that hash in the database.

Obviously, the first solution is a terrible one, and the second isn't much better: Although the password is encrypted, that encryption is based on a secret key. If the Web application must perform this encryption and decryption, the application must somehow store this secret key. If a hacker gains control of the application and the application can decrypt passwords, the hacker too can decrypt any passwords.

WARNING

Hashes are called *one-way functions* because you can derive a hash from a password but you cannot reverse the algorithm to produce the original password from the hash. Nevertheless, hashes are not completely impervious to attack and should still be carefully protected. If an attacker can obtain a hash, he or she can go through a large list of words, run each through the same hashing algorithm, and compare the two hashes until a match is found. This method of attack became popular in password crackers such as John the Ripper and l0pht crack.

One important reason for not storing actual passwords is that by if you do so, no one at your organization ever has access to user passwords. This is important because it is not uncommon for users to reuse passwords for many different systems. If some people in your organization have access to passwords in your application, it could mean that those people also have access to a user's accounts on other Web systems.

If passwords are stored in a database, an attacker can potentially gain access to all user accounts, even if the passwords are encrypted. This puts all users at risk, especially if they use the same passwords on other systems, as many users do. Some hackers collect large lists of username and password combinations to use in brute-force attacks of other systems.

Identify the hashing algorithm that would work best for your organization. Because hashes are still vulnerable to brute-force attacks, the best solution usually is not the algorithm with the best performance. In this case, a slower algorithm means the brute-force process will take longer. Design the system so that you never have to actually retrieve a password. Passwords should only be set or reset.

In rare instances, however, the application must store a password for later use. For example, I once audited an application that had to authenticate to a third-party data provider. Because the data provider required authentication, the application had to store the password using reversible encryption. Because the application required a retrievable password, the company had to compensate by taking extra measures to protect the encryption key, which it did by placing the encryption and decryption code in a COM component.

One weakness with using reversible encryption in a Web application is that in the real world, the encryption key rarely changes. The problem is that if you ever want to change the encryption key, you must decrypt all ciphertext in the database and then re-encrypt it using the new key—something that few Web or database applications are designed to handle. If you plan to use reversible encryption, plan also to have a mechanism to regularly change the encryption key and update all encrypted data.

WARNING

If you plan on using reversible encryption, always use a strong encryption algorithm such as DES, Blowfish, or some other algorithm that has been proven secure. Never use XOR, ROT-13, or a homegrown encryption code; these usually provide little protection and are easier to break than people realize. Weak encryption algorithms are roughly equivalent to the tiny locks that come with most luggage—hardly a deterrent to even the most casual thieves.

Use one-way hash functions and store the hash in the database. When a user logs in, run the hash function on the password the user enters, and compare that hash to the one in the database. One advantage of hash functions is that they consist of only numbers and letters, allowing users to enter any keyboard character as their password without you having to take extra measures to handle special characters.

TIP

If you have an existing system that stores plaintext passwords, the process of switchover to hashes is relatively painless. To do this, create a new hash field next to your existing password field. Next, hash all existing passwords and save them in the new hash field. Next, add the hash function to your authentication code and to your password-setting code. Finally, instead of storing and checking against the password field, update your code to first hash the password, then store and check using the hash field.

See Chapter 4, "Encrypting Private Data," for more information on using the encryption features provided by the .NET Framework.

Security Policies

■ Never store a password in plaintext or using reversible encryption.

■ Use strong hashing algorithms such as MD5, SHA-1, SHA256, or SHA512.

Password Aging and Histories

Summary: **Old or reused passwords provide more opportunity for attackers**

Threats: **Brute-force attacks, account hijacking**

As an application ages, so do user passwords, because users normally don't make the effort to regularly change their passwords. It is not uncommon to see users with passwords as old as the system itself, sometimes going several years without changing a password. This is especially true with Internet service provider (ISP) e-mail accounts that provide no easy method for changing passwords. You should always require users to change their passwords at regular intervals, a practice that few Web sites follow.

But setting the right interval isn't always easy. If the maximum password age is six months, the risk of compromised passwords increases. However, if you go the other extreme and require password changes every 30 days, you will find users writing down their passwords more and developing patterns such as sequential passwords or passwords based on dates. Requiring users to change their passwords too frequently can actually make the system less secure. Furthermore, if users log in to your Web application only once every few months and find they have to change their passwords each time, they are likely to get annoyed.

To determine the optimal maximum password age, ask yourself the following questions:

■ How sensitive is the protected data?

■ How often do users log in to the application?

■ How long would it take to guess a password based on your password complexity requirements?

If your Web application is an online banking system, you might want to consider maximum password ages of three to six months. On the other hand, if you provide an online flower shop, you may get away with letting users keep their same passwords for a year or more.

TIP

If you want to encourage users to change their passwords occasionally but do not want to force maximum password aging, consider warning users at regular intervals via e-mail that their password is getting old, along with a quick link to change their password. Another idea is to let users select their own password-aging requirements.

Related to password aging are password histories, which are historical lists of previous passwords a user has selected. Password histories prevent users from alternating between the same two or three passwords every time one password expires. A system should reject any password that matches those in the history list. Many systems will remember the last three to five passwords, but some may keep a history of 20 or more passwords. Keeping a password history doesn't require a significant amount of resources, so it usually makes sense to keep as many as possible.

WARNING

If you keep password histories, store only the hashes of the passwords, not the passwords themselves, as explained earlier in the section "Storing Passwords."

Despite password aging and history lists, some users are still determined to reuse the same passwords. They circumvent these security measures by resetting their password enough times to fill up the history list and then setting their password back to the original that just expired. The countermeasures are to keep long history lists and to set minimum password-aging requirements. Minimum password ages are the least amount of time that must pass before users can again change their passwords.

TIP

Minimum password aging can sometimes be inconvenient, but it doesn't take much to be effective: A day or even an hour could be enough to prevent users from resetting their passwords several times in an effort to flush the history list. If you do enforce minimum password ages, be sure to allow administrators to override this policy.

Passwords are nothing more than an obscure secret word or phrase. Given enough time, an attacker could eventually guess a password through brute-force methods or through exposure from operating system or application vulnerabilities. As passwords age, the risk of an attacker compromising that password increases. Furthermore, if an intruder has obtained a password without alerting the user, the intruder will have access for as long as the password is valid. Without password aging, the intruder will have access until the user manually changes his or her password.

Password aging and histories require extra database fields to track when a password was set and to keep a list of recent passwords. There is also the extra processing requirement of hashing the password and comparing it to each entry in the history list. You might want to allow different aging policies for individual users or groups, or choose a systemwide policy. One advantage of systemwide policies is that you can immediately expire all passwords in case there is a major security incident such as a server intrusion.

You should check a password's expiration date immediately after a user successfully authenticates to the system but before allowing access to the system. If you centralize your authentication to a single include library, you can more easily perform the password-aging check. If the password has not yet expired but is getting close, you might want to warn the user several days ahead of time. Figure 1.5 is an example of a password expiration screen.

You should check password histories and minimum password ages when validating a user's new password.

Figure 1.5 Example of an Expired Password Screen

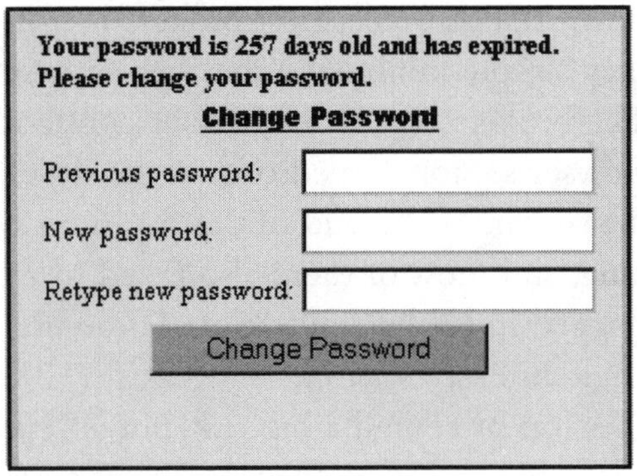

Security Policies

- Set a maximum password age that is appropriate for your application and for users.

- Keep a list of recent passwords to prevent password reuse.

- If possible, enforce a small minimum time interval between password resets.

Changing Passwords

Summary: **Make it easy and encourage users to regularly change their passwords**

Threats: **Brute-force attacks, account hijacking**

Many security experts warn against using "security through obscurity"(the practice of securing something by hiding it) as a defense mechanism. But passwords or authentication credentials—the center of many security systems—are nothing more than security through obscurity. A password's strength completely depends on our expectation that no one else will be able to guess or otherwise discover the password.

Given enough time, attackers *can* discover passwords, either by exploiting some system vulnerability or through the process of a brute-force guessing attack. Our only defense is to regularly change passwords, hopefully before anyone has a chance to discover the current one. Therefore, an important feature to include in any Web application is the ability to change passwords.

I once knew of a company with a financial trading application that required users to log in to perform trades. Since most brokers performed many trades throughout the day, they simply minimized the Web browser on their screens and remained logged in. The brokers complained about constantly having to authenticate because their browser sessions timed out, so the developers eliminated all session timeouts on the server. At the end of the day, most of the brokers left their computers running, and most of them also failed to exit the browser application, leaving them logged in to the application. Some users would sometimes go all week using a single browser session.

Keeping an open session presented a big risk, but an even greater risk was how the application managed password changes. To set a new password, users browsed to the preferences page, clicked on a link to change the password, and then entered the new password. But consider this scenario: Another broker waits until a target goes to lunch and then sets a new password using the target's open session, having no knowledge of the previous password. The target session remains logged in for the next week, but the other broker has full access to the account with the new password. It is not until the target is forced to log in again that he or she discovers that the password has changed.

If users do not regularly change their passwords, they face an increasing probability that others will be able to discover their passwords and therefore gain access to their accounts. The harder it is for users to change passwords, the less likely users are to change their passwords. This situation is worsened if users are not reminded or forced to regularly change passwords. Without techniques such as entering previous passwords, expiring sessions, and notifying users of changes, an attacker might be able to use an account for an extended period of time without detection.

Design the system so that changing passwords is a simple and intuitive process. Avoid practices that discourage changing passwords, such as overly oppressive password complexity requirements. Always require authentication before and after changing passwords.

After a user logs in, provide quick links to the most common account management tasks, including changing passwords. If your security policy does not require users to change old passwords, consider a simple warning including a link, like the one shown in Figure 1.6.

Figure 1.6 Example Warning for Old Passwords

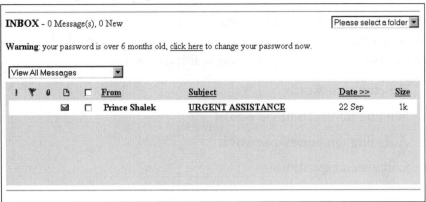

A password-change page should consist of three text boxes: one to enter the previous password, one to enter the new password, and a third to verify the new password. Figure 1.3 demonstrates a sample password reset screen.

To prevent anonymous brute-force attacks; make the password change page available only to active sessions of authenticated users.

Security Policies

- Always allow users to change passwords themselves.

- Make it intuitive and easy for users to change passwords.

- Remind or force users to regularly change their passwords.

- Require knowledge of the previous password to change a new password.

- Require the user to enter the new password twice to ensure accuracy.

- Confirm account changes via e-mail or some other means of communication.

- Expire all active sessions and require authentication after changing a password.

Resetting Lost or Forgotten Passwords

Sooner or later, some of your users will lose or forget their passwords. Because of the potential security risk, you must carefully consider how to deal with lost or forgotten passwords. In this section, you will learn about:

- Resetting passwords
- Sending information via e-mail
- Assigning temporary passwords
- Using secret questions

Resetting Passwords

Summary: **Follow a well-planned procedure for resetting lost or for-gotten passwords**

Threats: **Brute-force attacks, account hijacking**

To avoid the customer support overhead of dealing with lost passwords, many Web sites allow users to conveniently retrieve or reset their own passwords. However, password reset features, if not implemented correctly, can introduce security weaknesses to your Web application.

You should always treat a lost password as a security event, taking extra precautions to protect the user's account from intruders. Too many Web sites take a casual approach to lost passwords: Users enter a username or e-mail address (as shown in Figures 1.7 and 1.8), and in a few minutes they receive an e-mail containing the original password. Indeed, users who infrequently visit a site sometimes use the convenient password retrieval process instead of other methods to record or remember their passwords.

Figure 1.7 Password Retrieval Using E-Mail Only

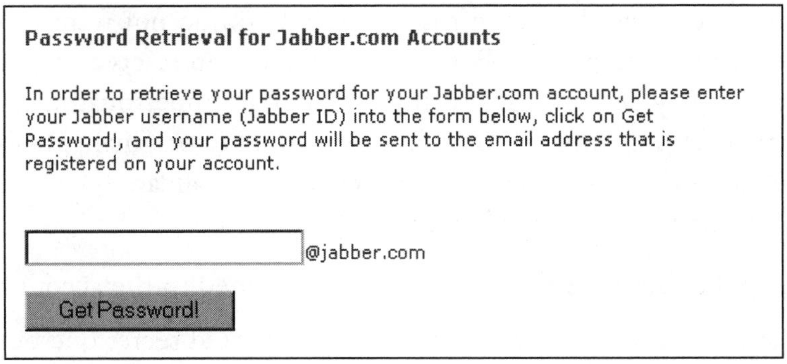

Figure 1.8 Another Password Retrieval Method Using E-Mail Only

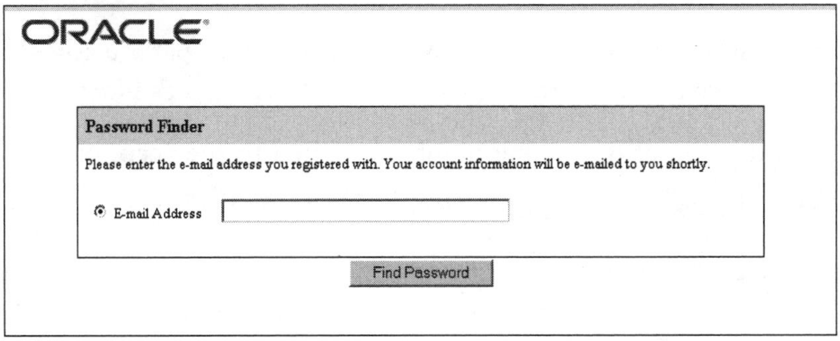

But retrieving passwords means that your Web application is either storing passwords in plaintext or using reversible encryption, both poor practices, as described earlier in the section "Storing Passwords." If a lost password event occurs, you should always abandon the old password and require the user to set a new password. You should never allow users to retrieve a lost password, only to set a new password. Password hints that remind a user of the actual password are not much better, especially if the hint is the password itself.

Tip

Another benefit of not sending the old password and forcing a reset is to prevent an attacker from retrieving a user's password without his or her knowledge. Although a skilled attacker may be able to obtain enough information and access to reset a user's password, this is hardly a stealthy attack, and the user certainly will be alerted the next time he or she tries to log in to the account and the old password no longer works.

The difficulty in resetting passwords is that you want to provide users the convenience of resetting their own passwords, but you do not want to weaken password security in the process. Before your application resets a password, you should be reasonably certain that it is the user, not an impersonator, on the other end of the transaction. Since the user no longer has the original password to prove his or her identity, you must take other steps to validate the user's identity. Here are some ways to accomplish this:

- Send the user an e-mail to the address assigned to the account.

- Ask the user to answer one or more preselected secret questions.

- Ask the user to provide one or more bits of information associated with the account (such as ZIP code or birth date).

For highly secure environments or when dealing with particularly sensitive information, you may even take further steps to verify a user's identity:

- Call the user at the phone number assigned to the account.

- Send the user a fax to a preselected fax number.

- Send the user a letter through the postal service.

- Ask the user to appear in person and present identification at your main or branch office.

The purpose of asking the user to answer a secret question or provide other information is to verify that they know something about the account, as shown in Figure 1.9. This helps prevent random anonymous attacks against users, but it does not protect a user from attack from an individual who has knowledge of the user. Sending the user an e-mail will prove that the person requesting the password reset has access to the user's e-mail account. It is possible for an attacker to have obtained access to the user's e-mail account, but if the attacker can answer a user's secret question and has access to the user's e-mail, the user likely has a much bigger problem that you really cannot do much about anyway. Nevertheless, you still should never reveal the old password in the e-mail, only provide a link to reset the password.

Figure 1.9 Example Password Retrieval Using Personal Information

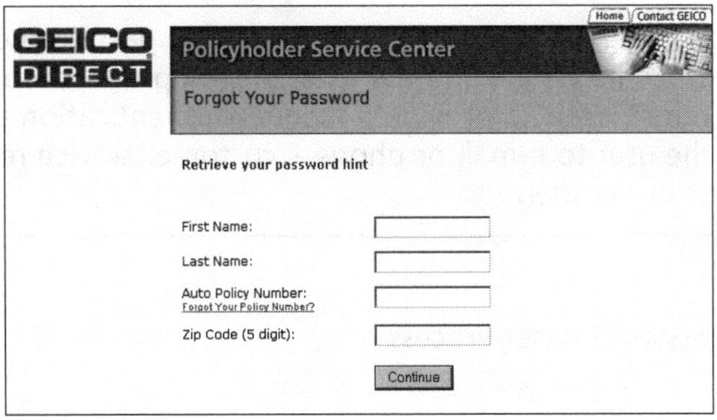

Design the system with a clear flow of events through the password reset process. Use secure session tokens with short expiration periods throughout the process. Never put usernames, e-mail addresses, or other identifying information on any URL.

The process for resetting a password should be as follows:

1. Ask the user to provide an account name and answer one or more questions that demonstrate knowledge of the account, as shown in Figure 1.10. Log the IP address of the client that initiated the request, and assign a secure token for the password reset session. Set a short expiration period for the session—24 hours or less.

2. Send an e-mail to the address assigned to the account explaining that a password reset has been requested; include the client IP address that initiated the request. Provide a secure link to your Web site using a temporary token linked to the reset process. Always provide an e-mail address or URL for the user to report a security incident if they were not the ones who initiated the password reset.

3. After the user clicks the link, ask the user to provide a new password and optionally a new security question and answer. Always check the session token to be sure it has not expired.

TIP

Sometimes a user loses both the username and password or no longer have access to the e-mail address used to set up the account. In this case, you might need to provide a manual authentication process, requiring the user to e-mail or phone a customer service representative to verify his or her identity.

Figure 1.10 Password Reset Process

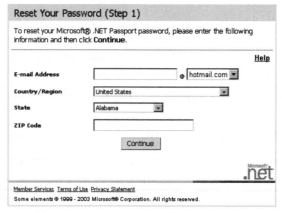

Figure 1.11 shows an example of a password reset process. This particular screen shows that the site correctly requires setting a new password rather than retrieving the old one. Although the site asks for an e-mail address and some personal information, a credit card number is by no means secure enough to verify a user's identity. Any merchant that has taken an online order from a user will likely have all the information necessary to complete this form. At first it might seem like this process is more secure because it sends the user an e-mail, but remember that *this is* the user's e-mail account, so it would be impossible to send the user an e-mail if her or she have forgotten the password. In this case, authentication will have to be sufficient to allow full access to the account. In addition to asking for the credit card information, this process should ask for additional personal information and ask the user to answer a secret question.

Figure 1.11 Example Password Reset Process

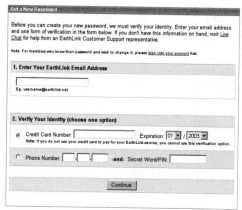

A common flaw in the password reset process is for a Web application to use hidden form fields or query strings to pass state information from one page to the next. For example, to ask users their secret questions, you must first find out who they are and then look up the secret questions. Therefore, most password reset processes begin with a user entering an e-mail address in a Web form. On the next page, the Web application presents a secret question and asks for an answer. Finally, the secret question is verified and action is taken to retrieve or reset the password. But sometimes a Web site will pass the user's e-mail address or username as a hidden form field that an attacker can modify. Sometimes this will result in the password being sent to the e-mail address of your choosing. Another common flaw is that you can begin the process with one account and modify a parameter halfway through to jump to another account and finish the process.

Review the password reset process, ensuring that the application sufficiently validates the user's identity before sending e-mail. Never send e-mail to any address other than the one assigned to the account. Walk through the reset process, watching every step to ensure that it is appropriately and securely linked to the previous step. Make sure that it is not possible to switch to the context of another account halfway through the reset process.

Security Policies

- Treat password resets as a security event, logging the client IP address and taking other practical security measures.

- Never retrieve a user's password; only allow a user to set a new password.

- Never use password hints to remind the user of the actual password.

- Ask the user to show some knowledge of the account through secret questions or by providing information associated with the account; never allow an anonymous password reset.

- Send the user an e-mail to confirm a password reset, providing a secure link to complete the process.

- If practical, after a password reset, clear any sensitive information stored with the account, such as credit card numbers.

- Expire all existing sessions after a password reset.

Sending Information Via E-Mail

Summary: **E-mail is insecure and you should not use it to convey sensitive information**

Threats: **Sensitive information leakage, account hijacking, user privacy**

Consider this e-mail I recently received after subscribing to a Web-based information service:

```
To: mburnett@xato.net

From: sales@example.net

CC: orders@example.net

Subject: Order confirmation


Dear M.,

Thank you for your subscription, below is the information for your account.
Please keep this e-mail for future reference:

Username: MBurnett

Password: 300Watt-Orange


Your credit card #1234-5679-1111-1111 will be charged $19.95 at the end of
your 30-day trial.
```

The problem with this e-mail is:

- It transmitted my username and password in plaintext across the Internet.

- It transmitted my credit card information in plaintext across the Internet.

- Whoever has access to the orders@example.net mailbox will receive a copy of this sensitive information.

- It instructs me to save the e-mail for future reference, potentially exposing sensitive information if someone gains access to my e-mail client.

- It tells me that they probably store my password and possibly my credit card information either in plaintext or using reversible encryption, not using a secure one-way hash.

E-mail is by nature an insecure medium: There is no guaranteed authentication of either the sender or the recipient, e-mail traffic is not encrypted as it traverses various networks in its path, many e-mail servers and clients do not encrypt stored messages, and there is no way to prevent others from receiving bounced, quarantined, or rejected copies of your e-mails. E-mail is also subject to attacks such as cross-site scripting, client vulnerability exploitation, scripting attacks, malicious attachments, and social-engineering attacks.

Another potential risk of e-mail is that a user is not guaranteed to always have the same e-mail address or domain. Some companies automatically forward e-mails addressed to departed employees to the new employee in that position. There is also the issue of expired domains that are registered by new owners, giving the new domain owner access to all e-mail sent to the entire domain (see www.auctionbytes.com/cab/abn/y03/m05/i15/s01).

Design the system so that it only relies on e-mail as a secondary form of identification and notification. If possible, take advantage of S/MIME or PGP signing and encryption to strengthen e-mail communications. Allow users to provide you with a public key to be used for all e-mail communication.

If you want a user to have some confirmation of an order or account registration, provide a secure, temporary link via which the user can view this information on your Web site. Rather than sending users their usernames and passwords, instruct them during the registration process to remember this information. If you must provide confirmation of a credit card order, only provide the last few digits of the card number, and do not provide any other identifying information.

When composing e-mails, always consider the effect on the user if this information is intercepted or viewed by others.

> **TIP**
>
> One feature I have yet to see any Web site implement is taking advantage of public-key encryption technologies such as PGP to sign or encrypt e-mails. It would be simple to allow a user to paste in or even permanently store a public key to use for all e-mail communications. You should also provide a public key for your organization and sign all outgoing e-mails. For a list of free PGP tools and development libraries, visit www.pgpi.org.

Security Policies

- Never send sensitive information such as user credentials or credit card information via e-mail.

- Never rely on e-mail alone to verify a user's identity.

- Do not use e-mail to save the results of a Web form submission that contains sensitive information.

- If possible, digitally sign or encrypt e-mail communications.

Assigning Temporary Passwords

Summary: **Users will not change temporary passwords unless forced to do so**

Threats: **Account hijacking, password guessing**

I once signed up for an account at an online book Web site, but I did not use the site until a couple months later. By that time I had forgotten my password, and despite several attempts to guess it, I was forced to click the Forgot Password link.

To my surprise I was not taken to a Web form, but instead my e-mail client popped up with a blank e-mail addressed to the site's customer service representatives. I was surprised that such a large site would rely on such a manual process, but I composed an e-mail and sent it off. A few hours later, I received an e-mail from a support representative telling me that my password had been reset, but she did not give me any instructions on how to log in to my account. I e-mailed her back and asked her how I set a new password. She promptly responded and told me my new password, which sounded suspiciously like a password she used often. I logged in to my account and could not find any place to change my password. After all, the password reset process was manual; could I possibly expect them to provide a password change feature? Because I was under a tight deadline, I gave up and simply used the assigned password. It wasn't until a month later that I actually figured out how to change my password to something new. Chances are there are hundreds of customers who never got around to changing their passwords for that site.

Temporary passwords are normally not a good solution, and you can usually find a better method to accomplish your goal. Temporary passwords created by humans tend to be repetitive and easily guessed. Automatically generated passwords also tend to follow patterns or are difficult to remember. Users are not likely to change temporary passwords unless forced to do so.

Building the Code

Design the system so that it does not depend on temporary passwords. If there is no alternative, provide a means for generating strong passwords, and limit each password so that the user must immediately change it to something else. A system with password-aging capabilities allows more flexibility with temporary passwords.

Never expect a randomly generated or temporary password to be temporary unless you force it to be temporary. One technique in generating passwords for users is to create the password but set the expiration date so that it is already expired, forcing the user to change the password the first time it is used. Be sure to add this password to the password history list.

Hacking the Code

If you find that an application uses temporary passwords, try creating several accounts to see if there is an obvious pattern. Also try resetting your password to see if it creates temporary passwords there.

As an auditor, determine if users are likely to immediately change those passwords. It is usually not enough to recommend that they change their passwords; the application should enforce this policy.

Security Policies

- Avoid having customer service representatives set temporary passwords.

- If you must use temporary passwords, use a strong random password generator.

- If you must use temporary passwords, provide a short expiration date or set the password as already expired.

Using Secret Questions

Summary: **Secret questions are not a replacement for passwords**
Threats: **Sensitive information leakage, account hijacking, user privacy**

To help verify a user's identity in the case of a lost password, many Web applications use secret questions. By answering a preselected question, a user can demonstrate some personal knowledge of the account owner. A classic example is asking to provide a mother's maiden name.

Answering secret questions requires some knowledge of the user account, but secret questions break all the rules for strong passwords and have some significant weaknesses:

- An attacker can sometimes discover the information with little research.

- The answer to the question is usually a fact that will never change.

- Users reuse the same secret questions and answers across multiple Web sites.

- Someone close to the individual could know the answers to many of the questions.

- People rarely change their secret questions.

- The answers are often case-insensitive and usually contain a limited character set.

- Some questions have a limited number of answers.

- With some questions, many people will have the same common answers.

Secret questions usually ask for an obscure fact that hopefully only the account owner would know and supposedly would never forget. Many Web sites assume that the user providing the answer to the question is sufficient to identify the user. But many secret questions ask for facts that anyone could discover with little research. To make things worse, if someone discovers this information, you can't just change a fact from the past.

I have seen countless Web sites that provide great tips on avoiding easily guessed passwords but then turn around and ask for a pet dog's name or what city you were born in to answer a secret question.

Even if an attacker knows nothing about the target user, the nature of secret questions limits the possible range of answers. For example, consider the questions and ranges of answers shown in Table 1.1. As the table shows, many secret questions have so few possible answers that a brute-force attack against these secret questions is completely feasible. To make matters worse, some Web sites fail to detect or prevent brute-force attacks against secret questions. For years security experts have told people to avoid using pet names, family names, or dates in passwords, but secret questions go directly against that advice.

Table 1.1 Secret Questions and Ranges of Answers

Question	Range of Answers
What is the name of your favorite pet?	The top 20 dog names are Max, Buddy, Molly, Bailey, Maggie, Lucy, Jake, Rocky, Sadie, Lucky, Daisy, Jack, Sam, Shadow, Bear, Buster, Lady, Ginger, Abby, and Toby.
In what city were you born?	The top 10 largest U.S. cities are New York City, Los Angeles, Chicago, Houston, Philadelphia, Phoenix, San Diego, Dallas, San Antonio, and Detroit; one in three of all U.S. citizens live in the top 250 cities; the top 10 most common U.S. city names are Fairview, Midway, Oak Grove, Franklin, Riverside, Centerville, Mount Pleasant, Georgetown, Salem, and Greenwood.
What high school did you attend?	There are approximately 25,000 to 30,000 high schools in the United States; you can use Classmates.com to get a list by U.S. state and city.
What is your favorite movie?	For a list of the all-time top 250 films, see www.imdb.com/ top_250_films.

Continued

Table 1.1 Secret Questions and Ranges of Answers

Question	Range of Answers
What is your mother's maiden name?	There are approximately 25,000 common surnames; one in 10 U.S. citizens have the surname Smith, Johnson, Williams, Jones, Brown, Davis, Miller, Wilson, Moore, Taylor, Anderson, Thomas, Jackson, White, Harris, Martin, Thompson, Garcia, Martinez, Robinson, Clark, Rodriguez, Lewis, Lee, Walker, Hall, Allen, or Young.
What street did you grow up on?	The 15 most common street names are Second/2nd, Third/3rd, First/1st, Fourth/4th, Park, Fifth/5th, Main, Sixth/6th, Oak, Seventh/7th, Pine, Maple, Cedar, Eighth/8th, and Elm.
What was the make of your first car?	Most cars are built by Acura, Audi, BMW, Buick, Cadillac, Chevrolet, Chrysler, Daewoo, Dodge, Ford, GMC, Honda, Hummer, Hyundai, Infiniti, Isuzu, Jaguar, Jeep, Kia, Land Rover, Lexus, Lincoln, Mazda, Mercedes-Benz, Mercury, Mitsubishi, Nissan, Oldsmobile, Plymouth, Pontiac, Porsche, Saab, Saturn, Subaru, Suzuki, Toyota, Volkswagen, or Volvo.
When is your anniversary?	The average length of a marriage is 7.2 years, giving 2,628 likely dates.
What is your favorite color?	There are around 100 common colors, even considering colors such as taupe, gainsboro, and fuschia.

The key to properly using secret questions is to understand that they should never be the equivalent of a password. They should only be used to initiate a password reset, to prevent anonymous attacks against the password reset process. Providing the answer to a secret question should never be enough to validate a user, but combined with other factors, such as having access to the user's e-mail account, secret questions can be effective in helping to identify a user.

The greatest threat with secret questions is that the answer is usually fixed and an attacker can sometimes discover this information through research. Because there is usually a limited set of answers to secret questions, they are also vulnerable to brute-force attacks. Finally, secret questions are usually ineffective against attacks by people close to the user. Individuals such as ex-spouses, once-close business associates, or wayward teenage children may have sufficient information and sufficient motivation to break into a user's account.

Building the Code

The key to successfully and securely using secret questions is to clearly define their role as just one part of the password retrieval process. They prevent password resets without some personal knowledge of the user. Design the system to be flexible with secret questions and answers, allowing users to disable secret questions or requiring a telephone call for final confirmation. Another effective technique for security-sensitive Web applications is to allow or require users to answer more than one secret question. Consider the impact on the database of having multiple and perhaps a variable number of secret questions.

Avoid allowing users to select their own questions, since most users are not trained to select strong enough questions. Sites that allow users to select their own secret questions end up with insecure questions such as:

- What year were you born?

- What is your password?

- What is the capital of Georgia?

Select good questions, carefully considering the possible range of answers as well as the likelihood of common answers. Use unique questions, and try to avoid subjects that return short, one-word answers. Also try to avoid questions that others commonly use, such as mother's maiden name, pet name, or high school. But keep in mind that you should ask questions that users will always answer the same way.

Establish a large list of questions, but provide a short, random list for users to select from. For users more concerned with security, you might want to provide an advanced option to select from a larger list of secret questions.

If the user provides a predetermined number of incorrect answers to the security question, you might not want to return an error, but instead send the user an e-mail explaining that he or she answered incorrectly. This will prevent brute-force attacks against the secret question process and alert users to a possible attack against their accounts.

Here are some examples of good secret questions:

- What is the first and last name of your first boyfriend or girlfriend?
- Which phone number do you remember most from your childhood?
- What was your favorite place to visit as a child?
- Who is your favorite actor, musician, or artist?

Security Policies

- Secret questions by themselves are not secure and should never be used as a password equivalent.
- Allow users to change their secret questions and answers if necessary.
- Detect brute-force attacks against secret questions.

Empowering Users

A security system is never complete without user participation. Users have a unique perspective that allows them to spot security problems that administrators and developers may overlook. But to participate in security, users need knowledge and tools. It is up to you to provide the knowledge and tools they need. In this section, you will learn about:

- Educating users
- Involving users

Educating Users

Summary: **Users must know how to protect their accounts**
Threats: **Account hijacking, social engineering, identity theft**

With the increasing dependence on the Internet for financial and business transactions comes an increasing threat of Internet crime. Identity theft, fraud, and online scams are rampant, and Web site security can only go so far. At some point, users must take responsibility for protecting themselves.

Despite great advances in security technology and techniques, users consistently fall for the same scams they fell for since the very beginning of electronic communication. For example, users will click links on HTML pages and e-mails and will eagerly enter account information in an e-mail-based form, and many users will divulge their passwords to someone who claims to be an administrator or help-desk technician.

Many users of online financial institutions and other Web sites have fallen victim to spoofed e-mails intended to steal user account information, an attack know as *phishing*. In these cases, users receive an e-mail such as that shown in Figure 1.12, explaining an account problem and asking them to authenticate using the provided form. The form submits the personal information to a Web server controlled by the fraudster and then transparently forwards the information on to the real Web site. The user is not aware that his or her information has been stolen until it is too late. Fortunately, these e-mails are notorious for poor English grammar and spelling, such as the word *unnormally* in Figure 1.12.

Figure 1.12 Example eBay Scam E-Mail

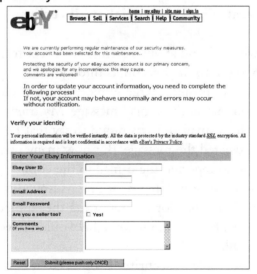

Another variation of the scam is to send users an e-mail that looks like plaintext but that is actually an HTML-based e-mail. Links appear to be one (legitimate) URL but take the user to another URL with a fake login form that looks identical to the original. Yet another variation is to encode or obscure the URL in such a way as to trick the user into thinking she is visiting one site while she is, in fact, visiting another.

If users are not aware of the techniques used by scammers, fraudsters, and identity thieves, the users will consistently fall victim to these social-engineering techniques. Users who are not smart about security may fall victim to account hijacking or identity theft and put themselves as well as others at risk.

Security Policies

- Through various media, educate users about the security risks involved with using your Web application.

- If possible, provide a user forum to discuss security issues.

- Never provide links or forms in e-mails sent to users; ask them to simply log in to their account.

Involving Users

Summary: **Involving users in security will raise awareness and help limit attacks**

Threats: **Account hijacking, social engineering**

Once I was talking with a friend about a scam e-mail sent to customers of a major bank, asking them to log in to their accounts through a form provided in the e-mail. I mentioned that a surprisingly large number of users fell for the scam, despite the obviously poor grammar in the e-mail message. My friend mentioned that he had actually received that e-mail and was proud to say that he immediately recognized it as a scam and deleted the message. But how many users could he have protected if he had instead reported the e-mail to the company?

Many users are aware of scams, fraud, or other suspicious incidents and never report them. My friend's reasons for not reporting the suspicious e-mail was that first, someone else probably will, and second, he wouldn't even know where to start to report the e-mail.

Users can play a great role in security if you make it easy for them. Since some users are already technically savvy and security-educated, you should give those users access to advanced security tools or security options. For example, some advanced users might want to set an option to only allow access to their accounts from specific IP address ranges. Advanced users might also want access to advanced security reports for their accounts.

If users have no way of identifying and reporting security incidents, the impact of a security incident could be larger than necessary. Design the system in such a way that all account actions are easily audited and reported. Provide conspicuous links for identifying and reporting security incidents. Create a modular design that allows users to easily customize their own security options.

Security Policies

- Allow users access to a history of account transactions and events.

- Provide users a clear and easy way to report security incidents, and ask them to report anything suspicious.

- If possible, provide a user forum to discuss security issues and incidents.

- Allow advanced security options for those who want to use them.

- Provide users a way to revoke or delete accounts they no longer want to use.

Coding Standards Fast Track

Establishing User Credentials

Enforcing Strong Passwords

- ☑ Access a password form field only once to validate it and assign it to a variable. After that use only the validated variable.
- ☑ Use a standard function to check password complexity requirements.

Avoiding Easily Guessed Credentials

- ☑ All temporary passwords should have a short expiration period or should be marked as already expired, forcing the user to change the password.

Preventing Credential Harvesting

- ☑ Never place the username on the URL's query string.
- ☑ Avoid user directories or other methods that others could use to harvest usernames.
- ☑ Do not automatically generate usernames or account IDs.

Managing Passwords

Storing Passwords

- ☑ Always use well-established hashing algorithms, such as those included with the System.Security.Cryptography class.
- ☑ Centralize all encryption code so that you can easily change algorithms and/or keys.

Password Aging and Password Histories

- ☑ Always check the password age immediately after authenticating the user.

Changing Passwords

- ☑ Password changes should be on a page of their own and accept the old password as well as the new password in a single step.

- ☑ Expire all user sessions immediately after changing a user's password, requiring the user to reauthenticate.

Resetting Lost or Forgotten Passwords

Resetting Passwords

- ☑ Treat lost passwords as a security event, taking measures such as logging event details, including client IP address.

- ☑ Carefully manage session state throughout the reset process; do not track session account identifiers on hidden form fields or query strings.

Sending Information Via E-Mail

- ☑ Never send sensitive information via e-mail.

- ☑ If possible, use PGP or S/MIME to digitally sign and/or encrypt e-mail communications.

Assigning Temporary Passwords

- ☑ If creating temporary passwords, use a strong random algorithm with sufficient entropy.

Using Secret Questions

- ☑ Use questions with enough possible answers to prevent guessing or brute-force attacks.

- ☑ Avoid questions for which many people will select the same common answers.

Empowering Users

Educating Users

☑ Avoid long or overly complex URLs, especially at the application entry points such as a login screen.

Code Audit Fast Track

Establishing User Credentials

Enforcing Strong Passwords

☑ Does the application allow for and enforce strong passwords?

☑ Does the application require both a username and password?

Avoiding Easily Guessed Credentials

☑ Does the application avoid using sequential user account numbers?

☑ Do account numbers or usernames follow predictable patterns?

☑ Do customer service personnel select passwords for users rather than users selecting their own?

☑ Does the system create default passwords?

Preventing Credential Harvesting

☑ Do account numbers or usernames follow predictable patterns?

☑ Are identifiable account numbers or usernames passed as query strings on URLs?

☑ Do account numbers or usernames unnecessarily appear on HTML pages?

Limiting Idle Accounts

☑ Does the system have large numbers of idle accounts?

☑ Is it possible to determine another user's account activity?

☑ Are users notified via e-mail after major account changes?

Managing Passwords

Storing Passwords

☑ Are password hashes rather than actual passwords stored?

☑ Are password hashes stored using well-established hashing algorithms?

☑ Can encryption keys be easily changed?

☑ Do password hashes use random salts?

Password Aging and Password Histories

☑ Does the application allow for password aging and do passwords expire after a set amount of time?

☑ Does the application enforce password histories to prevent users from reusing passwords?

Changing Passwords

■ Is it convenient for users to change their passwords?

■ Are users reminded to regularly change their passwords?

■ Does the password change process require the previous password?

■ Does the system confirm password changes via e-mail?

■ Does the system expire all active sessions after changing passwords?

Resetting Lost or Forgotten Passwords

Resetting Passwords

☑ Does the system allow only password resets, rather than retrieval?

☑ Does the system require users to answer secret or other questions to reset the password?

☑ Does the system send an e-mail to confirm the password change?

Sending Information Via E-Mail

☑ Does the system avoid sending sensitive information via e-mail?

Assigning Temporary Passwords

☑ If using temporary passwords, does the system use a strong random password algorithm?

☑ If your system uses temporary passwords, do they have a short expiration period?

Using Secret Questions

☑ Are secret questions treated as password equivalents?

☑ Do the secret questions have a great number of possible of answers?

☑ Does the system avoid secret questions with common answers?

☑ Does the system prevent users from setting their own secret questions?

Empowering Users

Educating Users

☑ Is a help page available to educate users on security?

☑ Does the Web site provide other methods to educate users?

Involving Users

☑ Are users able to view a history of transactions and events related to their account?

☑ Are users able to view a history of account logins, including dates, times, and IP addresses?

☑ Do users have an easy and intuitive way to report security incidents?

☑ Can advanced users customize their security options?

☑ Are users able to revoke or delete unused accounts?

Frequently Asked Questions

The following Frequently Asked Questions, answered by the authors of this book, are designed to both measure your understanding of the concepts presented in this chapter and to assist you with real-life implementation of these concepts. To have your questions about this chapter answered by the author, browse to **www.syngress.com/solutions** and click on the **"Ask the Author"** form. You will also gain access to thousands of other FAQs at ITFAQnet.com.

Q: Which hashing algorithms are bundled within the .NET Framework?

A: MD5, SHA1, SHA256, SHA384, and SHA512.

Q: Should I automatically generate passwords with totally random characters to make sure their passwords are secure?

A: Many people believe that generating completely random passwords will best protect users. But keep in mind that it is extremely difficult for users to remember a random password such as jD4nWpa8v, likely requiring them to write it down. Perhaps a better solution is to create a more memorable password made up of multiple random English words and punctuation. Users are more likely to remember these passwords, and you can even get away with giving users longer passwords.

Q: What should I allow for a maximum password length?

A: If you are using a hashing algorithm, the hash itself is a fixed length, regardless of the size of the password. In other words, a seven-character password produces a hash the same length as a 200-character password. So if you use password hashes, you do not need to enforce a maximum password length.

Q: My Web forum page is completely dependent on showing usernames. How can I prevent others from harvesting these usernames?

A: Some Web applications are based on user interaction and cannot completely prevent username harvesting. To counteract this potential danger, allow users to change their usernames and set aliases for their accounts.

Q: I operate a Web application that contains very sensitive user financial information. Should I force users to change their passwords every 30 days to ensure maximum password security?

A: This is the most secure policy, but it could cause users to find measures to circumvent this inconvenience by writing down passwords or following predictable patterns. A better solution is to encourage stronger passwords and allow users to keep them longer.

Q: After a password reset, what is the point of putting a link in the e-mail rather than the actual password? If a hacker can access the user's e-mail, he can just as easily access the link in an e-mail. Why not just e-mail the user a temporary password?

A: It is true that a link in an e-mail is just accessible as the password itself, but there are other reasons for doing this. First, it establishes a secure communication channel when the user clicks the link. Second, it allows the Web server to record the client's IP address and time of visit. Third, it prevents the user from saving an e-mail containing the password. And finally, if the user no longer owns the e-mail account or if the e-mail is routed incorrectly, it prevents others from obtaining the user's password.

Q: Are temporary passwords bad?

A: Temporary passwords are not bad, as long as you force them to be temporary. The best technique is to mark them as already expired so that when a user logs in she is forced to immediately change her password.

Q: What is the best way to get users involved in security?

A: The best way to get users involved is to allow users to discuss security in a public forum or via a mailing list. Such a forum is a great way for your organization and your users to discuss current security issues. But be careful to monitor the forum, since they are sometimes used as a way to social-engineer users into revealing their passwords. A fraudster once posted phony support phone numbers at an online payment support forum, instructing users to call those numbers to report security incidents. If someone called those support numbers, the fraudster on the other end first asked them to "authenticate" themselves by revealing their passwords.

Q: Where can I obtain some word lists for checking user passwords?

A: Visit www.gattinger.org/wordlists/download.html or http://neworder.box.sk/codebox.links.php?key=passdict.

Chapter 2

Authenticating and Authorizing Users

Solutions in this Chapter:

- **Authenticating Users**
- **Authorizing Users**

☑ Coding Standards Fast Track

☑ Code Audit Fast Track

☑ Frequently Asked Questions

Introduction

The real test of a secure Web application occurs when it comes time for users to log in and access your site. At first the process seems simple: provide the user with a login screen and let the user enter, if he or she supplies the correct username and password. But Web security can fail in many ways. In this chapter, we will discuss those failures and solutions to prevent them.

Authentication establishes a user's identity. Once this identity is proved valid, the user is authorized (or not authorized) to access various features of the Web application. ASP.NET has many advantages over classic ASP because it provides a much more robust authentication mechanism as well as tools to implement advanced authentication and authorization scenarios.

But with all the new authentication and authorization features of ASP.NET, programmers are still prone to making many of the same errors they did with past versions of ASP. This chapter focuses on the authentication and authorization portion of a Web application.

Understanding the Threats

The primary threats with user authentication are:

- **Account hijacking** This involves taking over the account of a legitimate user, sometimes denying the rightful user access to his or her account.

- **Man-in-the-middle** Intercepting Web traffic in such a way that the attacker is able to read and modify data in transit between two systems.

- **Phishing** A type of man-in-the-middle attack in which the attacker lures a legitimate user to enter a password through a fake e-mail or Web form designed to look like that of a legitimate Web site.

- **Unauthorized access** Gaining access to restricted content or data without the consent of the content owner.

- **Information leakage** Revealing or failing to protect information that an attacker can use to compromise a system.

- **Privilege escalation** Allowing an attacker to gain the access privileges of a higher-level account.

- **Sniffing** Using a network-monitoring utility to intercept passwords or other sensitive information that traverses a network.

Authenticating Users

The Web login screen is a chokepoint that forces a user to prove his or her identity by providing a valid username and password. It is important to carefully plan this login screen so that you can be sure of the user's identity. In this section, we will cover:

- Building login forms
- Using forms authentication
- Using Windows authentication
- Using Passport authentication
- Blocking brute-force attacks

Building Login Forms

Summary: **The login form should protect user credentials and resist attack**

Threats: **Account hijacking, information leakage, SQL injection, cross-site scripting**

Several years ago I sat in the hallway at a security conference watching another attendee's laptop screen as a list of usernames and passwords slowly scrolled down an open command prompt window. I immediately recognized that he was sniffing the network, gathering user logins—something I certainly could expect at this type of security conference. But what surprised me was when I started talking to him about it, he explained that those were only passwords from the Web-based e-mail services Hotmail and Yahoo! Within 10 minutes he had collected a long list of login credentials from people logging in to their e-mail accounts across an insecure, untrusted network connection.

Indeed, it used to be very easy to sniff these credentials. Both services offered SSL versions of their login screens, but few people actually used them. Fortunately, since then Hotmail has moved to authenticating with Passport over a secure connection, and Yahoo! creates an MD5 hash of your password before sending it over the wire. But many Web sites still fail to protect users' credentials when they log in.

Because the login form plays such an important role in authenticating users, it is important to protect the form itself from flaws. A poorly written login form is vulnerable to password sniffing, information leakage, and phishing. Furthermore, the form itself may be vulnerable to flaws such as SQL injection and cross-site scripting.

As you design and build a login form, keep it simple and avoid using a single form for multiple tasks. Always transmit credentials across a secure connection using SSL.

TIP

Try to establish a secure connection to the login form itself, not after users click the Login button to submit credentials. You want to assure the user that the login form is not only secure but authentic. See Chapter 4, "Encrypting Private Data," for more information on using SSL.

Because URLs are logged by proxy servers, browser caches, and typed URL histories, it is best to use the HTTP *POST* with Web forms method rather than the HTTP *GET* method. (See Chapter 6, "Building Secure ASP.NET Applications," for more information on creating forms.) It is important to always validate form input to prevent SQL injection and cross-site scripting attacks. (See Chapter 5, "Filtering User Input," for more information on filtering input.)

When handling failed logins, be careful how you return error messages. For example, inexperienced programmers sometimes return different error messages for bad usernames than for bad passwords. The error message should be generic enough to prevent credential harvesting based on the error messages returned. Figure 2.1 is an example of a proper failed-login message. With different error messages for bad usernames and bad passwords, an attacker could go through a list of usernames until the error message switches from indicating a bad username to indicating a bad password. After finding a valid username, the attacker could go on to guess the password.

Figure 2.1 Generic Failed-Login Message

When auditing a login screen, the first thing you should do is view the source code for the form. In particular, look for extra hidden tags within the form that could be modified or could reveal sensitive information. The next step is to try entering invalid information into the form fields to determine what attackers can learn from the error messages. Finally, try some of the SQL injection and cross-site scripting techniques mentioned in Chapter 5, "Filtering User Input."

When designing a login form, do not use hidden form fields to pass sensitive information. An attacker might be able to modify these hidden fields to gain unauthorized access or view them to gather information that will assist an attack. The following is an example of a hidden form field that might be vulnerable to attack:

```
<form method="POST">
  <input type="text" name="txtUsername"></p>
  <p><input type="text" name="txtPassword"></p>
  <input type="hidden" name="AdminArea" value="False">
  <p><input type="submit" value="Submit" name="B1"></p>
</form>
```

Security Policies

- Always transmit login criteria over an SSL connection.
- Use the HTTP *POST* method for sending form data.
- Always validate form input.
- Do not rely on hidden form fields to transfer data, because they can be modified by the client and may reveal sensitive information.

- Never reveal too much information in failed-login error messages.

Using Forms Authentication

Summary: **Insecure authentication form settings could weaken the Web application's security**

Threats: **Account hijacking, information leakage**

Thousands of poorly written ASP Web site login authentication schemes are implemented all over the world. Programmers consistently make the same security mistakes, especially when they are not properly trained in secure coding practices. ASP.NET introduces a new concept called *forms authentication*. Even though it is still not perfect, forms authentication at least provides a reasonably strong framework from which programmers can build secure login mechanisms.

Forms authentication provides good security and is very easy to use: Create a login page and change some settings in the web.config file. But its ease of use may also lead to poor security practices.

The biggest problem is that it allows you to add usernames and passwords right in the web.config file, even allowing you to use plain, unencrypted passwords, as shown in Figure 2.2. You can choose to store MD5 or SHA-1 hashes in the web.config file, as shown in Figure 2.3, but ASP.NET provides no easy method to create hashes of your passwords. Consequently, many developers will choose plaintext passwords simply because it is easier. The developers may intend to later encrypt these passwords, but it never seems to gain priority in their hectic schedules. If you set passwords in your web.config file, go ahead and use MD5 or SHA-1 right from the beginning.

Figure 2.2 Cleartext Passwords in Web.config

```
<credentials passwordFormat="Clear">
    <user name="Alice" password="test123"/>
    <user name="Bob" password="dragon"/>
    <user name="Charlie" password="superman"/>
    <user name="David" password="letmein"/>
</credentials>
```

Figure 2.3 Passwords Encrypted with SHA-1

```
<credentials passwordFormat="SHA1">
  <user name="Alice" password="7288EDD0FC3FFCBE93A0CF06E3568E28521687BC"/>
  <user name="Bob" password="AF8978B1797B72ACFFF9595A5A2A373EC3D9106D"/>
  <user name="Charlie"
password="18C28604DD31094A8D69DAE60F1BCD347F1AFC5A"/>
  <user name="David" password="B7A875FC1EA228B9061041B7CEC4BD3C52AB3CE3"/>
</credentials>
```

Use the C# code shown in Figure 2.4 or the VB.NET code shown in Figure 2.5 to compile a command-line utility to create password hashes. Another alternative is to use an online hash generator such as the one at www.securecode.net/HashCalc+main.html.

Figure 2.4 PassHash Utility: C#

```csharp
using System;
using System.Web.Security;
namespace Chapter02
{
  // Add System.Web to your references
  class PassHash
  {
    [STAThread]
    static void Main(string[] args)
    {
      string sMethod, sPass, sOut;
      if (Environment.GetCommandLineArgs().Length < 3)
      {
        ShowHelp();
      }
      else
      {
        sMethod =
            Environment.GetCommandLineArgs()[1].ToUpper().Substring(1,
            Environment.GetCommandLineArgs()[1].Length - 1);
        sPass = Environment.GetCommandLineArgs()[2];
```

Continued

Figure 2.4 PassHash Utility: C#

```csharp
        if ((sMethod == "SHA1" || sMethod == "MD5") && sPass.Length > 0)
        {
            sOut = FormsAuthentication.HashPasswordForStoringInConfigFile
                (sPass, sMethod);
            Console.WriteLine(sOut);
        }
        else
        {
            ShowHelp();
        }
    }
}
public static void ShowHelp()
{
    Console.WriteLine("Usage: PassHash [-MD5|-SHA1] <password>");
    Console.WriteLine("Example: PassHash -SHA1 letmein");
}
}
}
```

Figure 2.5 PassHash Utility: VB.NET

```vb
Imports System.Web.Security
Module PassHash
Sub Main()
    Dim sMethod As String, sPass As String
    Dim sOut As String
    If Environment.GetCommandLineArgs.Length < 3 Then
        ShowHelp()
    Else
        sMethod = UCase(Right(Environment.GetCommandLineArgs(1), _
            Environment.GetCommandLineArgs(1).Length - 1))
        sPass = Environment.GetCommandLineArgs(2)
        If (sMethod = "SHA1" Or sMethod = "MD5") And sPass.Length Then
            sOut=FormsAuthentication.HashPasswordForStoringInConfigFile(sPass,
                sMethod)
```

Continued

Figure 2.5 PassHash Utility: VB.NET

```
          Console.WriteLine(sOut)
     Else
          ShowHelp()
     End If
  End If
End Sub
Function ShowHelp()
  Console.WriteLine("Usage: PassHash [-MD5|-SHA1] <password>")
  Console.WriteLine("Example: PassHash -SHA1 letmein")
End Function
End Module
```

Some would argue that it is perfectly safe to use plaintext passwords in the web.config because ASP.NET prevents outside users from viewing this file. This is true to some extent; however, experience has taught us that those files are not always secure. In the future someone may discover a flaw in ASP.NET that allows viewing web.config files, or someone might access the file through other methods such as a poorly configured file share or FTP server. Too many developers have learned the hard way that you cannot guarantee that files on a server are safe from viewing.

But even if you do use MD5 or SHA-1 hashes, these too can be cracked through a dictionary or brute-force attack. Tools such as Cain & Abel at www.oxid.it/cain.html are able to crack MD5 and SHA-1 hashes. Although this method can be very slow with strong passwords, Cain can usually crack common passwords such as those shown in Figure 2.6 in a matter of minutes. You should weigh the risk of relying on web.config files to store security credentials before you roll any Web application to a production system.

WARNING

Because web.config files are plain hashes that do not make use of a salt, they are more vulnerable to cracking from precomputed hash lists. See Chapter 4, "Encrypting Private Data," for more information on hashing with a salt.

Figure 2.6 Cain & Abel Performing a Dictionary Attack on SHA-1 Hashes

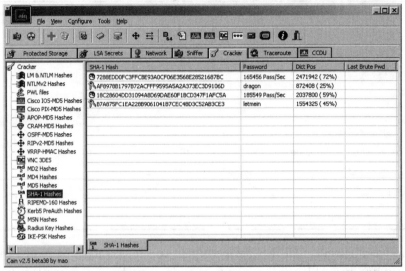

When using forms authentication, remember that it only applies to those resources managed by ASP.NET. That includes any files with the extensions:

- .asax

- .aspx

- .ascx

- .ashx

- .asmx

- .axd

- .vsdisco

- .rem

- .soap

- .config

- .cs

- .csproj

- .vb

- .vbproj

- .webinfo

- .licx

- .resx

- .resources

- .jsl

- .java

- .vjsproj

If you use forms authentication and request a file in a protected directory with any of these extensions, you will be forwarded to the login page. If you request a file with any other extension, you will get the file directly, with no request for authentication. For instructions on how to secure all files, see the sidebar "Mapping Non-ASP.NET Resources" later in this section.

Although forms authentication is a great improvement over features available in ASP, you still must use it carefully. Forms authentication is most secure when used with custom authentication against a SQL database, a protected data file, LDAP, or an operating system account. Storing the passwords or hashes in the web.config file itself may be safe, but it carries great risk. Another alternative is to use a custom XML file in a protected directory to handle authentication. For an example of how to implement this solution, see http://msdn.microsoft.com/library/en-us/cpguide/html/cpconcookieauthenticationusinganxmlusersfile.asp.

Hacking the Code...

Mapping Non-ASP.NET Resources

Most ASP.NET security features only protect ASP.NET resources, so you must take extra measures to protect non-ASP.NET files. To do that, you have to map these resources to the ASP.NET ISAPI filter using IIS 5 or IIS 6. Using IIS 5:

1. In the Internet Services Manager, select the properties for the application to configure.

2. From the **Home Directory** tab, click the **Configuration** button.

3. From the **App Mappings** tab, click the **Add** button.

4. Click the **Browse** button, and locate the .NET ISAPI filter (typically located at C:\Winnt\Microsoft.NET\Framework\<version>\aspnet_isapi.dll).

5. Enter the extension you want to map to ASP.NET (or enter .* to map all extensions).

Using IIS 6:

1. In the Internet Services Manager, select the properties for the application to configure.

2. From the **Home Directory** tab, click the **Configuration** button.

3. From the **Mappings** tab, click on the **Add** button.

4. Click the **Browse** button and locate the .NET ISAPI filter (typically located at C:\Winnt\Microsoft.NET\Framework\<version>\aspnet_isapi.dll).

5. Enter the extension you want to map to ASP.NET.

6. To add a wildcard mapping, click **Insert** from the **Mappings** tab, and enter the path to the .NET ISAPI filter.

Note that adding wildcard application maps cause ASP.NET to handle all file extensions. This will work fine for most static content, but you will not be able to do this for extensions mapped to other applications, such as Perl or Cold Fusion. Wildcard mappings might have some effect on server performance, depending on the type of content in your Web directories. ASP.NET does have a special handler for static content, but you might want to run performance tests for your particular Web site.

Configuring Forms Authentication

Some attributes in the Forms element of the web.config file do have some effect on security. These settings are:

- **name="[cookie name]"** Select a unique name that does not conflict with other form names.

- **protection="[All | None | Encryption | Validation]"** Although some of the settings might offer better performance, you should always set this to All to gain maximum cookie protection.

- **timeout="[minutes]"** This is the timeout in minutes for a cookie to be valid, measured from the time of the last request. The default value is 30 minutes, but you might want to select a shorter timeout, such as 10 or 15 minutes.

- **requireSSL="[true | false]"** This setting, when set to *true*, will mark the cookie as secure, causing the browser to not transmit the cookie unless a secure SSL session is established. Setting this value to *true* and using SSL offers the only true protection from cookie hijacking.

Security Policies

- Never use *passwordFormat="Clear"* on a production system or deployment.

- Understand the risks of storing any cleartext credentials in the web.config file.

- When using forms authentication, take extra measures to protect files not handled by ASP.NET.

- Carefully plan the settings for the authorization cookie to limit exposure to hijacking.

Using Windows Authentication

Summary: **Windows authentication can be secure, but only when configured properly**

Threats: **Account hijacking, man-in-the middle, information leakage**

In addition to Forms authentication, ASP.NET provides support for native IIS authentication methods, collectively referred to as *Windows Authentication*. When Windows Authentication is used, the browser prompts the user for a username and password, as shown in Figure 2.7.

Figure 2.7 Windows Authentication Prompt

To implement Windows authentication, modify the web.config file as follows:

```
<authentication mode="Windows" />
  <authorization>
    <deny users="?" />
  </authorization>
```

You must then open the Internet Services Manager and select the properties for the protected content directory. Uncheck **anonymous access** and select an authentication method.

IIS provides four standard methods for authentication:

- Basic authentication
- Digest authentication
- Integrated Windows authentication
- Client certificate mapping

Basic Authentication

Basic authentication works by prompting a Web site visitor for a username and password. This method is widely used because most browsers and Web servers support it. The benefits are:

- It works through proxy servers.

- It is compatible with nearly every Internet browser.

- It allows users to access resources that are not located on the IIS server.

Basic authentication also has some drawbacks:

- Information is sent over the network as cleartext. The information is encoded with base64 encoding (see RFC 1521 for more information on base64 encoding), but it is sent in an unencrypted format. Any password sent using basic authentication can easily be decoded.

- By default, users must have the Log On Locally right to use basic authentication.

- Basic authentication is vulnerable to replay attacks.

Because basic authentication does not encrypt user credentials, it is important that traffic always be sent over an encrypted SSL session. A user authenticating with basic authentication must provide a valid username and password. The user account can be a local account or a domain account. By default, the IIS server will look locally or in Active Directory for the user account. If the user account is in a domain other than the local domain, the user must specify the domain name during logon. The syntax for this process is *domain name\username,* where *domain name* is the name of the user's domain. Basic authentication can also be configured to use user principal names (UPNs) when you use accounts stored in Active Directory.

To prevent exposing user credentials to others on the network, it is essential that you always use SSL with basic authentication. Note that basic authentication causes the browser to send user credentials to every page on the same site or within the same realm, not just the login page. If you don't use SSL on every page, user credentials will be visible on the network. One way to prevent these credentials from being sent on unprotected content is to use a unique realm for protected and unprotected content. See Chapter 4, "Encrypting Private Data," for more information on using SSL.

Digest Authentication

Digest authentication has many similarities to basic authentication, but it overcomes some of the problems. Digest authentication does not send usernames or passwords over the network. It is more secure than basic authentication, but it requires more planning to make it work.

Some of the similarities with basic authentication are:

- Users must have the Log On Locally right.
- Both methods work through firewalls.

Like all authentication methods, digest authentication does have some drawbacks:

- Users can only access resources on the IIS server. Their credentials can't be passed to another computer.
- The IIS server must be a member of a domain.
- All user accounts must store passwords using reversible encryption.
- The method works only with Internet Explorer 5.0 or higher.
- Digest authentication is vulnerable to replay attacks, to a limited extent.

Digest authentication is secure due to the way it passes authentication information over the network. Usernames and passwords are never sent. Instead, IIS uses a message digest (or hash) to verify the user's credentials. In order for digest authentication to work, all user accounts must be stored using reversible encryption in Active Directory, which may be a potential risk. After this setting is enabled for a user account, the user's password must be changed to create the plaintext copy.

Digest authentication does provide more security, but for most Web sites, the limitations of this method outweigh the benefits. One interesting peculiarity with IIS is that when you send authentication headers to a client, it will send the basic authentication header before the digest one. Many Internet browsers use the first header they encounter and therefore opt for the weaker basic authentication.

Integrated Windows Authentication

Integrated Windows authentication is also a secure solution because usernames and passwords aren't transmitted across the network. This method is convenient because, if a user is already logged on to the domain and if the user has the correct permissions for the site, the user isn't prompted for his or her username and password. Instead, IIS attempts to use the user's cached credentials for authentication. The cached credentials are hashed and sent to the IIS server for authentication. If the cached credentials do not have the correct permissions, the user is prompted to enter a different username and password.

Depending on the client and server configuration, integrated Windows authentication uses either the Windows NT LAN Mangager (NTLM) or Kerberos for authentication. You cannot directly choose which one is used; IIS will automatically choose a method based on the server and client configuration. The Web browser and the IIS server negotiate which one to use through the negotiate authentication header. Both Kerberos and NTLM have their own advantages and disadvantages. Kerberos is faster and more secure than NTLM. Unlike NTLM, which authenticates only the client, Kerberos authenticates both the client and the server. This helps prevent spoofing. Kerberos also allows users to access remote network resources not located on the IIS server. NTLM restricts users to the information located on the IIS server only.

Kerberos is the preferred authentication method for an intranet Web server. However, the following requirements must be met for Kerberos to be used instead of NTLM:

- Both the client and server must be running Windows 2000 or later.

- The client must be using Internet Explorer 5 or later.

- The client and server must be in either the same domain as the IIS server or in a trusted domain.

Integrated Windows authentication has a few limitations:

- It works only with Internet Explorer 3.01 or later.

- It does not work through a firewall. The client will use the firewall's IP address in the Integrated Windows hash, which will cause the authentication request to fail.

Client Certificate Mapping

Client certificate mapping is the process of mapping a certificate to a user account. Certificates can be mapped by Active Directory or by IIS. Both of these methods require Secure Sockets Layer (SSL). There are three types of certificate mappings:

- One-to-one mapping
- Many-to-one mapping
- UPN mapping

Certificate mapping is the process of linking a certificate to a specific user account. Normally, if we wanted to give a user authenticated access to the intranet, we would either create a user account or allow the user to log in using his domain account. Creating duplicate accounts is time-consuming, yet if users use their domain accounts, there is the concern that their domain passwords could become compromised.

To provide better security and reduce the administrative workload, we could choose to issue each user a certificate. Certificates can be used to verify a user's integrity. It is actually more efficient to use a certificate than a user account because certificates can be examined without having to connect to a database. It is generally safer to distribute certificates than user accounts. Furthermore, it is much easier to guess or crack someone's password than it is to forge a certificate.

Authenticating Users

If you are securing an intranet application for which you have control over the server and client configuration and the corresponding clients and server(s) are in the same domain, integrated Windows authentication is probably the best solution. For a public Web site, the most widely supported method is basic authentication over an SSL connection. Because basic authentication is secure only if you use SSL, you might want to enforce this policy on your server. You can do this through an HTTP module, as shown in Figure 2.8 (C#) and Figure 2.9 (VB.NET). Every time an authentication request is sent to the server, this code checks to see if the request is using basic authentication and if it is sent over an SSL connection. If both those criteria are not met, the code returns a "403.4 SSL Required error" message back to the client.

Figure 2.8 Blocking Basic Authentication Without SSL: C#

```
using System;
using System.Web;
using System.Security.Principal;
namespace HttpAuthModules
{
  public class AuthenticationModule : IHttpModule
  {
    public AuthenticationModule()
    {
    }
```

Continued

Figure 2.8 Blocking Basic Authentication Without SSL: C#

```csharp
public void Init(HttpApplication httpApp)
{
  // Register the event handler with Application object.
  httpApp.AuthenticateRequest +=
    new EventHandler(this.AuthenticateRequest);
}
private void AuthenticateRequest(object obj, EventArgs ea)
{
  HttpApplication objApp = (HttpApplication) obj;
  HttpContext objContext = (HttpContext) objApp.Context;
  // Deny access if user is using basic authentication without SSL
  if (objApp.User.Identity.AuthenticationType == "Basic" &&
    objContext.Request.IsSecureConnection == false)
  {
    objContext.Response.StatusCode = 403;
    objApp.Response.End();
  }
}


public void Dispose()
{
}
}
}
```

Figure 2.9 Blocking Basic Authentication Without SSL: VB.NET

```vbnet
Imports System.Web
Public Class AuthenticationModule
  Implements IHttpModule
  Public Sub Init(ByVal app As HttpApplication) Implements IHttpModule.Init
    AddHandler app.AuthenticateRequest, AddressOf Me.AuthenticateRequest
  End Sub
  Public Sub Dispose() Implements IHttpModule.Dispose
  End Sub
```

Continued

Figure 2.9 Blocking Basic Authentication Without SSL: VB.NET

```
Private Sub AuthenticateRequest(ByVal obj As Object, ByVal ea As
    System.EventArgs)
  Dim objApp As HttpApplication
  Dim objContext As HttpContext
  objApp = obj
  objContext = objApp.Context

  ' Deny access if user is using basic authentication without SSL
  If objApp.User.Identity.AuthenticationType = "Basic" And _
    objContext.Request.IsSecureConnection = False Then
    objContext.Response.StatusCode = 403
    objApp.Response.End()
  End If
  End Sub
End Class
```

TIP

Note that code in an HTTP module runs only on files handled by ASP.NET. If you want ASP.NET to handle all files, follow the instructions in the sidebar "Mapping Non-ASP.NET Resources."

Another problem with authenticating to the operating system or domain is that there is no direct control over which account is used to log in. If you provide a login box, anyone with an account on that system can try to log in. They might not be able to gain access to the resource, but they can authenticate to the server. This gives attackers the opportunity to launch brute-force attacks against privileged accounts such as Administrator.

Depending on the network and server configuration, Windows authentication might also allow relaying attacks from the Web server to other trusted domains or servers on the internal network. Windows authentication allows the user to enter a domain-qualified name in the format *domain\username* to authenticate to other trusted domains. If an attacker knows the name of other trusted domains that the Web server can see, he or she can potentially relay attacks by trying to authenticate to the internal domain. Basic authentication can also be configured to leverage UPNs when you use accounts stored in Active Directory, again providing more opportunity for data relay attacks.

When using Windows authentication, you might want to restrict which users can log in to the server. You can use file or URL authorization to prevent access, but this doesn't prevent the user from trying to authenticate—it just prevents the user from accessing the content. Both of these methods enforce access based on the username, so a user must first be authenticated. If you don't want to expose a privileged user account to a brute-force attack through your authentication mechanism, you can simply prevent that user from authenticating at all through the Web application. One way to accomplish this goal is through an HTTP module, as shown in Figure 2.10 (C#) and Figure 2.11 (VB.NET). This code checks the username whenever an authentication request is sent to see if it contains the user *Administrator* and returns an "HTTP 401 error" message if it does. This prevents anyone from even attempting to authenticate as *Administrator*.

Figure 2.10 Blocking Administrator Logins: C#

```csharp
using System;
using System.Web;
using System.Security.Principal;
namespace HttpAuthModules
{
  public class AuthenticationModule : IHttpModule
  {
    public AuthenticationModule()
    {
    }
    public void Init(HttpApplication httpApp)
    {
      // Register the event handler with Application object.
      httpApp.AuthenticateRequest +=
        new EventHandler(this.AuthenticateRequest);
    }
    public void AuthenticateRequest(object obj, EventArgs ea)
    {
      HttpApplication objApp = (HttpApplication) obj;
      HttpContext objContext = (HttpContext) objApp.Context;
```

Continued

Figure 2.10 Blocking Administrator Logins: C#

```csharp
      // If user identity is not administrator, return 403 code
      if ( objApp.User.Identity.Name.IndexOf("administrator") >= 0)
      {
        objContext.Response.StatusCode = 403;
        objApp.Response.End();
      }
    }
    public void Dispose()
    {
    }
  }
}
```

Figure 2.11 Blocking Administrator Logins: VB.NET

```vbnet
Imports System.Web


Public Class AuthenticationModule
  Implements IHttpModule
  Public Sub Init(ByVal app As HttpApplication) Implements IHttpModule.Init
    AddHandler app.AuthenticateRequest, AddressOf Me.AuthenticateRequest
  End Sub


  Public Sub Dispose() Implements IHttpModule.Dispose
  End Sub


  Public Sub AuthenticateRequest(ByVal obj As Object, ByVal ea As
  System.EventArgs)
    Dim objApp As HttpApplication
    Dim objContext As HttpContext


    objApp = obj
    objContext = objApp.Context


    ' If user identity is not administrator, return 403 code
    If objApp.User.Identity.Name.IndexOf("administrator") >= 0 Then
```

Continued

Figure 2.11 Blocking Administrator Logins: VB.NET

```
        objContext.Response.StatusCode = 403
        objApp.Response.End()
    End If
  End Sub
End Class
```

Security Policies

- Always use SSL with every page that uses basic authentication.

- Use unique realms for protected and unprotected content.

- Use Integrated Windows authentication if possible in an intranet environment.

- Block privileged users from brute-force attacks by preventing them from authenticating.

Using Passport Authentication

Summary: **Passport authentication has many strengths, but you must also be aware of the risks**

Threats: **Account hijacking**

In mid-1999, Microsoft released its Passport service, a single sign-on and e-commerce solution for the Web. Despite widespread privacy and security concerns, the Passport service is constantly growing, with support from large companies such as eBay, McAfee, and Citibank.

But many consumers feel uneasy with the concept of such a large central database controlled by a private company. With so much centralized control over this data, the potential for abuse is great. Another concern is security. Microsoft's Passport service has had problems and has not gone long enough without security flaws to prove itself a reliable service.

Nevertheless, Passport does have its benefits. For consumers, it's fewer passwords to remember; for Web sites, it involves no hassle setting up a user database. One could argue that having a single authentication service with a few flaws might even be better than a thousand poorly secured Web sites. But the risk is with the single point of failure: If someone hijacks your Passport account, that person gains access to every service you use with Passport.

One problem is that Microsoft has not proven that the service is secure; all we really have to go by is that the company says it is secure. Being a proprietary system, it has not gone through a public review. Microsoft doesn't make much effort to publish third-party audits of the Passport services, nor does the company justify its security with details of the security measures it employs. Consequently, only time will tell us how secure Passport is. Another problem is that as more sites begin to use Passport, the more attractive it will become as a target.

The Passport login forms from different sites are not consistent in appearance or format—sometimes appearing inline, as at Hotmail.com and MSN.com; appearing on their own pages at the same site, as at eBay.com (see Figure 2.12), or appearing as a customized branded page at login.passport.net (see Figure 2.13). Depending on your operating system, you might also be prompted for a .NET Passport from a Windows dialog box or wizard. The problem with this lack of consistency is that it makes it more difficult for users to discern a real login box from a fake login box. In fact, anyone can probably put a fake .NET Passport sign-in box on a Web site and simply collect the usernames and passwords people enter.

Figure 2.12 eBay's Passport Login Form.

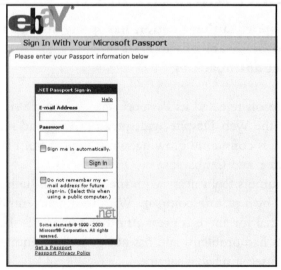

Figure 2.13 Citibank's Passport Login Form

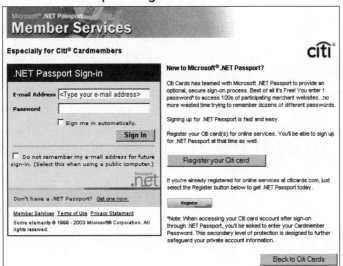

Although Passport lets you set various parameters for security, there is no guarantee that other participating sites are going to use the same level of security. In other words, although you might choose to use more secure settings, the user's password is no more secure than the security implemented by the least secure participating Passport site.

Despite these shortcomings, there are many uses for Passport. Web sites that use Passport for user customization or sites that do not store personal information are particularly well-suited for Passport authentication. In fact, it is beneficial for sites such as these to use Passport authentication rather than giving a user yet another username and password to have to remember. Many Web developers are not qualified to create secure account management features, and in these cases, Passport is a more secure option.

But for Web sites with sensitive financial and personal information, you should carefully consider the risks of Passport or any single sign-on mechanism. The Citibank example in Figure 2.13 says that after authenticating with .NET Passport, you'll be asked to enter another password. Although this is a good security measure and makes up for many of Passport's shortcomings, it makes me wonder why anyone would even bother with a single sign-on solution if you are going to make the user remember another password anyway.

TIP

Even if you do not use Passport on your site, you might still benefit from using it to help users prove their identity if they ever lose their account credentials for your Web site. Used in combination with the techniques described in Chapter 1, Passport would make for a reasonably strong verification of user identity. For example, if a user forgets her password, you can have her authenticate using Passport and then send her an e-mail with further instructions on how to reset her password for your site. This way you still keep user authentication private but benefit from Passport's centralized authentication features.

Security Policies

■ Avoid using Passport on Web sites that store sensitive financial and personal information.

■ If using Passport on a sensitive site, consider implementing additional methods to authenticate the user.

Blocking Brute-Force Attacks

Summary: **Brute force attacks are difficult to block completely but you can limit their effectiveness**

Threats: **Account hijacking, denial of service, resource starvation**

As we saw in Chapter 1, a brute-force attack is an attempt to discover a password by systematically trying every possible combination of letters, numbers, and symbols until you discover the one correct combination that works. An attacker will always discover a password through a brute-force attack, but the downside is that it could take years to find it. Depending on the password's length and complexity, there could be trillions of possible combinations. To speed things up a bit, a brute-force attack could start with dictionary words or slightly modified dictionary words because most people will use those rather than a totally random password. These attacks are commonly referred to as *dictionary attacks* or *hybrid brute-force attacks*. Brute-force attacks put user accounts at risk and flood your site with unnecessary traffic.

Hackers launch brute-force attacks using widely available tools that utilize wordlists and rule sets to intelligently and automatically guess user passwords. Although such attacks are easy to detect, they are not so easy to prevent. For example, many HTTP brute-force tools can relay requests through a list of open proxy servers. Since each request appears to come from a different IP address, you cannot block attacks simply by blocking the IP address. Thousands of Akamai proxy servers were leveraged in an attack of this nature against a popular e-commerce site right after the turn of the century. To further complicate things, some tools try a different username and password on each attempt, so you can't lock out a single account for failed password attempts.

WARNING

Adult Web sites are notorious targets for brute-force attacks, often seeing hundreds or thousands of unique attacks each day. Many tools are available specifically for launching brute-force attacks against adult Web sites. One technique hackers use is to collect large lists of username and password combos. The logic is that if a person has an account on one adult Web site, there is a good chance that person has an account at another site and might be using the same password on both sites. Tools such as Combomania (available at www.securibox.net/phpBB2/dload.php?action=viewall) scour the Internet for username and password combos to quickly build combo lists. Although tools like Combomania were designed to hack adult Web sites, the concept applies to all types of Web sites.

Locking Accounts

The most obvious way to block brute-force attacks is to simply lock out accounts after a defined number of incorrect password attempts. Account lockouts can last a specific duration, such as one hour, or the accounts could remain locked until manually unlocked by an administrator. But account lockout is not the best solution, because someone could easily abuse it and lock out hundreds of user accounts. In fact, some Web sites are attacked so much that they are unable to enforce a lockout policy because they would constantly be unlocking customer accounts.

The problems with account lockouts are:

- An attacker can cause a denial of service (DoS) by locking out large numbers of accounts.

- Because you cannot lock out an account that doesn't exist, only valid account names will lock. An attacker could use this fact to harvest usernames from the site, depending on realized error responses.

- An attacker can cause a diversion by locking out many accounts and flooding the help desk with support calls.

- An attacker can continuously lock out the same account, even seconds after it is unlocked by an administrator, effectively disabling the account.

- Account lockout is ineffective against slow attacks that try only a few passwords every hour.

- Account lockout is ineffective against attacks that try one password against a large list of usernames.

- Account lockout is ineffective if the attacker is using a username/password combo list and guesses correctly on the first couple of attempts.

- Powerful accounts such as administrator accounts often bypass lockout policy, but these are the most desirable accounts to attack. Some systems lock out administrator accounts only on network-based logins.

- Even once an account is locked out, the attack may continue, consuming valuable human and computational resources.

Account lockout is sometimes effective, but only in controlled environments or in cases where the risk is so great that even continuous DoS attacks are preferable to account compromise. In most cases, however, account lockout is not the best option for stopping brute-force attacks. Consider, for example, an auction site on which several bidders are fighting over the same item. If the auction Web site enforced account lockouts, one bidder could simply lock the others' accounts in the last minute of the auction, preventing them from submitting any winning bids. The same technique could be used to block critical financial transactions or e-mail communications.

> **WARNING**
>
> When I talk to administrators and developers about the problems with account lockouts, their first response is to suggest increasing the number of failed attempts before locking the account. This solution does prevent someone from accidentally locking out an account, but even if you allow 20 attempts, it is simple for an attacker to lock out an account. Another suggestion I hear is to decrease the lockout time to just a few minutes. In fact, Microsoft's Passport uses this strategy. Although this solution does limit brute-force attacks, it doesn't completely prevent DoS attacks, because an attacker can simply lock your account again after the few minutes pass. Ultimately, you have to decide yourself what works best for your Web site.

Finding Other Countermeasures

As described, account lockouts are not always practical solutions, but because of the automated nature of brute-force attacks, there are other things you can do. First, since the success of the attack is dependent on time, an easy solution is to randomly inject pauses when checking a password. Adding even a few seconds' pause can greatly slow a brute-force attack but will not bother most legitimate users as they log in to their accounts. The code in Figure 2.14 (C#) and Figure 2.15 (VB.NET) shows an example of how to implement this pause using an HTTP module.

Figure 2.14 Password Authentication Delay: C#

```
private void AuthenticateRequest(object obj, EventArgs ea)
    {
        HttpApplication objApp = (HttpApplication) obj;
        HttpContext objContext = (HttpContext) objApp.Context;
        // If user identity is not blank, pause for a random amount of time
        if ( objApp.User.Identity.Name != "")
    {
        Random rand = new Random();
        Thread.Sleep(rand.Next(minSeconds, maxSeconds) * 1000);
    }
    }
```

Figure 2.15 Password Authentication Delay: VB.NET

```
Public Sub AuthenticateRequest(ByVal obj As Object, ByVal ea As
    System.EventArgs)
  Dim objApp As HttpApplication
  Dim objContext As HttpContext
  Dim ran As Random
  objApp = obj
  objContext = objApp.Context

  ' If user identity is not blank, pause for a random amount of time
  If objApp.User.Identity.Name <> "" Then
    ran = New Random
    Thread.Sleep(ran.Next(ran.Next(minSeconds, maxSeconds) * 1000))
  End If
End Sub
```

Note that although adding a delay could slow a single-threaded attack, it is less effective if the attacker sends multiple simultaneous authentication requests.

Another solution is to lock out an IP address with multiple failed logins. The problem with this solution is that you could inadvertently block large groups of users by blocking a proxy server used by an ISP or large company. Another problem is that many tools utilize proxy lists and send only a few requests from each IP address before moving on to the next. Using widely available open proxy lists at Web sites such as http://tools.rosinstrument.com/proxy/, an attacker could easily circumvent any IP blocking mechanism. Because most sites do not block after just one failed password, an attacker can use two or three attempts per proxy. If the attacker has a list of 1,000 proxies, he can attempt 2,000 or 3,000 passwords without being blocked. Nevertheless, despite this method's weaknesses, many Web sites—adult Web sites in particular—do choose to block proxy IP addresses because they are so often attacked. Companies such as Pennywize (www.pennywize.com) offer solutions to help block brute-force attacks.

One simple yet surprisingly effective solution is to simply design your Web site to not use predictable behavior for failed passwords. For example, most Web sites return an "HTTP 401 error" code with a password failure, but some sites instead return an "HTTP 200 SUCCESS" code but direct the user to a page explaining the failed password attempt. This fools some automated systems, but it is also easy to circumvent. A better solution might be to vary the behavior enough to eventually discourage all but the most dedicated hackers. You could, for example, use different error messages each time or sometimes let a user through to a page and then prompt him again for a password.

TIP

Some automated brute-force tools allow the attacker to set certain trigger strings to look for that indicate a failed password attempt. For example, if the resulting page contains the phrase "Bad username or password," the tool would know the credentials failed and would try the next in the list. A simple way to fool these tools is to also include those phrases as comments in the HTML source of the page they get when they successfully authenticate.

After one or two failed login attempts, prompt the user not only for the username and password but also to answer a secret question. This not only causes problems with automated attacks, it prevents an attacker from gaining access, even if they do get the username and password correct. You could also detect high numbers of attacks systemwide and under those conditions prompt all users for the answer to their secret questions.

Other techniques you might want to consider are:

- For advanced users who want to protect their accounts from attack, give them the option to allow login only from certain IP addresses.

- Assign unique login URLs to blocks of users so that not all users can access the site from the same URL.

- Use a CAPTCHA to prevent automated attacks (see the sidebar "Using CAPTCHAs").

- Instead of completely locking down an account, place it in a lockdown mode with limited capabilities.

Most of these techniques can sometimes be circumvented, but by combining several techniques, you can protect your site from many brute-force attacks. It might be difficult to stop an attacker who is determined to specifically obtain a password on your site, but these techniques certainly can be effective against many attackers, including just about all novice attackers. These techniques also require more work on the attacker's part, which gives you more opportunity to detect the attack and maybe even identify the attacker. Intrusion detection systems provide realized value in situations such as these.

Hacking the Code...

Using CAPTCHAS

A *completely automated public Turing test to tell computers and humans apart,* or CAPTCHA, is a program that allows you to distinguish between humans and computers. First widely used by Alta Vista to prevent automated search submissions, CAPTCHAs are particularly effective in stopping any kind of automated abuse, including brute-force attacks. They work by presenting some test that is easy for humans to pass but difficult for computers to pass; therefore, they can conclude with some certainty whether there is a human on the other end.

For a CAPTCHA to be effective, humans must be able to answer the test correctly as close to 100 percent of the time as possible. Computers must fail as close to 100 percent of the time as possible. Ez-gimpy (www.captcha.net/cgi-bin/ez-gimpy), perhaps the most commonly used CAPTCHA, presents the user with an obscured word that the user must type to pass the test. But researchers have since written pattern recognition programs that solve ez-gimpy with 92 percent accuracy. Although these researchers have not made their programs public, all it takes is one person to do so to make ez-gimpy mostly ineffective. Researchers at Carnegie Mellon's School of Computer Science continually work to improve and introduce new CAPTCHAs (see www.captcha.net/captchas).

If you are developing your own CAPTCHA, keep in mind that it is not how hard the question is that matters—it is how likely it is that a computer will get the correct answer. I once saw a CAPTCHA with a picture of three zebras, and the user was presented with a multiple-choice question asking how many zebras were in the picture. To answer the question, you clicked one of three buttons. Although it would be very difficult for a computer program to both understand the question and interpret the picture, the program could just randomly guess any answer and get it correct 30 percent of the time. Although this might seem a satisfactory level of risk, it is by no means an effective CAPTCHA. If you run a free e-mail service and use a CAPTCHA such as this to prevent

Continued

spammers from creating accounts in bulk, all they have to do is write a script to automatically create 1,000 accounts and expect on average that 333 of those attempts will be successful.

Nevertheless, a simple CAPTCHA may still be effective against brute-force attacks. When you combine the chance of an attacker sending a correct username and password guess with the chance of guessing the CAPTCHA correctly, combined with other techniques described in this chapter, even a simple CAPTCHA could prove effective.

Although brute-force attacks are difficult to stop completely, they are easy to detect because each failed login attempt records an HTTP 401 status code in your Web server logs. It is important to monitor your log files for brute-force attacks—in particular the intermingled 200 status codes that mean the attacker found a valid password.

Here are conditions that could indicate a brute-force attack or other account abuse:

- Many failed logins from the same IP address

- Logins with multiple usernames from the same IP address

- Logins for a single account coming from many different IP addresses

- Excessive usage and bandwidth consumption from a single use

- Failed login attempts from alphabetically sequential usernames or passwords

- Logins with a referring URL of someone's mail or IRC client

- Referring URLs that contain the username and password in the format http://user:password@www.*example*.com/login.htm

- If protecting an adult Web site, referring URLs of known password-sharing sites

- Logins with suspicious passwords hackers commonly use, such as own-syou (ownzyou), washere (wazhere), zealots, hacksyou, and the like (see www.securibox.net/phpBB2/viewtopic.php?t=8563)

Security Policies

- Use account lockout policies only in controlled environments or where the risk of a compromised account is greater than the risk of continual DoS attacks.

- Insert random delays in the authentication process to slow brute-force attacks.

- Consider blocking IP addresses with multiple failed login attempts, but take into consideration the impact of blocking a proxy used by multiple clients.

- Vary responses to both failed and successful password authentication.

- Ask users to answer their secret questions after seeing multiple failed logins.

- Provide user options to limit account login to specific IP addresses.

- Use unique login URLs for different blocks of users.

- Use a CAPTCHA to prevent automated attacks.

- Limit an account's capabilities if an attack is suspected.

Authorizing Users

Once you have verified a user's identity, you must determine whether that user has access to the requested resource. Authorizing a user is the process of verifying a user's rights to access a resource. Perhaps the greatest security improvements in ASP.NET are in the area of user authorization. In this section, we will cover:

- Deciding how to authorize

- Configuring file authorization

- Implementing URL authorization

- Authorizing through code

Deciding How to Authorize

Summary: **In-depth authorization strategies are the basis for sound application security**

Threats: **Unauthorized access, privilege escalation**

Classic ASP had no built-in authorization features—you either handled it entirely with custom code or let the underlying operating system handle it with little interaction from your ASP code. ASP.NET introduces a robust authorization infrastructure with so many new features and concepts that it is almost overwhelming to users who are new to ASP.NET.

Unfortunately, this robustness could be intimidating enough to cause some to avoid learning and implementing these features, but it is critical that you understand ASP.NET authorization to be able to build a solid security groundwork for your applications.

ASP.NET applications will work fine without any authorization, and some developers might not understand the need for authorization once the user has been authenticated. In fact, many ASP applications simply imply that users are authorized because they are authenticated. For example, Web sites commonly have an admin area for site maintenance and other privileged functions. To gain access to these functions, you provide an administrative username and password. The drawback is that this method either allows all access or denies all access. Authorization allows you to granularly define roles and the way those roles can interact with your application's operations or resources. Authentication concerns allowing access, but authorization precisely defines what access is allowed.

Identities, Principals, and Roles

Authentication is a key part of authorization. Before allowing or denying permissions to a user, you first must know the identity of that user. The .NET Framework represents users with *identity* and *principal* objects. A principal object corresponds to a user and contains an identity object that represents that user's details. Users can be categorized into different groups, or *roles*, such as administrators and users.

The principal object implements the *IPrincipal* interface that allows you to check role membership and provides an *IIdentity* object:

```
public interface IPrincipal
{

   bool IsInRole(string role);
   IIdentity Identity {get;}

}
```

The *Identity* object implements the *IIdentity* interface and provides additional details of the user's identity:

```
public interface IIdentity
{

   string authenticationType {get;}
   bool IsAuthenticated {get;}
   string Name {get;}

}
```

The .NET Framework contains several objects that implement the *IPrincipal* and *IIdentity* interfaces. The objects you use depend on which method you use to authenticate users. Table 2.1 shows which objects to use for different authentication scenarios. Note that in addition to these built-in objects, you can also create and manage your own custom principal and identity objects.

Table 2.1 Authentication Types with Associated Principal and Identity Objects

Authentication Method	Principal Object	Identity Object	Credentials	Roles
Forms	GenericPrincipal	FormsIdentity	Stored in web.config or custom authentication code	Established with custom code
Windows	GenericPrincipal	WindowsIdentity	Provided by underlying operating system or domain	Windows or Active Directory Groups
Passport	GenericPrincipal	PassportIdentity	.NET Passport	Established based on custom groups of Passport users

Roles and Resources

There are two basic approaches to user authorization in ASP.NET: role-based and resource-based. *Role-based access control (RBAC)* authorizes users based on membership in logical groups, or roles. *Resource-based authorization*, similar discretionary access control (DAC), works by granting or revoking access on individual resources based on individual users or groups. In many ways these two approaches are similar, but the primary difference is that resource-based authorization is specific to tangible resources and is specific to users and groups on the underlying operating system or network. Role-based authorization is more abstract and is independent of the operating system or its resources.

Therefore, resource-based authorization is similar to applying a discretionary access control list (DACL) granting BUILTIN\Users Read access to the c:\inetpub\wwwroot\members\ directory and its files. Role-based authorization is similar to granting members, through code or the web.config file, permission to access the Members application. Resource-based authorization depends on how Windows defines the BUILTIN\Users group and the physical location of the Members directory. Role-based authorization depends on the way the application defines the Members role and the Members application.

Because role-based authorization is more abstract and independent of the underlying infrastructure, it provides more flexibility and scalability than resource-based authorization. Even so, it is common to implement resource-based authorization as a means of implementing role-based authorization. The abstraction of role-based authorization also makes it a natural representation of an organization's structures, rules, and processes.

TIP

With role-based authorization, you can easily enable or disable application functions based on role membership. For example, you might want to provide an Advanced User role and provide enhanced user interface options for members of that role. Further, you could establish a Locked Down role for user accounts suspected of security breaches and disable certain account operations while users are members of that role.

In ASP.NET, there are several approaches to role-based authorization, which are described in more detail later in this chapter:

- URL authorization

- Declarative user-based security

- Imperative user-based security

- Explicit role checks

Security Policies

- Implement strong authorization groundwork early in the application design.

- Develop a solid role-based authorization scheme.

- Use resource-based authorization to enhance role-based authorization.

- Always use multiple layers of role-based and resource-based authorization.

Employing File Authorization

Summary: **File authorization provides a layered and granular approach to security**

Threats: **Unauthorized access, privilege escalation**

File authorization is the process of allowing access to file resources by setting appropriate access control lists (ACLs) to Web content files. There is nothing to configure in ASP.NET, and in fact every ASP.NET application automatically uses file authorization; you cannot turn it off. File authorization is not controlled by ASP.NET but is a function of the NTFS file system.

You may wonder, therefore, why ASP.NET even provides a file authorization module if it is already handled by the operating system. The reasons ASP.NET includes file authorization are:

- Impersonation is not required for file authorization to work. The operating system therefore only sees the file request coming from the context of the ASP.NET process. ASP.NET handles the appropriate access checks for the requesting user.

- ASP.NET may not access the file directly but instead accesses the compiled assembly for the file.

■ Because ASP.NET checks the NTFS permissions, it is able to handle and recover from any security exceptions due to failed access.

You configure file authorization by accessing the security properties of the file in Windows Explorer, using a tool such as xcacls.exe, through security templates, or through Group Policy. Because ASP.NET enforces file authorization based on file ACLs, it requires a valid Windows identity; therefore, it works only with Windows authentication. In fact, if no *WindowsIdentity* is associated with the request, it will not perform any access check at all. The same is true for any file types not mapped to ASP.NET. IIS and the underlying operating system will, however, still perform these checks. It is thus important that you understand the security context of the threads that will access files so that you can set appropriate permissions.

It is valuable to always use some form of file authorization, even if you don't have a complete understanding of ACLs and security contexts. *At a minimum, you should allow users only read access to Web content.* NTFS provides many granular settings; the more you take advantage of these settings, the more robust your application's security becomes.

TIP

Every object in Windows has three ACLs: one for itself, one to pass on to child objects (files), and one to pass on to child containers (directories). One technique for achieving extra-tight security is to set the inheritable permissions on a directory so that new child objects have little or no access. This forces you to explicitly set NTFS permissions for all new files and directories, but it also restricts access if an attacker is somehow able to create a new file or directory.

Although file authorization is resource-based access control, you can also take advantage of Windows or Active Directory groups to implement a role-based strategy.

Security Policies

■ Always set restricted NTFS permissions on Web content files, even if not using Windows authentication and file authorization.

- Use file authorization to implement both resource-based and role-based security.

- Apply specific and detailed NTFS permissions to increase application security.

- Users should only be allowed read access to Web content.

Applying URL Authorization

URL authorization is a mechanism to control access based on the user, role, resource, or HTTP verb used. URL authorization is based on the principal associated with the request, so it works with any form of authentication. It also allows setting restrictions for unauthenticated users.

URL authorization is an effective means of enforcing least privilege to a Web application by precisely defining who can access what and how. You can configure URL authentication by editing the web.config for the application you want to protect. Each application's web.config will override the settings of any parent applications.

Users and Roles

The following section from a web.config file is an example of URL authorization:

```
<authorization>
   <deny users="?"/>
   <allow users="*"/>
</authorization>
```

Note that URL authorization uses the question mark (?) to indicate any unauthenticated users and the asterisk (*) to indicate all users. In this example, the code denies any unauthenticated users and allows those who have authenticated. The following examples are all valid formats for identifying users:

```
<allow users="?"/>
<allow users="*"/>
<allow users="Admin"/>
<allow users="Alice, Bob"/>
<allow users="BUILTIN\Administrator"/>
<allow users="Local.Domain\Joe"/>
```

Roles are identified in a similar manner:

```
<allow users="Managers"/>
<allow users="BUILTIN\Administrators"/>
<allow users="Local.Domain\Administrators"/>
```

ASP.NET processes URL authorization settings from the top to the bottom, stopping with the first match it finds and ignoring any subsequent elements. Therefore, you should carefully consider the order of the elements. If you are configuring URL authorization for protected content, there are two basic techniques for controlling access. One technique is to begin by denying unauthenticated users, followed by denying specific users or roles, and ending by allowing all users. The following example demonstrates this method:

```
<authorization>
   <deny users="?"/>
   <deny roles="Expired"/>
   <allow users="*"/>
</authorization>
```

This example basically forces users to authenticate, denies expired users, and allows everyone else. In this example, it is crucial that you deny unauthenticated users with the first line. Otherwise, the configuration would look like this:

```
<authorization>
   <deny roles="Expired"/>
   <allow users="*"/>
</authorization>
```

By not denying unauthenticated users, the system will begin by checking to see if the user is a member of the Expired role. Since the user is not yet authenticated, he or she is not a member of any role, and therefore this element will not match. The next element allows all users, which will match, and they will be allowed access to the application.

Another of the more popular techniques is to deny unauthenticated users, allow specific users or roles, and then deny everyone else:

```
<authorization>
   <deny users="?"/>
   <allow roles="Managers"/>
   <deny users="*"/>
</authorization>
```

This example forces all users to authenticate, allows those users who are Managers to access the application, but denies everyone else. With this method it is crucial that you include the last line that denies all users. If the user does not match any of the authorization elements, he or she is by default granted access, unless the web.config in a parent directory explicitly denies access.

HTTP Verbs

You can also use URL authentication to block certain HTTP verbs. For example, if you have a Web form and want to ensure that users always use the *POST* method, you can do this:

```
<authorization>
  <allow users="*" verbs="POST"/>
  <deny users="*"/>
</authorization>
```

Note that in this example, we allow any requests from any users using the *POST* verb. In the next line we deny all requests from all users. We do this because any verb besides *POST* would not match the first line and therefore would be allowed. In other words, the *allow* element explicitly defines verbs that are allowed, but it does not define verbs that are not allowed. When specifying verbs with the *allow* element, you must always follow it with a *deny* element. The following example accomplishes the same as the previous one:

```
<authorization>
  <allow users="*" verbs="POST"/>
  <deny users="*" verbs="GET, HEAD, DEBUG"/>
</authorization>
```

Note that not specifying the *verbs* attribute is equivalent to allowing or denying all verbs supported by ASP.NET (*GET, HEAD, POST,* and *DEBUG*).

WARNING

You might want to use URL authorization to block CGI vulnerability scanners that use the HTTP *HEAD* verb. Although you can block the scanner from sending *HEAD* requests to files that exist, it will still return a "404 Not Found" error message if the file doesn't exist. Therefore, the scanner simply needs to know that the status code 401 Unauthorized rather than the usual 200 OK means the file exists.

There are some limitations with using URL authorization to restrict HTTP verbs:

■ You cannot specify wildcards in the *verbs* attribute.

■ You easily specify different settings for different types of files (unless you use the location element described later).

■ A blocked verb returns a 401 Unauthorized status code rather than the more correct 405 Method Not Allowed status code. By returning a 401, if a request uses a denied verb, the user will be prompted to enter credentials, but even the correct credentials will return yet another 401 error.

The *HttpMethodNotAllowedHandler* gives you more control over blocking verbs. You can add this handler to your web.config file as shown here:

```
<system.web>
  <httpHandlers>
    <add verb="*"
         path="*.mdb"
         type="System.Web.HttpMethodNotAllowedHandler"/>
  </httpHandlers>
</system.web>
```

This example blocks all verbs to any file with the .mdb extension. Note that for this example to work, the file extension *.mdb must be explicitly mapped to the aspnet_isapi.dll or have a wildcard mapping in the application for aspnet_isapi.dll. The path attribute can contain wildcard characters in any part of the path as follows:

```
<system.web>
  <httpHandlers>
    <add verb="*"
         path="/members/a??/def*.*"
         type="System.Web.HttpForbiddenHandler"/>
  </httpHandlers>
</system.web>
```

It is interesting to note that the *verb* attribute can also handle wildcard characters, unlike the *verbs* attribute that URL authentication uses. The *HttpMethodNotAllowedHandler* does not provide any authorization for particular users; it simply returns a "405 Method Not Allowed" error message for any requests that match the given verb and path. It is useful for flexible blocking of HTTP verbs but does not provide per-user settings. The best approach is to use a combination of the URL authorization *verb* attribute and *HttpMethodNotAllowedHandler*.

Files and Paths

You can also use URL authorization to set restrictions on individual files and paths using the *location* element, as shown here:

```
<configuration>
    <location path="">
      <system.web>
        <authentication mode="Windows"/>
        <authorization>
          <deny users="?"/>
          <allow users="*"/>
        </authorization>
      </system.web>
    </location>
    <location path="default.aspx">
      <system.web>
        <authorization>
          <allow users="*"/>
        </authorization>
      </system.web>
    </location>
</configuration>
```

In this example, the first element leaves the path blank, which refers to the current directory and denies all unauthenticated users from accessing any files in that directory. The second *location* element defines the path to the default.aspx file and allows all users to access that file. This allows unauthenticated users to access a homepage but requires authentication before accessing any other files. It is interesting to note that the order of the location elements has no effect on how they are processed. This is because the default.aspx file is a child of the current application and therefore treats the configuration as a hierarchy. (Configuration hierarchies are explained in more detail later in this chapter.)

You can use *location* elements to completely block access to a specific file:

```
<location path="settings.mdb">
  <system.web>
    <authorization>
      <deny users="*"/>
    </authorization>
  </system.web>
</location>
```

Note that you cannot use wildcards in the path settings, so you can set the location path to either the entire directory or to each individual file you want to have different authorization settings. If you want to completely block all users from accessing a file by wildcard, you can add the following to the web.config file:

```
<system.web>
  <httpHandlers>
    <add verb="*" path="*.mdb" type="System.Web.HttpForbiddenHandler"/>
  </httpHandlers>
</system.web>
```

For this example to work, the file extension *.mdb must be explicitly mapped to the aspnet_isapi.dll or have a wildcard mapping in the application for aspnet_isapi.dll. The *path* and *verb* attributes both support wildcards such as *HttpMethodNotAllowedHandler* already mentioned. See the <httpHandlers> section in the machine.config file for examples of how ASP.NET uses *HttpForbiddenHandler* to block certain file extensions.

TIP

In addition to *HttpForbiddenHandler* and *HttpMethodNotAllowedHandler* we've mentioned, ASP.NET provides two others: *HttpNotFoundHandler* and *HttpNotImplementedHandler*.

Configuration Hierarchy

With ASP.NET, you can create a web.config file for an application and a unique web.config for each child application. In addition, a machine.config handles global settings for all applications. When handling authorization, ASP.NET handles the various config files cumulatively, starting with the lowest-level child application. In other words, it checks the authorization section from the web.config file of the current application. If there is no match, it checks the authorization section of the machine.config files in any parent applications, eventually ending up in the machine.config file, which, by default, allows access to all verbs and all users. ASP.NET treats the various config files as if you appended the authorization sections from each, starting at the current level and working your way up.

To avoid unintentionally allowing access to a user, it is always a good practice to end each authorization with an element either allowing or denying all users. When ASP.NET encounters this line, it always matches and does not process any more authorization elements. The one exception to this rule is if you want to make one application have a subset of the parent application's authorization settings. In this case, you should carefully plan the parent configuration to prevent unintended access.

TIP

You can prevent a child application from overriding a parent's configuration by adding the *allowOverride="false"* attribute to the location element.

Security Policies

- Use URL authorization to limit access to Web site resources.

- Block unused HTTP verbs using the *verbs* attribute or *HttpMethodNotAllowedHandler*.

- Use *HttpForbiddenHandler* or *HttpNotFoundHandler* to block everyone's access to certain files.

Authorizing Users Through Code

The most flexible aspect of ASP.NET authorization is the ability to authorize users programmatically. There are three ways you can accomplish this task:

- Declarative authorization
- Imperative authorization
- Explicit authorization

Declarative Authorization

Declarative security allows you to set permission demands at the class level as well as on individual methods, properties, or events. You do this by setting an attribute, as shown in Figure 2.16 (C#) and Figure 2.17 (VB.NET), where the methods only allow access to members of the local Administrators group.

Figure 2.16 Declarative Security: C#

```
[PrincipalPermissionAttribute(SecurityAction.Demand, Role=@"
BUILTIN\Administrators ")]
public DoSomething
{
}
```

Figure 2.17 Declarative Security: VB.NET

```
<PrincipalPermissionAttribute(SecurityAction.Demand, Role:=
"BUILTIN\Administrators")> _
Public Sub DoSomething()
End Sub
```

Declarative security has the advantage of conveniently setting permissions on selective members or on the class as a whole with a single attribute. The .NET Framework checks declarative security immediately before invoking a method, before it runs any code.

Imperative Authorization

Declarative security allows you to set permissions on a class or its members, whereas imperative security allows you to demand permission from within your code. Figure 2.18 (C#) and Figure 2.19 (VB.NET) demonstrate imperative security.

Figure 2.18 Imperative Security: C#

```
public DoSomething()
{
   PrincipalPermission ppCheck = new PrincipalPermission(null,"Admins");
   ppCheck.Demand();
   // Admin code
}
```

Figure 2.19 Imperative Security: VB.NET

```
Sub DoSomething()
   Dim Perm As New PrincipalPermission(Nothing, "Admins", True)
   Perm.Demand()
   // Admin code
End Sub
```

Explicit Authorization

Similar to using imperative security, you can explicitly check for role membership using the *IPrincipal.IsInRole* method. The primary difference between imperative security and explicitly checking role membership is that you can check role membership within your code as an *If-Then* statement without raising exceptions when access fails. This method is useful, for example, when you're enabling or disabling features based on the current user's role, as shown in Figure 2.20 (C#) and Figure 2.21 (VB.NET).

Figure 2.20 Explicit Authorization: C#

```
If (User.IsInRole("Admins")
{
    Response.Write("<a href=/admin.aspx>Admin Menu</a>");
}
```

Figure 2.21 Explicit Authorization: VB.NET

```
If User.IsInRole("Admins") then
  Response.Write("<a href=/admin.aspx >Admin Menu</a>")
End If
```

Code-based authorization allows you to enforce granular security checks throughout your application. For the best protection, use a combination of declarative, imperative, and explicit authorization techniques.

Security Policies

- Use declarative, imperative, and explicit role checks to provide multiple layers of authorization.

- If utilizing the .NET Framework, you should implement robust declarative authorization techniques.

Coding Standards Fast Track

Authenticating Users

Building Login Forms

- ☑ Always use SSL for transmitting user credentials.
- ☑ Always use the HTTP *POST* method for transmitting user credentials.
- ☑ All form input must be validated against SQL injection and cross-site-scripting attacks.
- ☑ Do not rely on hidden form fields to transfer sensitive data.
- ☑ Use the same error message for failed username or failed password; do not reveal any other information in an error message.

Using Forms Authentication

- ☑ If possible, keep authenticated users on an SSL connection to prevent cookie hijacking.
- ☑ Avoid storing credentials in the web.config file, but if you do so, at least use MD5 or SHA-1 hashes.
- ☑ Configure the site so that all protected resources are handled by ASP.NET using wildcard application mappings.

Using Windows Authentication

- ☑ Always use SSL with basic authentication.
- ☑ Isolate protected and unprotected content and use unique realms for each.
- ☑ Block privileged users from brute-force attacks by preventing them from authenticating.

Using Passport Authentication

- ☑ Use the strongest security settings available when using Passport authentication.

Blocking Brute-Force Attacks

☑ Carefully consider the benefits and risks of an account lockout policy.

☑ Insert random delays in the authentication process to slow brute-force attacks.

☑ Vary responses to both failed and successful password authentication, varying the HTTP status code and the error message text.

☑ Ask users to answer their secret questions after seeing multiple failed logins.

☑ Provide advanced users the option to limit account login to specific IP addresses.

☑ Use unique login URLs for different blocks of users.

☑ Consider using a CAPTCHA after a predefined number of failed logins.

☑ Provide the capability to selectively limit features or temporarily suspend an account without having to completely shut down a user.

Authorizing Users

Deciding How to Authorize

☑ Build the application around well-defined security roles.

☑ Set strict file ACLs and enforce other authorization limitations so that you can identify these settings early in the development process.

Employing File Authorization

☑ Set restricted NTFS permissions on Web content files, even if you're not using Windows authentication and file authorization.

☑ Use file authorization to implement both resource-based and role-based security.

☑ Apply specific and detailed NTFS permissions to increase application security.

Applying URL Authorization

- ☑ For protected content, always start the authorization section with *<deny users="?"/>*.

- ☑ End the authorization section with *<deny users="*">* or *<allow users="*">*.

- ☑ If you're using the *verbs* attribute with allow elements, always follow it with a *deny* element.

- ☑ Use *HttpForbiddenHandler* or *HttpNotFoundHandler* to block everyone's access to certain files.

- ☑ Carefully plan the web.config hierarchy to avoid unintentionally allowing access to files.

Authorizing Users Through Code

- ☑ Use declarative, imperative, and explicit role checks to provide multiple layers of authorization.

Code Audit Fast Track

Authenticating Users

Building Login Forms

- ☑ Does the login form transmit data across a secure connection?
- ☑ Does the login form use the HTTP *POST* method instead of *GET*?
- ☑ Does the application validate the login form input?
- ☑ Does the form reveal sensitive information through hidden form fields?
- ☑ Do error messages reveal too much information?

Using Forms Authentication

- ☑ Does the web.config file contain user credentials when other alternatives would be more secure?
- ☑ Does the web.config file contain cleartext user credentials?

☑ Does the web.config file use the most secure settings for cookies?

Using Windows Authentication

☑ If you're using basic authentication, is the traffic encrypted with SSL?

☑ Does the site design allow credentials to be sent when moving from an SSL page to an unencrypted page?

☑ Can an attacker launch brute-force attacks against privileged accounts?

☑ Can an attacker relay brute-force attacks from the Web server to other systems?

Using Passport Authentication

☑ Is Passport authentication sufficient given the nature of the Web site?

Blocking Brute-Force Attacks

☑ Does the site enforce account lockout? What risks are involved with this policy?

☑ Does the site have any features to slow brute-force attacks?

☑ Does the site have any features to fool automated brute-force tools?

☑ Does the site have any features to stop automated attacks, such as asking for a secret question or using a CAPTCHA?

☑ Does the application provide advanced user settings to restrict access to an account?

☑ Does the application have any way to limit or suspend an account suspected of abuse?

Authorizing Users

Deciding How to Authorize

☑ Does the system have a solid roles-based security framework?

☑ Does the system use multiple layers of authentication?

Employing File Authorization

☑ Does the system define the minimum NTFS file permissions required to run the application?

☑ Does the system use file authorization to implement both resource-based and role-based security?

Applying URL Authorization

☑ Does the authorization section of the web.config for protected content start by denying unauthenticated users?

☑ Does the authorization section end with a default rule allowing all or denying all users?

☑ Are all *allow* verb elements followed with *deny* verb elements?

☑ Does the application use *HttpForbiddenHandler* or *HttpNotFoundHandler* to block everyone's access to certain files?

Authorizing Users Through Code

☑ Does the application use declarative, imperative, and explicit role checks to provide multiple layers of authorization?

Frequently Asked Questions

The following Frequently Asked Questions, answered by the authors of this book, are designed to both measure your understanding of the concepts presented in this chapter and to assist you with real-life implementation of these concepts. To have your questions about this chapter answered by the author, browse to **www.syngress.com/solutions** and click on the **"Ask the Author"** form. You will also gain access to thousands of other FAQs at ITFAQnet.com.

Frequently Asked Questions

Q: I have configured my web.config file to use forms authentication and deny unauthenticated users, but it doesn't redirect me to the login form when I access protected content.

A: Check the properties of the application in the Internet Services Manager to be sure that anonymous access is disabled. If anonymous access is enabled, IIS will never attempt to authenticate the user.

Q: Instead of using HTTP modules shown in this chapter, can I use the *Application_OnAuthenticateRequest* event in the global.asax file?

A: You do not need to create an HTTP module to handle global ASP.NET events. You can also add event handlers to global.asax. HTTP modules are much like binary versions of global.asax.

Q: I have my site configured for Windows authentication, and I enter the correct password, but it keeps prompting me to enter the password again.

A: There may be various reasons for this. First, make sure that you include the principal with the username in the format *domain\username* or *localsystem\username*. Also be sure that the user account you are using has NTFS permissions to access the Web content.

Q: What is the difference between the different HTTP error handlers such as *HttpMethodNotAllowedHandler* and *HttpForbiddenHandler*?

A: The difference is the HTTP status code it returns: *HttpForbiddenHandler* returns a 403, *HttpNotFoundHandler* returns a 404, *HttpMethodNotAllowedHandler* returns a 405, and *HttpNotImplementedHandler* returns a 501.

Chapter 3

Managing Sessions

Solutions in this Chapter:

- **Maintaining State**
- **Using ASP.NET Tokens**

- ☑ **Coding Standards Fast Track**
- ☑ **Code Audit Fast Track**
- ☑ **Frequently Asked Questions**

Introduction

For many Web sites, the user experience depends on the continuity of the user session. Since HTTP is a connectionless protocol, it is usually up to the Web developer to maintain some form of session persistence. When users browse through a Web site, they usually access multiple pages with different content on each page. Initially they visit one page, browse the contents of that page, then visit another page and continue until they are finished using that Web site. At that point they either close their browser or keep the browser open and continue on to a different Web site. To the user, it appears as one continuous session with the Web site they visit. But behind the scenes, the process is very different.

For each page visit, the browser makes several requests of the server for those elements required to render the page in the browser window. After retrieving those elements, the client closes the connection with the server. When retrieving the next page, the browser repeats the process, but the server has no idea that this request is connected to the previous request.

For that reason, the server needs to issue some kind of unique token that the browser can present with each visit to know which sessions are related. A *token* is an identifying string that is unique to each session. Using these session tokens, the server can treat a series of disconnected requests as if they were one continuous connection.

A server can assign two basic types of tokens:

- Session tokens
- Authentication tokens

Session Tokens

Session tokens create continuity between HTTP requests. A session token's life usually begins with the first request a client makes to a server and ends either with the client closing the browser or after a specified timeout period. Session tokens are most often maintained through cookies, either as session cookies or persistent cookies, and are often automatically handled by the server application. The purpose of a session token is to track the entire interaction between client and server to provide the appearance of a seamless connection with the server. Session tokens apply to all requests, including anonymous requests.

Web developers use session tokens to maintain user preferences, track session variables, connect multiple forms, and maintain lists such as items in a shopping cart. Session tokens usually take the form of cookies because they provide an easy method to store information about a client.

Session tokens should be secure, but security is normally not critical for basic session management.

Authentication Tokens

Once a user authenticates to the server, rather than asking for credentials with each request, the server issues an *authentication token* that the user can submit with each request to prove his or her identity. The authentication token uniquely identifies an authenticated user. It is important to note that the authentication token is almost as sensitive as the user's actual credentials except that the authentication token has a limited life span.

It is important to distinguish between session and authentication tokens. By keeping them separate, you can better optimize the settings of each and limit exposure to some types of attacks. For example, you can use the built-in ASP.NET state management features for session tokens and use more advanced techniques for authentication tokens.

In order to remain secure, a token must have certain properties. A token must:

- Uniquely identify a client to the server, but not to anyone else

- Not be usable by the client outside the scope of the application

- Not be usable by anyone else

This chapter teaches you how to secure both session and authentication tokens in an ASP.NET application.

Understanding the Threats

The primary threats against token schemes that we address in this chapter are:

- **Token hijacking** Being able to access another user's token and potentially gain access to that user's account.

- **Account hopping** Manipulating an existing token to gain access to another user's account.

- **Session fixation** Providing another user with a known fixed token to authenticate and then gaining access to that user's session.

- **Token prediction** Guessing or predicting a valid session token because the token scheme uses a sequential or predictable pattern.

- **Token brute-force attacks** Discovering a valid session token by submitting all possible combinations within the token's key space.

- **Token keep-alive** The process of periodically sending Web requests to keep a session token from expiring; often used with session fixation attacks.

- **Token manipulation** Modifying a token on the URL or in a cookie to gain unauthorized access to an application.

- **Cross-site scripting** An attack that involves injecting HTML or script commands into a trusted application with the purpose of hijacking a user's cookie, session token, or account credentials.

- **Information leakage** Improper token mechanisms may leak information about users or user configurations.

- **Phishing** A form of man-in-the-middle attack in which the attacker lures a legitimate user to enter a password through a fake e-mail or Web form designed to look like that of a legitimate Web site.

The trouble with token schemes is that it is very difficult to design one that perfectly assures you that the token is from a legitimate user login and not an attacker. For example, a user might have a valid token, but it could be coming from a hacker who somehow discovered the token. You can determine if the token is coming from the same IP address to which you issued the token, but it might not actually be coming from the user's computer, because that IP address could be a firewall or shared proxy server. Even if you do determine that the request is coming from the user's computer, it might not be coming from the user's login session. And even if you do determine *that*, it might not be coming from the user's browser but instead from a Trojan, a virus, or a worm. And if you determine that it is coming from the user's browser, the user might not have intended to send it but was the victim of a phishing or cross-site scripting attack. Finally, you don't know if it is even the real user at the other end; it could be a coworker who knows the user's credentials or who is using the browser session of a user who is out to lunch.

It is entirely possible with our current technology to create a mechanism that almost completely deals with these issues, but then new issues arise of compatibility, user acceptance, deployment, user training, developer training, and infrastructure support. Consequently, most Web applications end up with vulnerable token schemes saved as cleartext cookies sent over an unsecured connection. This chapter demonstrates how to get the most out of cookie security.

Maintaining State

ASP.NET greatly simplifies the process of managing both session and authentication tokens. A developer can use the default ASP.NET session management features or expand on those to provide more robust and secure token management features. In this section, we will cover:

- Designing a secure token
- Selecting a token mechanism
- Using state providers

Designing a Secure Token

Summary: **To be secure, a token must meet certain criteria**
Threats: **Session hijacking, account hijacking, session fixation, information leakage**

Web developers have long used session and authentication tokens in their Web applications. However, lack of understanding of session management has led to the compromise of many Web applications. It is important to keep session tokens secure, but it's even more important to keep authentication tokens secure. For an authentication token to be secure, it should pass a number of tests, as outlined in the following sections.

Is the Token Tightly Bound to the User's Session?

This is the most common failure of tokens, often allowing attackers to hijack another user's session by manipulating a token. Most token schemes have no binding to a particular user, relying on the assumption that possession of the token is proof of ownership.

Does the Server Transmit the Token to the Client in a Secure Manner?

Essentially, this means using SSL or IPSec to encrypt the traffic when sending the token. If the traffic is not encrypted, the token could be visible to others. When you use a cookie, it is important to mark it as secure so that the client's browser handles it properly.

Does the Application Use a Sufficiently Large Keyspace?

To prevent brute-force attacks on the session token, you should use a large enough token to ensure that an attacker cannot easily come across a valid token. For example, a 128-bit number allows for 340,282,366,920,938,463,463,374,607,431,768,211,456 (or 2^{128}) possible unique session tokens.

Does the Application Use a Strong Random-Number Generator for Tokens?

A strong random-number generator ensures that a token utilizes the available keyspace and does so in an unpredictable manner. It is impossible for a computer to generate a truly random number, but many pseudo-random-number generators are good enough that you cannot easily reproduce the same results twice.

Does the Application Create New tokens for Each Login?

A user should never be allowed to reinstate a session with an old token. Each time the user authenticates, always destroy any old tokens and initiate a new session with a new token.

Will the System Accept Any Token Provided by the Client?

If a system accepts a client-provided token, it could be vulnerable to what is called a *session fixation attack*. With this kind of attack, the attacker sends the victim a URL that contains a session token. The victim clicks the URL and enters his or her login credentials, validating the session. The attacker then browses to the site using that same session ID and gains access to the user's account. Not only should you reject such tokens, you should also log them as a security incident.

Is It Possible for a User to Manipulate the Token to Hop to Another Account?

Many Web applications use a weak session token that, when modified, allows an attacker to hop to another authenticated user's account. The token should always be bound to a specific account and session, and you should always avoid sequential or predictable session tokens.

Can the Application Detect a Modified or Invalid Token?

To prevent others from modifying a token to somehow exploit an application, the system should be able to identify a cookie that has been changed from its original state. The application should always be able to identify a token that it did not issue itself or that a user has changed since issuing by using a digital signature or hash of the token.

Does the Token Uniquely Identify the Client?

The token should always be a random number that in no way identifies the client. The token should be a random number generated by the server and stored on the server side in association with the user ID. When the client provides the token to the server, the server looks up that session and identifies the client.

Does the Token Properly Limit Its Scope?

An application should associate a token only within a limited application scope to prevent users from overstepping their bounds or from inadvertently transmitting their tokens across an insecure connection. This is especially important for cookies so that the cookie is not sent when moving from a secure to an insecure page. It also prevents cookie-hijacking attacks from servers with the same domain name.

Does the Token Have Both Relative and Absolute Timeouts?

A session token should be valid for only a short period of time since the user's last request. Because it is possible for a user to keep a token alive indefinitely, tokens should also have an absolute expiration. At this point, all information regarding this token should be destroyed and a new token issued if the session is still active.

Does the Client Store the Token After the Session Ends?

This is a problem because the user may be connecting from a shared computer. The client's browser stores persistent cookies, keeps a history of URLs, and caches visited pages, making this a challenge for all types of tokens.

Does the User Have the Option to Terminate a Session?

Although a session should eventually time out, users should also have the option to terminate sessions themselves. When they do so, all information regarding the token should be destroyed. It is also important that you delete any old sessions from that user who may remain in the database.

Can You Revoke a Token from the Server?

Sometimes you need to revoke a single session or even all sessions due to a security incident. The token must rely on the server for its validity. For example, with the built-in ASP.NET session tokens, the server can only determine if it issued the token based on its hash, but because the server does not maintain a list of sessions, there is no mechanism to revoke a token.

Unfortunately, few token schemes meet all these criteria and in fact, the HTTP protocol itself makes it difficult to meet all these perfectly. Every token method has its weaknesses and no single method is perfect. Moreover, many developers trade security for greater compatibility with their wide range of customers.

Security Policies

- Where possible, use extra measures to bind the token to the client session.
- Transmit tokens using SSL whenever possible.
- Always use a sufficiently large keyspace for session tokens.
- Always use a strong random-number generator for session tokens.
- Never accept new tokens submitted by a client.
- Never include visible plaintext user identifiers in the token.
- Always limit the token's scope to the current application.

- Use both relative and absolute timeouts for tokens.

- Take measures to prevent the client from storing the session token after the session ends.

- Allow users to manually terminate a session.

- Always issue a new token with each session login.

Selecting a Token Mechanism

Summary: **Carefully choose a token mechanism that provides users with the best security**

Threats: **Session hijacking, account hijacking, session fixation, information leakage**

URL-Based Tokens

URL-based tokens are tokens that exist on the URL as part of the URI path or as part of the query string, as shown in these examples:

```
http://www.example.com/inbox.aspx?sessionID=6861636B696E67746865636F6465
http://www.example.org/user.aspx?sid={6861-636B-696E-6774-6865-636F-6465}
http://www.example.net/(o5lmpx45ylxps255o3bxzoib)/Default.aspx
```

This method is perhaps the most common because it is the most universally compatible. The drawback with this method is that it is easy for others to discover your session token. The token may appear in your browser history, your browser cache, or logs of any intermediary proxy servers or filters and can be sniffed by others, provided that it is not secured via SSL, and it will show up as the referrer when you click links to other sites. One old trick that used to work with many free Web-based e-mail systems is to embed an image link that you control in an e-mail and wait for the person to view the message. Once they do, their session token will appear in your Web logs under the referer[sic] field. All you have to do is enter that URL and you have access to that person's account.

If you use URL-based tokens, there is also the risk of users sharing, copying, or bookmarking URLs that contain session tokens. Another problem with URL-based tokens is that they are more susceptible to session fixation attacks because it is easier for an attacker to send you a URL that already contains a session token. (Session fixation attacks are explained in more detail later in this chapter.)

Cookie-Based Tokens

Another common method for communicating tokens is using an HTTP cookie mechanism. Most browsers support cookies, but some users block them for privacy reasons or in the belief that they are a security risk. But an increasing number of Web sites require the use of cookies to authenticate to their sites. The argument of privacy is weak because users are already identifying themselves with their credentials.

Cookies are somewhat more secure than other methods because:

- They are sent as part of the body, which is rarely stored in a log file.
- Session cookies do not persist across browser sessions (unless marked as persistent).
- They have built-in mechanisms for expiration, scope, and using secure connections.

However, cookies do not guarantee immunity from session-hijacking attacks. If not sent over an SSL connection, cookies are still vulnerable to sniffing and man-in-the-middle attacks, and the attacker may be able to physically steal the cookie if he has access to the user's computer. Microsoft introduced an HttpOnly cookie in Internet Explorer 6 Service Pack 1 that stops one specific type of cookie-hijacking attack but does not completely eliminate the problem. Most security problems related to cookies are due to poor security policy and development practices. Later in this chapter, we look at how to properly configure and use cookies for authentication tokens.

ASP.NET forms authentication uses cookie-based tokens, but it also offers the option to use encryption and verification of the session token.

Form-Based Tokens

Some Web sites embed tokens as hidden fields within HTML forms. The browser submits the session token in the request body when moving to a new page. Here is an example of using a token in a hidden form field:

```
<INPUT TYPE="hidden" NAME="sessionID "
VALUE="6861636B696E67746865636F6465">
```

The security of hidden form fields is about the same as cookies, but it does not provide as many features as cookies. Normally this method works best for limited authentication state management, such as using a shopping cart.

ASP.NET provides a form-based mechanism called *ViewState* that enhances the hidden form field technique to include encryption and a more structured storage. *ViewState* overcomes some of the problems of form-based tokens, but it still is not a perfect solution. We look at *ViewState* and some techniques for making it more secure later in this chapter.

The basic obstacle here is that none of these state management techniques was designed for secure token management, nor are they entirely appropriate for that use by themselves. None of these methods provides the robust security and privacy features required for sensitive Web-based applications. To make matters worse, although SSL can compensate for many of these limitations, many large Web sites still fail to use it, and it is very rare to see a Web site utilizing client-side certificates.

Security Policies

- If using URL-based tokens, take extra measures to bind the token to the client session.

- With cookie-based tokens, make sure you follow proper security guidelines.

- Whenever possible, use SSL to help protect authentication tokens.

Using State Providers

Summary: **Properly secure the state provider you select**
Threats: **Session hijacking, account hijacking, session fixation,**
              information leakage

ASP.NET supports three methods for storing session state on the server: in-process, ASP.NET State Service, or SQL Server. The decision to use one method over the other is based on reliability and scalability requirements. In-process state management is similar to what was available with IIS 5 and classic ASP. In-process state management is handled locally within the ASP.NET worker process. It is the fastest of the three, but all session information is lost if IIS or the Web application restarts. The ASP.NET State Service is an external service that maintains state even if IIS restarts, and it can be shared by multiple servers. You can run the ASP.NET State Service locally or on a remote computer. SQL Server state management is the most scalable and reliable solution but the slowest and most difficult to configure.

Securing In-Process State

There is not much to do to customize local state management, but there are a few steps you should take if you are using it. To use in-process state management, edit your web.config file as follows:

```
<sessionState
  mode="InProc"
  cookieless="false"
  timeout="15"
/>
```

If you use in-process state management, be sure to disable the ASP.NET State Service using the Services administrative tool. If you have Windows Server 2003, you can also disable it using this command from a command prompt:

```
C:\>sc config aspnet_state start= disabled
```

Securing the ASP.NET State Service

The ASP.NET State Service is essentially a miniature HTTP server that specifically handles session state *PUTs* and *GETs*. Figure 3.1 shows a packet capture of the type of traffic ASP.NET sends to the service.

Figure 3.1 ASP.NET State Service Packet Capture

```
***AP*** Seq: 0xE6F3358D  Ack: 0x85F6237  Win: 0x4470  TcpLen: 20
0x0000: 00 D0 B7 8F 6A F0 00 A0 24 E6 4C 8E 08 00 45 00    ....j...$.L...E.
0x0010: 00 ED 0A 66 40 00 80 06 DA 97 0A 55 00 63 0A 55    ...f@......U.c.U
0x0020: 00 01 08 72 00 50 E6 F3 35 8D 08 5F 62 37 50 18    ...r.P..5.._b7P.
0x0030: 44 70 CA E1 00 00 50 55 54 20 2F 2F 4C 4D 2F 57    Dp....PUT //LM/W
0x0040: 33 53 56 43 2F 31 2F 52 6F 6F 74 2F 73 74 61 74    3SVC/1/Root/stat
0x0050: 65 2F 46 6F 72 6D 73 28 52 79 6A 6B 41 63 46 59    e/Forms(RyjkAcFY
0x0060: 58 42 70 37 2B 4D 52 78 45 64 70 68 78 64 6E 41    XBp7+MRxEdphxdnA
0x0070: 50 36 63 3D 29 2F 74 76 6C 64 77 74 79 33 79 34    P6c=)/tvldwty3y4
0x0080: 64 79 76 6E 6E 61 32 6E 73 33 76 32 35 35 20 48    dyvnna2ns3v255 H
0x0090: 54 54 50 2F 31 2E 31 0D 0A 48 6F 73 74 3A 20 31    TTP/1.1..Host: 1
0x00A0: 30 2E 38 35 2E 30 2E 31 0D 0A 54 69 6D 65 6F 75    0.85.0.1..Timeou
0x00B0: 74 3A 32 30 0D 0A 43 6F 6E 74 65 6E 74 2D 4C 65    t:20..Content-Le
0x00C0: 6E 67 74 68 3A 33 34 0D 0A 4C 6F 63 6B 43 6F 6F    ngth:34..LockCoo
```

Continued

Figure 3.1 ASP.NET State Service Packet Capture

```
0x00D0:  6B 69 65 3A 30 0D 0A 0D 0A 14 00 00 00 00 01 00    kie:0..........
0x00E0:  01 00 00 00 FF FF FF FF 08 54 65 73 74 49 74 65    .........TestIte
0x00F0:  6D 01 07 57 6F 6F 68 6F 6F 6F FF                   m..Woohooo.
```

The weakness with the ASP.NET State Service is that it uses an unencrypted and unauthenticated connection to the Web server or with anyone else who can reach the open port. Unfortunately, the service has only a limited facility to restrict IP addresses. In fact, all it can do is allow or block all external connections through an undocumented registry setting. This works well if you use the ASP.NET State Service on only one computer, but it will not work in a Web farm. If you run the service for a single local Web server, you can set that key as follows:

- **Key** HKEY_LOCAL_MACHINE\SYSTEM\CurrentControlSet\ Services\aspnet_state\Parameters\

- **Value** AllowRemoteConnection

- **Type** DWORD

- **Settings** 0 to block remote connections, 1 to allow remote connections

To effectively limit access to this service, you must configure an external packet filter or use IPSec rules to restrict (and encrypt) traffic to authorized servers only. Note that you can also use an obscure port for the service to make it more difficult to locate. You can do this with the following registry setting:

- **Key** HKEY_LOCAL_MACHINE\SYSTEM\CurrentControlSet\ Services\aspnet_state\Parameters\

- **Value** Port

- **Type** DWORD

- **Settings** Any unused port number from 1 to 65535

TIP

Note that if you change the default listening port, be sure to make the same change in your web.config file.

To configure ASP.NET to use the state service, set the following in your web.config file:

```
<sessionState
  mode="StateServer"
  stateConnectionString="tcpip=10.185.0.31:3104"
  cookieless="false"
  timeout="15"
/>
```

If you want to further obscure the location and port of the state service, you can encrypt the connection string and save it in the registry with the aspnet_setreg.exe (available at http://support.microsoft.com/default.aspx?scid=329290). To use this tool, enter a command such as this:

```
C:\>aspnet_setreg -k:Software\YourApp\State
-d:stateConnectionString="tcpip=10.185.0.31:3104"
```

After that, change the *stateConnectionString* attribute in your web.config file to this:

```
stateConnectionString
="registry:HKEY_LOCAL_MACHINE\SOFTWARE\YourApp\State\ASPNET_SETREG,
stateConnectionString"
```

Securing SQL Server State Management

To use SQL Server to manage session state, set your web.config file as follows:

```
<sessionState
  mode="StateServer"
  sqlConnectionString="data source=10.185.10.4;Trusted_Connection=yes"
  cookieless="false"
  timeout="15"
/>
```

You must also configure SQL Server with the appropriate tables to save session state. For more information on how to do this, see http://support.microsoft.com/?scid=317604.

After configuring the SQL Server tables, create a new low-privilege account on the database server dedicated to state management. As with the state service configuration, you can use aspnet_setreg.exe to encrypt your database connection string:

```
C:\>aspnet_setreg -k:Software\YourApp\State
-d: sqlConnectionString="data source=10.185.10.4;Trusted_Connection=yes"
```

After that, change the *sqlConnectionString* attribute in your web.config file to this:

```
sqlConnectionString="registry:HKEY_LOCAL_MACHINE\SOFTWARE\YourApp\State\
ASPNET_SETREG, sqlConnectionString"
```

For more information on securing database connections, see Chapter 6 "Accessing Data."

General Settings

The cookieless option tells ASP.NET to add the session token to the URL, rather than using a session cookie. Some flaws with the ASP.NET session tokens might make them inappropriate to use on the URL. ASP.NET will accept any syntactically valid token and therefore is vulnerable to session fixation. It also provides no encryption or hashing to ensure the token originated from the server and that no one has modified it. Cookie-based tokens have the same problems, but they are somewhat easier to control. For session state, ASP.NET uses a session cookie, so the browser should not save this cookie to disk.

The timeout value is the number of minutes to keep the session alive. Keep this number as low as is practical for your application to reduce exposure to session-hijacking attacks.

Security Policies

- If you're not using the ASP.NET Session State service, disable it from the services admin tool.

- If you're using the service, set the *AllowRemoteConnection* registry key if managing state only for the local system.

- If you're using the state service with multiple servers, use IPSec or another packet-filtering mechanism to limit access to the port.

- Set a nonstandard port with the state service.

- With state service or SQL Server state management, always encrypt the connection string using aspnet_setreg.exe.

- Avoid using cookieless tokens.

- Set short cookie timeouts that are appropriate for your application.

Using ASP.NET Tokens

After establishing a method for tracking and managing state, you can focus on the specifics of state management. Neither cookies nor URLs were designed to securely transport session or authentication tokens, but there are some techniques you can employ to protect them from attack.

Using Cookies

Summary: **Cookies were not designed to be secure, but with careful configuration you can help protect them**

Threats: **Session hijacking, account hijacking, session fixation, information leakage**

HTTP cookies are a mechanism to store user state to create the effect of a seamless connection with a Web server. Cookies were designed to handle user preferences and to track session variables, and they do that well. But when it comes to security, some problems do arise. Much of the specification depends on servers, client browsers, and any proxies in between following the rules. Unfortunately, that is not always the case. Furthermore, there is no requirement for the user agent to even accept cookies, although some Web sites will not grant users access if they don't.

Normally, to save a cookie with ASP.NET, you use the *Response.Cookies* collection. However, ASP.NET automatically writes some cookies without you writing any code. If you enable session state, ASP.NET creates a session cookie with a unique token for each user who connects to the server. If you use forms authentication with cookies, ASP.NET also adds a forms authentication token to this cookie.

To access these cookies, you can use the *Response.Cookies* collection. For the forms authentication cookie, the *FormsAuthenticationTicket* object provides access to the cookie properties as well as other properties associated with forms authentication.

Cookies will always be somewhat vulnerable, but some settings limit that vulnerability. The properties that have security significance are:

- Domain
- Path
- Expires
- Secure
- Value

Cookie Domain

The optional domain property of the cookie determines which servers can access the information in the cookie. If this property is left blank, the browser is supposed to allow access to only the host that issued the cookie. However, you might still want to specify this value.

The cookie domain allows access to all hosts that match the domain name, including all subdomains. In other words, it matches from right to left, so the cookie domain set to example.com would match *.example.com. The domain name *must contain a minimum of two dots*, to prevent a server from setting the domain to something like *.com*. Try to be specific as possible on the domain. For example, if you have a host named ro.cker.org and set the cookie domain to *.cker.org,* the hosts cra.cker.org, atta.cker.org, and just.about.any.script.kiddie. ha.cker.org can all access the cookie. This is important because an attacker might be able to find and exploit flaws on these systems to gain access to cookies from the target system. Figures 3.2 and 3.3 demonstrate how to set the domain on all cookies.

In addition to providing a specific host name, you might also want to check the cookie domain you receive. Say, for example, that the host ro.cker.org sets the domain property to *ro.cker.org*. However, the host ha.cker.org sets the domain property to *.cker.org*. Now suppose the user browses to ha.cker.org and the server sends a session cookie with this header:

```
Set-Cookie: ASP.NET_SessionId=nkih5piv3zdeuc55xj2np555; domain=.cker.org.
```

Now the user browses to ro.cker.org, and the browser sees that the host ro.cker.org matches the domain .cker.org, so it sends back the cookie it received from ha.cker.org:

```
Cookie:  ASP.NET_SessionId=nkih5piv3zdeuc55xj2np555;
```

The ro.cker.org server does not check the domain and simply accepts the cookie. This kind of flaw may expose the server to a number of attacks, including session fixation, account hopping, and token manipulation. To prevent this type of attack, always check the cookie's domain, as shown in Figure 3.2 (C#) and Figure 3.3 (VB.NET). Note that you should always run the verification code in Figure 3.4 (C#) and Figure 3.5 (VB.NET) before you set the domain on all cookies, as shown in Figures 3.2 and 3.3.

Figure 3.2 Setting the Domain on All Cookies: C#

```
private void settingTheDomainOnAllCookies()
{
  foreach (string key in Response.Cookies.Keys )
  {
    Request.Cookies[key].Domain = "te.st.ing";
  }
}
```

Figure 3.3 Setting the Domain on All Cookies: VB.NET

```
Private Function settingTheDomainOnAllCookies()
  Dim key As String

  For Each key In Response.Cookies.Keys
    Request.Cookies(key).Domain = "te.st.ing"
  Next
End Function
```

Figure 3.4 Verifying the Cookie Domain: C#

```
private void verifyingTheCookieDomain()
{
  foreach (string key in Response.Cookies.Keys )
  {
    HttpCookie cookie = Request.Cookies[key];
    if (cookie.Domain != "te.st.ing")
    {
```

Continued

Figure 3.4 Verifying the Cookie Domain: **C#**

```
        cookie.Expires = DateTime.Now.AddYears(-1);
    }
  }
}
```

Figure 3.5 Verifying the Cookie Domain: VB.NET

```
Private Function verifyingTheCookieDomain()
  Dim key As String

  For Each key In Response.Cookies.Keys
    Dim cookie As HttpCookie = Request.Cookies(key)
    If cookie.Domain <> "te.st.ing" Then
      cookie.Expires = DateTime.Now.AddYears(-1)
    End If
  Next
End Function
```

Cookie Path

Similar to the domain, cookies also have a path property to limit their scope. After passing the domain check, the server checks the cookie path. The path matches from left to right, matching any path and the paths below it. So if you set the path to / (slash), the cookie applies to all paths on the server. A path of */shopping* limits the cookie to all items in the shopping directory and all its sub-directories.

It is helpful to set the path as specifically as possible because a browser will send the cookie to all URLs that match the path. By keeping the scope narrow, you can prevent the browser from sending the cookie when it shouldn't do so, such as when browsing non-SSL pages. It also limits exposure to cross-site scripting attacks if an attacker finds a flaw in one part of the application. For instance, suppose that you have a Web application for members only at www.example.com/protected/ but provide a demo application that anyone can log in to at www.example.com/demo/. Now suppose that someone plays around with the demo and finds a cross-site scripting flaw that allows him to use the demo application to steal all members' authentication cookies. In this instance, setting a specific cookie path for the protected and demo directories would likely limit exposure to the attack, so someone would need access to the protected directory to exploit the flaw against actual members, whereas everyone has access to the demo directory. Although this is by no means a solution for the cross-site scripting problem, it does limit exposure to the attack.

TIP

Security strategies usually have varying levels of effectiveness. Some techniques are absolutely effective; other techniques mitigate attacks by limiting scope. Yet other techniques serve only to obscure things to slow an attack and discourage less dedicated hackers. Mitigating and obscuring techniques do not provide solid protection, but they do have the effect of improving overall exposure to attack, especially when you combine many techniques.

Always set a specific cookie path, and always check the path on cookies the client sends your application. For forms authentication, set the path attribute for the forms element in the web.config file.

Cookie Expiration

Cookie expiration in ASP.NET is sometimes confusing, but it is important to keep the lifetime of a cookie as short as possible, to limit exposure to cookie hijacking. Cookies have an *Expires* property that sets a limit on how long the browser should keep the cookie. If the expiration is left blank, the client browser is supposed to discard the cookie when it closes and not save it to disk. Although the expiration date tells a browser when it should stop using the cookie, there is no guarantee that it will remove expired cookies. So, even though this is not a reliable security measure, you should still take advantage of the feature.

When ASP.NET issues a session ID cookie, it does not set an expiration date, so the browser should discard the cookie when it closes. ASP.NET itself handles the expiring and reissuing of session tokens based on the session timeout setting in the *sessionState* element of the web.config file, as shown here:

```
<sessionState
  mode="InProc"
  sqlConnectionString="data source=127.0.0.1;Trusted_Connection=yes"
```

```
  cookieless="false"

  timeout="20"

/>
```

ASP.NET also handles the expiration of forms authentication tickets. The cookies for forms authentication tokens will not have an expiration date unless the Web application sets the cookie as persistent. The *FormsAuthentication.RedirectFromLoginPage* method has a parameter to indicate whether you want to use a persistent cookie or not, like this:

```
FormsAuthentication.RedirectFromLoginPage(UserName.Text, Persist.Checked)
```

Note that the *FormsAuthenticationTicket* class also has an *IsPersistent* property that you can set. Some Web applications provide users with a "Remember Me" feature so they don't have to enter their credentials with each visit. This is an unsafe security practice, and you should never provide it on a Web site that stores personal user information or allows users to perform any significant financial, personal, or communication actions.

The *FormsAuthenticationTicket* class has an *Expiration* property that indicates when the authentication token expires, but this does not set the expiration date of the cookie itself. The cookie sent to the browser will have no expiration date unless you mark it as persistent. Once ASP.NET detects an old authentication token, it will revoke that token and issue a new one.

Forms authentication provides two settings that control how it handles token expiration: *timeout* and *slidingExpiration*. *Timeout* specifies the number of minutes until a cookie expires. *SlidingExpiration*, if set to *true*, updates the cookie's expiration date with each browser request, providing that at least half the specified time has elapsed. In other words, setting the timeout to 20 and the *slidingExpiration* to *true* allows a user to go up to 20 minutes since the last page request before having to authenticate again. Setting *slidingExpiration* to *false* requires the user to reauthenticate 20 minutes after the *first* request.

WARNING

Timeout settings have no effect on persistent cookies. If you set an authentication ticket as persistent, ASP.NET gives the cookie an expiration date *50 years* from the time the server issued the cookie—even more reason not to use persistent cookies with forms authentication.

Although it is nice to be able to choose relative or absolute timeouts, it would be nicer to have both. That way you can timeout after a certain amount of idle time but also timeout after a set number of minutes. Without an absolute timeout, if someone leaves his browser open to a page that automatically refreshes, the session will never end. Attackers can also take advantage of this flaw by keeping a token alive for a session fixation attack.

Secure Cookies

A server can mark a cookie as secure to indicate to the client that it should take measures to protect the cookie. Although the RFC does not specify what security measures the browser should take, it usually means only sending the cookie over an encrypted SSL session. Nevertheless, marking a cookie as secure is only a suggestion from the server and the client browser does not have to honor that setting. In theory, the browser should provide the same level of security that the provided when issuing the cookie. Most common Web browsers do honor this setting.

If you protect your Web site with SSL, you should also mark your cookies as secure so that the client will not send them to a non-SSL page on your Web site.

You can configure forms authentication to always use a secure cookie with the *requireSSL* setting in the web.config file like this:

```
<forms name=".ASPXAUTH"
  loginUrl="/protected/login.aspx"
  protection="All"
  path="/protected/
  timeout="15"
  slidingExpiration="false"
  requireSSL="true"
>
```

Note that if you mark the forms authentication cookie as true, you must provide an SSL connection for the entire protected area of the Web application. Otherwise, if the user visits a non-SSL page the browser will not send the cookie and the user will have to authenticate again to create a new FormsAuthenticationTicket and therefore a new cookie. If you require security for forms authentication cookies, make sure the entire protected area is SSL-enabled. Likewise, you may not want to mark session cookies as secure unless your entire Web application is SSL-enabled.

Cookie Values

The most common use for cookies is storing user variables, such as items in a shopping cart or user preferences. However, some developers use cookies to store sensitive information such as usernames, passwords, or even credit card details. You should never store sensitive information in a cookie, and you should always encrypt the other information that is appropriate to store

Security Policies

- Always set a specific domain attribute and check the domain attribute when reading cookies.

- Always set a specific cookie path and check the path on cookies the client sends your application.

- Use short timeouts on session cookies to limit exposure to session-hijacking attacks.

- If you are using SSL, mark cookies as secure.

- Never store sensitive information such as authentication credentials or credit card numbers, and always encrypt what you do store.

Working with View State

Summary: View State can be secure if you use the right settings
Threats: Parameter manipulation, session fixation, information leakage

View State is an ASP.NET feature that allows you to persist form properties when a page posts back to itself. ASP.NET takes the current state of all form controls and stores them as an encoded string in a hidden form field. The risk of View State is that an attacker might be able to view or modify these form values to accomplish a variety of attacks. Fortunately, ASP.NET allows you to protect the View State data with encryption and detect tampering with hashes.

Enabling View State

You can enable View State on the machine, application, page, or control level. It might be tempting to enable View State for your entire site, but you might want to be more selective, to reduce exposure to attacks. Table 3.1 shows how to configure View State at various levels. In general, if you are not using View State for a page or control, you might want to disable it.

Table 3.1 Enabling View State

Scope	Configuration
Machine	In the machine.config file, set *<pages enableViewState="true"/>*.
Application	In the web.config file, set *<pages enableViewState="true"/>*.
Page	In the page source, use *<% @ Page enableViewState="true" %>* or in code set *Page.EnableViewState=True*.
Control	In the page source, set the control property *EnableViewState="True"*.

Protecting View State

View State appears in the HTML source as a hidden form field, as shown in Figure 3.6. Although it looks cryptic, it is merely using base 64 encoding. You can decode this data and view it graphically using the ViewState Decoder tool shown in Figure 3.7, which is available at http://staff.develop.com/onion/resources.htm.

Figure 3.6 Sample View State Field

```
<input type="hidden" name="__VIEWSTATE"
value="dDwxNTQyMjY4Nzg2O3Q802w8aTw3PjtpPDk+Oz47bDx0PDtsPGk8MT47PjtsPHQ8QDA8c
DxwPGw8RGF0YUtleXM7XM7XyFJdGVtQ291bnQ7PjtsPGw8PjtpPDEwPjs+Pjs+Ozs7Ozs+O2w8a
TwwPjtpPDE+O2k8Mj47aTwzPjtpPDQ+O2k8NT47aTw2PjtpPDc+O2k80D47aTw5Pjs+O2w8dDw7b
DxpPDA+Oz47bDx0PEA8MzEhU29ydGluZy9GaWx0ZXJpbmcgRml4ZWWQgRGF0YVN1dCBSZXN1bHRzO
z47Oz47Pj47dDw7bDxpPDA+Oz47bDx0PEA8MzA7VGhlIEJhc2ljcyBvZiBVc2luZyBTUUw7Pjs7P
js+Pjt0PDtsPGk8MD47PjtfPHQ8QDwyOTtVc2luZyBRdWVyeXN0cmluZyBSZXN1bHRzIGluIFNRT
CBTdGF0ZW1lbnRzOz47Oz47Pj47dDw7bDxpPDA+Oz47bDx0PEA8Mjg7VXNpbmcgdGhlIE1TIElFI
FRhY1N0cmlwwIENvbnRyb2w7Pjs7Pjs+Pjt0PDtsPGk8MD47PjtsPHQ8QDwyNztCZWdpbm5lcgR
3VpZGUgVkI2IENVbSBProYmXlY3RzIGluIEFFTUC5OZXQ7Pjs7Pjs+Pjt0PDtsPGk8MD47PjtsPHQ8Q
DwyNjtDcmVhdGluZyBhIExvdW5lbC0VtYWlsL0FjdGl2YXRpb24gUGFnZTs+Ozs+Oz4+O3Q802w8a
TwwPjs+O2w8dDxAPDI001RoZSBCZWdpbm5lcidzIEd1aWRlIIHRvIGFuIEFycmF5TGlzdDs+Ozs+O
z4+O3Q802w8aTwwPjs+O2w8dDxAPDIzOO0NvbmZpZ3VyaW5nIGEgVHJ1c3RlZCBTUUwgU2V6dmVyI
ENvbm51Y3Rpb247Pjs7Pjs+Pjt0PDtsPGk8MD47PjtsPHQ8QDwyMjtBZGRpbmcgRHluYW1pYyBDb
250ZW50IHRvIFlvdXIgUGFnZXM7Pjs7Pjs+Pjt0PDtsPGk8MD47PjtsPHQ8QDwyMTtDcmVhdGl33
yBhIE11bnUgVXN1ciBDb250cm9sIHdpdGGgUm9sbG92ZXJzOz47Oz47Pj47Pj47dDw7bDxpPP
DA+Oz47bDx0PEA8MDY3MjMyNTAxMjswNjcyMzI1MDEyOO0FTUC5ORVQgRGF0YSBXZWJcGJyYXD5Db
250cm9scyBLaWNrIFN0YXJ0IA0K01Njb3R0IE1pdGNoZWxsOz47Oz47Pj47Pj47Po/QlmEhBOdXC
ZBvDCRMGZGf0TBW" />
```

Figure 3.7 The ViewState Decoder

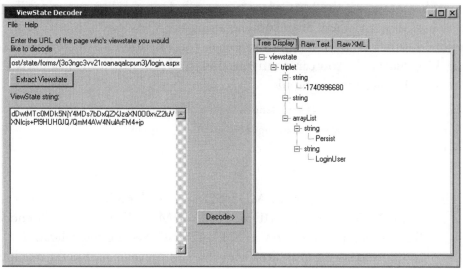

Because View State represents a form's control properties, an attacker would be able to modify the form by modifying the View State properties. For example, an attacker might be able to change a product's price on an online shopping cart or modify a parameter to perform an SQL injection attack. An attacker might try a number of other attacks such as cross-site scripting, unauthorized file access, or overflowing buffers.

To prevent attackers from manipulating View State, you can include a message authentication code (MAC). A MAC is essentially a hash of the data that ensures its integrity. You can enable the View State MAC on the machine, application, or page level. You can enable the MAC wherever you enable View State with this attribute:

```
enableViewStateMac="true"
```

WARNING

Although many documents recommend not using the View State MAC unless necessary for performance reasons, I advise you always use it. There is a very slight performance hit but not enough that a human would notice. The security benefits far outweigh the performance hit.

The MAC protects you from someone tampering with View State data, discarding the contents if the MAC does not match. However, anyone can still decode and view the View State contents using the ViewState Decoder tool mentioned earlier. To overcome this problem, you can also encrypt the contents of the *View State* field. You can configure this encryption with the *machineKey* element in the machine.config file:

```
<machineKey validationKey="AutoGenerate,IsolateApps"

   decryptionKey="AutoGenerate,IsolateApps"

   validation="3DES"

/>
```

The validation attribute can be MD5, SHA-1, or 3DES. The first two of these cause ASP.NET to create a MD5 or SHA-1 MAC hash, but 3DES encrypts the View State contents and creates an SHA-1 MAC. Setting the validation mode to 3DES protects the data from viewing and prevents parameter manipulation, but this still does not make View State completely secure. An attacker could prepopulate a form, save the *View State* field, and then trick another user into using that form. To prevent this type of attack, ASP.NET allows you to set a unique key for each user that makes the View State data valid for only that user. You can do this in the *page_init* event by setting the *ViewStateUserKey* property of the *page* object. With authenticated users, you can set this to the user's name or session ID, but with an anonymous user, you should create a random number and save it in the user's cookie. Figure 3.8 (C#) and Figure 3.9 (VB.NET) demonstrate how to employ the methods mentioned in this section.

Figure 3.8 Securing View State: C#

```
private void Page_Init(object sender, System.EventArgs e)
{
  EnableViewState = true;

  EnableViewStateMac = true;

  ViewStateUserKey = User.Identity.Name;

}
```

Figure 3.9 Securing View State: VB.NET

```
Private Sub Page_Init(ByVal sender As System.Object, ByVal e As
    System.EventArgs) Handles MyBase.Init
    EnableViewState = True
    EnableViewStateMac = True
    ViewStateUserKey = True


    InitializeComponent()
End Sub
```

To properly secure View State, you should use encryption, hashing, and unique user keys. You should always disable View State if you are not using it.

Security Policies

- Disable View State unless you specifically use it.
- Where you enable View State, always enable the View State MAC.
- Set the validation attribute in machine.config to 3DES.
- Set a unique View State user key for each user.

Enhancing ASP.NET State Management

ASP.NET state management is convenient, but it does not meet the criteria mentioned at the beginning of this chapter. For example, session and authentication tokens are not tightly bound to user sessions, and ASP.NET will accept any token the client provides. This section explains how to use the built-in state management features combined with client-side cookies to provide an additional layer of security. This section covers:

- Creating tokens
- Establishing sessions
- Terminating sessions

It is important to note that although it will not stop all attacks, using SSL will further enhance the techniques described in this section.

Creating Tokens

Summary: **Use additional code to increase token security**
Threats: **Session hijacking, account hijacking, session fixation, information leakage**

The token you use for session management should be a strong random number and should not directly identify a user, and the application should be able to prove that it is authentic.

Random numbers are an important aspect of security, but they must have certain properties to be considered truly random. For instance, the number should not be predictable or reproducible, and it should be large enough to prevent someone guessing it. When ASP.NET creates a session token, it uses a strong random-number generator to create a 120-bit key, which is certainly adequate for most purposes. This session token is stored in a cookie named *ASP.NET_SessionId* or on the URL if you're using a cookieless state. This session token is also available through the *SessionID* property of the *Session* object.

The only weakness with the ASP.NET session token is that it is just a random number and ASP.NET will accept any token you supply of the correct length, making it vulnerable to session fixation attacks. To compensate for this weakness, we must create a MAC for the session token based on a random number stored with the server's state mechanism, as shown in Figure 3.10 (C#) and Figure 3.11 (VB.NET).

Figure 3.10 Enhancing the Session ID with a MAC: C#

```
private void enhanceSessionIdWithMac()
{
  string SessionMacCookieValue;

  // Check if there is a SessionMac cookie
  if (Request.Cookies["SessionMac"] == null)
  {
    SessionMacCookieValue = null;
  }
  else
  {
    SessionMacCookieValue = Request.Cookies["SessionMac"].Value;
  }
```

Continued

Figure 3.10 Enhancing the Session ID with a MAC: C#

```csharp
// Create and store hash
if (Session["key"] == null && SessionMacCookieValue == null)
{
   Session["key"] = CreateKey();

   string hash = createHMASCHA1(Encoding.Unicode.GetBytes(
           Session.SessionID),
           Encoding.Unicode.GetBytes(
             (string)Session["key"]));
   HttpCookie SessionMac = new HttpCookie("SessionMac", hash);
   Response.Cookies.Add(SessionMac);
}
// Check against stored hash
else
{
   string createdHash = createHMASCHA1(
                Encoding.Unicode.GetBytes(
                  Session.SessionID),
                Encoding.Unicode.GetBytes(
                  (string)Session["key"]));
   if (createdHash != Request.Cookies["SessionMac"].Value)
   {
      Session.Abandon();
      Response.Redirect("default.aspx");
   }
}
}
```

Figure 3.11 Enhancing the Session ID with a MAC: VB.NET

```vbnet
Private Sub enhanceSessionIdWithMac()
  Dim SessionMacCookieValue As String

  ' Check if there is a SessionMac cookie
  If Request.Cookies("SessionMac") Is Nothing Then
```

Continued

Figure 3.11 Enhancing the Session ID with a MAC: VB.NET

```
    SessionMacCookieValue = Nothing
  Else
    SessionMacCookieValue = Request.Cookies("SessionMac").Value
  End If


  ' Create and store hash
  If Session("key") Is Nothing And SessionMacCookieValue Is Nothing Then
    Session("key") = createKey()
    Dim hash As String
    hash = createHMASCHA1(Encoding.Unicode.GetBytes(Session.SessionID), _
                Encoding.Unicode.GetBytes(Session("key")))
    Dim SessionMac As HttpCookie
    SessionMac = New HttpCookie("SessionMac", hash)
    Response.Cookies.Add(SessionMac)
  Else
    ' Check against stored hash
    Dim createdHash As String
    createdHash = createHMASCHA1(_
                Encoding.Unicode.GetBytes(Session.SessionID), _
                Encoding.Unicode.GetBytes(Session("key")))
    If (createdHash <> Request.Cookies("SessionMac").Value) Then
      Session.Abandon()
      Response.Redirect("default.aspx")
    End If
  End If
End Sub
```

This code creates a MAC based on the session ID using a random number stored on the server as the key. It saves this MAC in a cookie on the client. When a client request comes in, you again compute a MAC and see if it matches the MAC stored in the client cookie. If the two match, you know it is a valid session ID; otherwise, you abandon the current session and force the user to acquire a new session ID. After a session times out on the server, the key will no longer be available and the MAC based on that key will no longer be valid. If the client sends a cookie for a preexisting session without providing a MAC, the server abandons the session and starts over with a new session ID.

For forms authentication tickets, you don't need to add our own MAC if you always use encryption and validation using the *protection="All"* attribute of the *forms* element in the web.config file. This ensures that an attacker cannot view or modify the forms authentication ticket. The ticket is encrypted and hashed based on the *decryptionKey* and *validationKey* attributes of the *machineKey* element in the machine.config file. On a default installation, both of these are set to *"AutoGenerate,IsolateApps"*, which means that ASP.NET will generate random values for these keys. The *IsolateApps* setting is important because it ensures a unique key for every ASP.NET application on the server. This is especially important on a shared host because without it, one Web site could produce a valid forms authentication ticket for another site on the same server.

TIP

If you explicitly set custom *decryptionKey* and *validationKey* values to allow forms authentication in a Web farm, you can still use the *IsolateApps* setting to ensure unique keys for each application on the server.

Binding to the Client

Once you establish a secure token and send it to the client, you want to make sure that only that client can use that token. Although it is difficult to absolutely prevent someone else from hijacking that cookie, there are some things you can do to limit the scope enough to block many types of attacks.

There are various ways that an attacker can obtain the session token and hijack the user's session. Some techniques an attacker could use are:

- Man-in-the-middle attack involving ARP or DNS spoofing
- Obtaining the session token on the URL stored in the cache, in a proxy server's logs, or listed as the referrer in a server's Web logs
- Gaining access to the client's system and stealing the browser's cookie; Trojans fall into this type of attack, too
- Using cross-site scripting to obtain the browser's cookie or the token in the URL

The reason so few sites bind to the user's session is that it is difficult to reliably bind to a single session, and even if you can, it does not protect against all types of attacks. You need to not only obtain the token but make it difficult to use that token from another client.

There are several ways that you can create a stronger bind between the session and the client. The most obvious of these is using the client's IP address. The main problem with this choice is that some ISPs use load-balanced caching proxy servers. This means first that more than one user will have the same IP address and second that a user might not have the same IP address for each request. To overcome this, you might be able to use the first one or two octets of the IP address. So, if the client comes from 192.168.10.58, you can bind the session to the first two octets, 192 and 168. Another method is to bind to the *User Agent* string provided by the client. However, some proxies randomly change the *User Agent* string to help protect user privacy, and it is possible for an attacker to discover and fake this string. Yet another option is to bind to the current ASP session cookie. None of these methods is perfect, but using a combination of these certainly provides more security than using none.

Figure 3.12 (C#) and Figure 3.13 (VB.NET) show how to obtain information about the client and store it in the session state. With each request from that client, you compare the client information with the saved information and abandon the session if they do not match. You will likely need to test these to see if they work with your client base.

Figure 3.12 Binding to the Client: C#

```
private void bindingToTheClient()
{
  // get the first two octets
  string[] userIpArray = Request.UserHostAddress.Split('.');
  string firstTwoOctets = userIpArray[0] + "." + userIpArray[1];

  if (Session["firstTwoOctets"] == null &&
    Session["userAgent"] == null)
  {
    Session["firstTwoOctets"] = firstTwoOctets;
    Session["userAgent"] = Request.UserAgent;
  }
  else
```

Continued

Figure 3.12 Binding to the Client: C#

```
    {
      if ((string) Session["firstTwoOctets"] != firstTwoOctets ||
        (string) Session["userAgent"] != Request.UserAgent)
      {
        Session.Abandon();
        Response.Redirect("default.aspx");
      }
    }
}
```

SYNGRESS syngress.com

Figure 3.13 Binding to the Client: VB.NET

```
Private Function bindingToTheClient()
  Dim userIpArray() = Split(Request.UserHostAddress, ".")
  Dim firstTwoOctets As String = userIpArray(0) + "." + userIpArray(1)

  If Session("firstTwoOctets") Is Nothing And _
    Session("userAgent") Is Nothing Then
    Session("firstTwoOctets") = firstTwoOctets
    Session("userAgent") = Request.UserAgent
  Else
    If Session("firstTwoOctets") <> firstTwoOctets Or _
      Session("userAgent") <> Request.UserAgent Then
      Session.Abandon()
      Response.Redirect("default.aspx")
    End If
  End If
End Function
```

Security Policies

- Always use a strong random-number generator for session tokens.
- Use a token that does not identify the user to anyone but the server.
- Use an additional MAC to ensure the authenticity of a session token.

- When using forms authentication on a shared server, always use the *IsolateApps* setting of the *machineKey* element in the machine.config file.

- Save client variables to help ensure binding to the same client.

Terminating Sessions

Summary: **Carefully choose a token mechanism that provides users with the best security**

Threats: **Session hijacking, account hijacking, token keep-alive**

At some point a session must end, at which time you should destroy the session token. There are several ways a Web session can end:

- The client closes the Web browser.

- The client keeps the browser open but browses to a different Web site.

- The client browser sits idle long enough for the token to expire.

- The server revokes the token.

When the client closes the browser, the browser discards any session tokens not marked as persistent. However, if the user just browses to a different Web site, the session tokens remain in the browser's memory. This means that if users browse back to your site, their session tokens may still be valid. This could be a risk on a shared public computer or if the user leaves a browser window open for an extended period of time. To counter this danger, ASP.NET automatically expires a session after a predefined time, usually 20 minutes.

But if the user is on a Web page that automatically refreshes every few minutes, the session never sits idle long enough to expire. An attacker can use this capability with a session fixation attack to keep the token alive long enough to carry out the attack.

The best countermeasures are to provide three different expiration factors:

- After a specific amount of idle time

- After an absolute time since the token was issued

- After a specified number of uses

Using these factors, you could, for example, expire a session after idle for 10 minutes, after two hours have passed since issuing the token, or after 50 hits to your Web site. Under any of these conditions, you should create a new session token or reauthenticate the user. This type of practice is commonly implemented in online banking Web sites.

Since ASP.NET automatically handles idle session timeouts, we can use session state to store the other two variables. Figure 3.14 (C#) and Figure 3.15 (VB.NET) show how to use, store, and check the absolute expiration and hit counter.

Figure 3.14 Expiring Sessions: C#

```csharp
private void expiringSessions()
{
  if (Session["absoluteExpiration"] == null &&
    Session["maxHitCount"] == null)
  {
    Session["absoluteExpiration"] =
      DateTime.Now.AddHours(2); // Two hours from now
    Session["maxHitCount"] = 3; // Fifty hits to the website
    Session["hitCount"] = 0;
  }
  else
  {
    Session["hitCount"] = (int) Session["hitCount"] + 1;
    // Check if session has expired, or exceeded max hit count
    if (DateTime.Now > (DateTime) Session["absoluteExpiration"] ||
      (int) Session["hitCount"] > (int) Session["maxHitCount"])
    {
      Session.Abandon();
      Response.Redirect("default.aspx");
    }
  }
}
```

Figure 3.15 Expiring Sessions: VB.NET

```vbnet
Private Function expiringSessions()
  If Session("absoluteExpiration") Is Nothing And _
    Session("maxHitCount") Is Nothing Then
```

Continued

Figure 3.15 Expiring Sessions: VB.NET

```
    ' Two hours from now
    Session("absoluteExpiration") = DateTime.Now.AddHours(2)
    ' Fifty hits to the website
    Session("maxHitCount") = 50
    Session("hitCount") = 0
  Else
    Session("hitCount") = Session("hitCount") + 1
    ' Check if session has expired, or exceeded max hit count
    If DateTime.Now > Session("absoluteExpiration") Or _
      Session("hitCount") > Session("maxHitCount") Then
      Session.Abandon()
      Response.Redirect("default.aspx")
    End If
  End If
End Function
```

This code checks to see if the current session has an absolute expiration and hit count. If it doesn't, the code creates one and saves it with the session state. When the next request comes in, it again checks those values until the client exceeds either. At that point, we expire the session and require the user to again authenticate to the server.

Security Policies

- Use timeouts to expire idle sessions.
- Use absolute timeouts to set a limit on active sessions.
- Use hit counters to limit the use of any single token.

Coding Standards Fast Track

Maintaining State

Designing a Secure Token

☑ Where possible, use extra measures to bind the token to the client session.

☑ Always transmit authentication credentials using SSL or IPSec.

☑ Always use a sufficiently large keyspace (at least 120 bits) for session tokens.

☑ Always use a strong random-number generator for session tokens.

☑ Never accept new tokens submitted by a client.

☑ Never include visible plaintext user identifiers in the token.

☑ Always limit the token's scope to the current application.

☑ Use both relative and absolute timeouts for tokens.

☑ Take measures to prevent the client from storing the session token after the session ends.

☑ Allow users to manually terminate a session.

☑ Always issue a new token with each session login.

Selecting a Token Mechanism

☑ Avoid using URL-based token mechanisms.

☑ Use cookie-based tokens whenever possible.

☑ Use *HttpOnly* tokens with Internet Explorer clients.

☑ Use SSL whenever possible to protect session tokens.

Using State Providers

☑ Disable the ASP.NET State Service if you are not using it.

☑ Use aspnet_setreg.exe to encrypt the state connection string.

☑ Avoid using cookieless tokens.

☑ Set short cookie timeouts as appropriate for your application.

Using ASP.NET Tokens

Using Cookies

☑ Always set a specific domain and path on all cookies.

☑ Always check the domain and path on incoming cookies to block cookies with the incorrect scope.

☑ Do not set an expiration on cookies to have them expire when the browser closes.

☑ If using persistent cookies, use a short expiration date.

☑ If using SSL, mark cookies as secure to prevent transmitting them over non-SSL connections.

☑ Never store sensitive information in a cookie, and always encrypt what you do store.

Working with View State

☑ Disable View State on all pages where you do not specifically use it.

☑ Wherever you enable View State, also enable the View State MAC.

☑ Set the validation attribute of the *machineKey* element in machine.config to 3DES.

☑ Set a unique View State user key for each user.

Enhancing ASP.NET State Management

Creating Tokens

☑ Always use a strong random-number generator for session tokens.

☑ Use a MAC based on a random number to ensure the authenticity of the session token.

☑ Use the *IsolateApps* settings to ensure unique keys between applications.

☑ Use client variables to tightly bind to the client session.

Terminating Sessions

- ☑ Use absolute timeouts in addition to idle timeouts to enforce a maximum token age.

- ☑ Use hit counters to limit the use of any one token.

Code Audit Fast Track

Maintaining State

Designing a Secure Token

- ☑ Is the token tightly bound to the user's session?
- ☑ Does the server transmit the token to the client in a secure manner?
- ☑ Does the application use a sufficiently large keyspace?
- ☑ Does the application use a strong random-number generator for tokens?
- ☑ Will the system accept any token provided by the client?
- ☑ Is it possible for a user to manipulate the token to hop to another account?
- ☑ Does the token identify the client?
- ☑ Does the token properly limit its scope?
- ☑ Does the token have both relative and absolute timeouts?
- ☑ Does the client store the token after the session ends?
- ☑ Does the user have the option to terminate a session?
- ☑ Does the application create new tokens for each login?

Selecting a Token Mechanism

- ☑ Does the application use a secure mechanism for transferring cookies?
- ☑ Does the application use *HttpOnly* tokens with Internet Explorer clients?
- ☑ Does the application use SSL when appropriate?

Using State Providers

☑ If you're not using the ASP.NET Session State service, is the service disabled?

☑ If you're using the ASP.NET Session State service, does the system use a nonstandard port?

☑ If you're using the ASP.NET Session State service, does the system use appropriate controls to limit access to the service port?

☑ Does the web.config file contain encrypted session state connection strings created with aspnet_setreg.exe?

☑ Does the application avoid cookieless tokens?

☑ Does the application use short cookie timeouts?

Using ASP.NET Tokens

Using Cookies

☑ Does the code set a specific domain and path on all cookies?

☑ Does the code check the domain and path on incoming cookies to block cookies with the incorrect scope?

☑ Does the application set the appropriate cookie expiration properties?

☑ Does the application mark cookies as secure when they're sent over SSL connections?

☑ Does the application avoid saving sensitive information in cookies?

☑ Does the application encrypt all data stored in cookies?

Working with View State

☑ Does the application disable View State on pages where it is not used?

☑ Does the application enable the View State MAC when using View State?

☑ Does the *machineKey* element in the machine.config file use 3DES as the validation method?

☑ Does the application set a unique View State user key for each user?

Enhancing ASP.NET State Management

Creating Tokens

☑ Does the application use a strong random-number generator for session tokens?

☑ Does the application ensure the authenticity of the session token?

☑ Does the system use the *IsolateApps* setting to ensure unique keys between applications?

☑ Does the application use client variables to tightly bind to the client session?

Terminating Sessions

☑ Does the application use absolute timeouts in addition to idle timeouts to enforce a maximum token age?

☑ Does the application use hit counters to limit the use of any one token?

Frequently Asked Questions

The following Frequently Asked Questions, answered by the authors of this book, are designed to both measure your understanding of the concepts presented in this chapter and to assist you with real-life implementation of these concepts. To have your questions about this chapter answered by the author, browse to **www.syngress.com/solutions** and click on the **"Ask the Author"** form. You will also gain access to thousands of other FAQs at ITFAQnet.com.

Q: Does SSL add enough security to make it worth the extra load?

A: SSL does not solve all problems, but it does protect the user from many types of attacks, and you should therefore use it whenever possible. On a slow server, SSL can sometimes double the processor load, but it has a less significant impact with a more powerful CPU. Furthermore, you can offload SSL handling with specialized hardware. If your site deals with sensitive user financial, personal, or communications data, utilizing SSL should be mandatory.

Q: Can I create a different *machineKey* setting in each application's web.config file instead of a single setting in the machine.config?

A: Yes, this is actually the preferred method for securing a server with multiple users, such as with a Web hosting service. To configure this, use the *IsolateApps* setting as follows:

```
<machineKey validationKey="AutoGenerate,IsolateApps"
decryptionKey="AutoGenerate,IsolateApps" validation="SHA1"/>
```

Q: Is it more secure to manage and store session state on the client or on the server?

A: It is best to store and manage session state information on *both* the client and the server. If you rely only on the server, it is easier for an attacker to take over a client's session without knowing about the client. If you do it only on the client, it is more difficult to protect from session fixation, and there is no way to revoke a user's session after a security incident.

Q: Why is it so important to use a strong random-number generator for the session token?

A: The main reason for a strong random-number generator is to prevent guessing or brute-force attacks of the session token. For example, an attacker could create a script to submit thousands of session IDs until it finds a valid session. The stronger the random number, the more difficult it is to find a valid session. To be effective, the random numbers must be large, unpredictable, and evenly spread across the entire keyspace. If you have a 120-bit random number and 10,000 active sessions, you should feel safe knowing that for every active session, 132,922,799,578,491,000,000,000,000,000,000,000 session IDs are not valid. Even using an automated script, it would very difficult to come across a valid session ID.

Q: I run a Web-based e-mail Web service, and for business reasons I must place the session token on the URL. How can I prevent the client's browser from sending the URL token in the *Referer* field when a user clicks an external hyperlink?

A: If you place the session ID on the URL and the user clicks a link, the destination Web site will be able to see the original URL, including the session token, by looking at the HTTP *Referer* field. Sometimes an attacker can use this flaw to take over a user's session. The easiest way to prevent this attack is to wrap all URLs with a URL of your own, passing the original URL as a parameter. So, for example, you could end up with something like this:

```
http://www.example.com/externallink.aspx?original=www.
externalURL.com.
```

Next, have externallink.aspx grab the original URL parameter and forward the client to that site with a client-side redirect. The external site will only see the link coming from externallink.aspx.

Chapter 4

Encrypting Private Data

Solutions in this Chapter:

- Using Cryptography in ASP.NET
- Working with .NET Encryption Features
- Protecting Communications with SSL

☑ Coding Standards Fast Track

☑ Code Audit Fast Track

☑ Frequently Asked Questions

153

Introduction

With so much resting on digital security in our modern world, it's a wonder that such a small percentage of Web sites use encryption. Perhaps the complexity and lack of application support make it difficult, but security is all about protecting data, and you cannot protect data without cryptography. Fortunately, ASP.NET provides an impressive set of cryptography-related classes to protect even the most sensitive data. Best of all, ASP.NET makes it easy to implement cryptography throughout your application.

But cryptography is about more than just ensuring the confidentiality of your data. In fact, cryptography plays many roles in data security, such as:

- Ensuring data integrity
- Guaranteeing privacy
- Authenticating senders and recipients
- Preventing repudiation

Data integrity involves proving that data has remained unmodified since a certain point in time. *Privacy* and *confidentiality* prevent others from accessing your data without your permission. *Authentication* is proving that the data came from the stated source and that it is accessible to only the stated recipient. Finally, *repudiation* is denying an action or ownership of data. Cryptography forces a user to acknowledge an action or concede ownership of data.

As you read this chapter, you will find concepts sometimes unique to the science of cryptography. Although a full discussion of the workings of cryptography is beyond the scope of this book, it is important to understand some of these concepts:

- **Plaintext** The original unmodified, unprotected data., also known as cleartext.
- **Ciphertext** The plaintext transformed in such a manner that it is not usable without a proper key.
- **Encryption** The process of transforming plaintext into ciphertext.
- **Decryption** The process of transforming ciphertext into plaintext.
- **Cipher** The algorithm or process used to encrypt sensitive data.
- **Key** The secret used to encrypt and decrypt sensitive data.

- **Keyspace** The set of all possible keys available to a specific cipher.

- **Pseudorandom-number generators (PRNGs)** Because computers cannot be truly random, we depend on pseudorandom-number generators to closely simulate true randomness. Random numbers play an important role in cryptography.

Although cryptography is an important element of data security, it is not impervious to attack. In fact, there are a number of ways to attack a cryptographic system, such as:

- **Brute force** Guessing a key by trying all possible keys. The success of a brute-force attack depends on the speed of current computing technology and the time allocated for such an attack.

- **User weaknesses** Humans are vulnerable to social engineering, physical threats, and blackmail, and they make poor security choices.

- **Cryptanalysis** Many people study cryptographic algorithms to find flaws within such code.

- **Side-channel leakage** Sometimes it is possible to discover a cryptographic key or find flaws in a cipher by measuring and analyzing timing, power consumption and dissipation, electromagnetic radiation, heat radiation, or other side channels.

- **Physical attack** An attacker may gain physical access to your computer and discover your private key or install a key logger or other monitoring device to discover your password.

- **Poor implementation** Many developers do not understand how to properly implement cryptography in their applications and so can inadvertently introduce weaknesses.

Using Cryptography in ASP.NET

Before you integrate cryptography into your ASP.NET application, you should first understand when to use the various available ciphers. ASP.NET has three main categories of cryptographic cipher:

- Symmetric algorithms
- Asymmetric algorithms

- Hashing and signature algorithms

Each of these plays a unique role in the overall security of an ASP.NET application. It is important to understand which type of cipher to use in various situations. Table 4.1 shows some of the different uses for the various categories of ciphers.

Table 4.1 Encryption Algorithms Available with the .NET Framework

Category	Algorithms	Suggested Uses
Symmetric	DES, 3DES, Rjindael (AES), RC2	Bulk data encryption
Assymetric	RSA	Authentication, data integrity
Hashing and signatures	MD5, SHA1, SHA256, SHA384, SHA512, DSA	Data integrity

> **WARNING**
>
> With so much built-in support for well-accepted encryption algorithms, there is no excuse to try to "roll your own." In fact, because so few people are actually qualified to write strong encryption algorithms, you should never trust your own code. Furthermore, data obfuscation algorithms such as XOR, ROT-13, and base-64 encoding provide little if any realized protection. Despite our best efforts to educate everyone on this, programmers consistently and predictably use these flawed techniques to protect secret data.

Employing Symmetric Cryptography

Summary: Symmetric cryptography is useful for bulk encryption, but scalability and key management issues limit its use

Threats: Information leakage, data corruption, man-in-the-middle attacks, brute-force attacks

Symmetric cryptography, known also as *secret key cryptography*, is the use of a single shared secret to share encrypted data between parties. Ciphers in this category are called symmetric because you use the same key to encrypt and to decrypt the data. In simple terms, the sender encrypts data using a password, and the recipient must know that password to access the data.

Symmetric encryption is a two-way process. With a block of plaintext and a given key, symmetric ciphers will always produce the same ciphertext. Likewise, using that same key on that block of ciphertext will always produce the original plaintext. Symmetric encryption is useful for protecting data between parties with an established shared key and is also frequently used to store confidential data. For example, ASP.NET uses 3DES to encrypt cookie data for a forms authentication ticket.

Table 4.2 shows the characteristics of the symmetric encryption algorithms available in the .NET Framework. Although these algorithms work differently, the .NET Framework provides a standardized model through the *SymmetricAlgorithm* abstract base class.

Table 4.2 .NET Framework Symmetric Encryption Algorithms

Name	Block Size	Cipher Modes	Key Lengths
DES	64	CBC, ECB, and CFB	56 bits
Triple DES (3DES)	64	CBC, ECB, and CFB	Two or three 56-bit keys
Rijndael (AES)	128, 192, 256	CBC and ECB	128, 192, or 256 bits
RC2	64	CBC, ECB, and CFB	40, 48, 56, 64, 72, 80, 88, 96, 104, 112, 120, or 128 bits

In addition to providing access to different encryption algorithms, the .NET Framework also allows you to customize the cipher modes, key lengths, block sizes, and padding mode, as well as other parameters. The cipher mode determines the cipher's mode of operation. Although the *CipherMode* enumeration includes five different modes, only three are supported with existing algorithms, as shown in Table 4.2. The *CipherMode* options are:

- **Electronic Codebook Mode (EBC)** The simplest and fastest mode, EBC allows ciphertext to be broken one block at a time and allows for codebook compilation. Encrypted blocks can be replaced without affecting the entire message. This mode is useful only where performance is the highest priority, at the expense of security.

- **Cipher Block Chaining Mode (CBC)** This mode uses an initialization vector (IV) to add feedback to the block transformation. This prevents the problems seen with EBC mode. Decryption requires knowing the IV, but this is not a secret and you can transmit it over an insecure connection.

- **Cipher Feedback Mode (CFB)** Uses an IV as CBC does but works with partial blocks, making it well suited for encrypting streaming data.

TIP

Although the symmetric algorithms available with the .NET Framework are all block ciphers, you can access them through a stream-oriented design. However, they are still block ciphers, and you should not confuse them with stream ciphers that are not always as secure.

You can see a full implementation of all the symmetric algorithms and settings in action with the symmetric.aspx file found in the \Ch04 directory of the supplemental code download available at this book's Web site (www.syngress.com/solutions). Figure 4.1 shows an example of how this page looks.

Figure 4.1 Symmetric Cryptography Sample

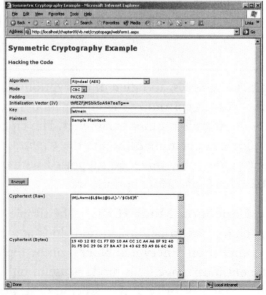

DES and 3DES

The U.S. government developed Data Encryption Standard (DES) in 1977 as an official cryptography standard; it is still used widely. DES formed the basis of the first automated teller machine (ATM) personal identification number (PIN) code authentication and until recent years existed as the primary authentication encryption method for UNIX machines. DES is a block cipher using a 64-bit block size with a 56-bit key length. In early 1990 it was proven insufficiently secure given current hardware capabilities and that it was possible to exhaust all potential DES key combinations in less than a day. *Triple DES* (also known as 3DES) emerged to address DESs shortcomings. 3DES uses standard DES encryption cycled over itself three times, with one cycle using a different set of encryption keys. This was a simple yet easy way to effectively increase the key size from 56-bit to 168-bit, thus increasing its security, but it obviously takes three times longer than DES to encrypt the data.

DES is probably nearing the end of its useful life, and 3DES is not as efficient as other algorithms, but they both still dominate as the algorithms of choice. Many programmers feel more comfortable using these algorithms because of their compatibility and wide acceptance.

The .NET Framework provides access to these algorithms through the *DESCryptoServiceProvider* and *TripleDESCryptoServiceProvider* classes. Note that both of these classes are managed wrappers that call the unmanaged Win32 CryptoAPI functions. Figures 4.2 and 4.3 demonstrate the use of 3DES encryption.

TIP

Although DES and 3DES do not use managed code, you can get some open-source implementations of these classes that contain fully managed code. Open-source implementations of the .NET Framework include the mono project (www.go-mono.com) and DotGNU Portable .NET (www.southern-storm.com.au/portable_net.html). Note, however, that the native .NET Framework classes that call the CryptoAPI have been FIPS 140-1 certified (see http://csrc.nist.gov/cryptval/140-1/1401vend.htm).

Figure 4.2 3DES Encryption with ASP.NET: C#

```csharp
private void tripleDES()
{
   string plainText = "This is a secret for 3DES";
   Response.Write("plainText: " + plainText + "<br>");
   byte[] buffer = ASCIIEncoding.ASCII.GetBytes(plainText);
   TripleDESCryptoServiceProvider des =
      new TripleDESCryptoServiceProvider();
   des.GenerateKey();
   des.GenerateIV();

   string encryptedString = Convert.ToBase64String(
      des.CreateEncryptor().TransformFinalBlock(
        buffer, 0, buffer.Length));
   Response.Write("Encrypted string: " + encryptedString + "<br>");

   buffer = Convert.FromBase64String(encryptedString);
   string decryptedString = ASCIIEncoding.ASCII.GetString(
      des.CreateDecryptor().TransformFinalBlock(
      buffer, 0, buffer.Length));
   Response.Write("Decrypted string: " + decryptedString + "<br>");
}
```

Figure 4.3 3DES Encryption with ASP.NET: VB.NET

```vbnet
Private Function tripleDES()
     Dim plainText As String = "This is a secret for 3DES"
     Response.Write("plainText: " + plainText + "<br>")

     Dim buffer() As Byte = ASCIIEncoding.ASCII.GetBytes(plainText)
     Dim des As New TripleDESCryptoServiceProvider
     des.GenerateKey()
     des.GenerateIV()

     Dim encryptedString As String = _
         Convert.ToBase64String( _
```

Continued

Figure 4.3 3DES Encryption with ASP.NET: VB.NET

```
            des.CreateEncryptor().TransformFinalBlock( _
            buffer, 0, buffer.Length))
        Response.Write("encryptedString: " + encryptedString + "<br>")
        buffer = Convert.FromBase64String(encryptedString)
        Dim decryptedString As String = _
            ASCIIEncoding.ASCII.GetString( _
            des.CreateDecryptor().TransformFinalBlock( _
            buffer, 0, buffer.Length))
        Response.Write("Decrypted string: " + decryptedString + "<br>")
End Function
```

DES does have some keys that you must avoid because they are weak. In fact, there are four keys that produce the same subkeys in every round. This means that if you encrypt data with one of these keys and then encrypt that encrypted data again with the same key, you will end up with the original plaintext message. In addition to these weak keys are 12 semi-weak keys. Semi-weak keys work in pairs, where one key decrypts data encrypted with the first. ASP.NET allows you to check for these with the *IsWeakKey* and *IsSemiWeakKey* methods. You can view the actual source code for the *IsWeakKey* method in Figure 4.4 and the *IsSemiWeakKey* method in Figure 4.5.

TIP

You can download the source code for the .NET Framework cryptography base classes at www.gotdotnet.com/team/clr/samples/ eula_clr_cryptosrc.aspx.

Figure 4.4 .NET Framework Source Code for the *IsWeakKey* Method

```
public static bool IsWeakKey(byte[] rgbKey) {
    if (!IsLegalKeySize(rgbKey)) {
        throw new CryptographicException(
                Environment.GetResourceString(
                "Cryptography_InvalidKeySize"));
    }
```

Continued

Figure 4.4 .NET Framework Source Code for the *IsWeakKey* Method

```
UInt64 key = QuadWordFromBigEndian(rgbKey);
if ((key == 0x0101010101010101) ||
     (key == 0xfefefefefefefefe) ||
     (key == 0x1f1f1f1f0e0e0e0e) ||
     (key == 0xe0e0e0e0f1f1f1f1)) {
     return(true);
}
return(false);
}
```

Figure 4.5 .NET Framework Source Code for the *IsSemiWeakKey* Method

```
public static bool IsSemiWeakKey(byte[] rgbKey) {
    if (!IsLegalKeySize(rgbKey)) {
    throw new CryptographicException(
        Environment.GetResourceString(
        "Cryptography_InvalidKeySize"));
    }
    UInt64 key = QuadWordFromBigEndian(rgbKey);
    if ((key == 0x01fe01fe01fe01fe) ||
         (key == 0xfe01fe01fe01fe01) ||
         (key == 0x1fe01fe00ef10ef1) ||
         (key == 0xe01fe01ff10ef10e) ||
         (key == 0x01e001e001f101f1) ||
         (key == 0xe001e001f101f101) ||
         (key == 0x1ffe1ffe0efe0efe) ||
         (key == 0xfe1ffe1ffe0efe0e) ||
         (key == 0x011f011f010e010e) ||
         (key == 0x1f011f010e010e01) ||
         (key == 0xe0fee0fef1fef1fe) ||
         (key == 0xfee0fee0fef1fef1)) {
         return(true);
    }
    return(false);
}
```

Note that automatically generated keys and those from the *GenerateKey* method will never produce weak keys, and the chances of randomly selecting one of these are 1 in 18,014,398,509,482,000. Furthermore, the *DES* and *TripleDES* classes will throw a *CryptographicException* if you try to use a weak key.

Rijndael

Given that DES is reaching the end of its useful life and 3DES is really not much more than a temporary fix, many experts are looking to other algorithms. The National Institute of Standards and Technology (NIST) recently chose the Rijndael specification as its official replacement to DES. This specification, referred to as the Advanced Encryption Standard (AES), can be found at http://csrc.nist.gov/publications/fips/fips197/fips-197.pdf. Rijndael supports larger key sizes than DES but has improved performance over 3DES. The Rijndael specification supports key sizes of 128, 192, or 256 bits.

Because of government standardization on this algorithm, it is expected to become a widely used replacement for DES, although ASP.NET still relies heavily on DES and 3DES. However, Rijndael is the default algorithm used with the *SymmetricAlgorithm* class and is the only symmetric algorithm that fully runs in managed code. Figures 4.6 and 4.7 show an example using Rijndael encryption in ASP.NET. Note that Rijndael encryption does not have any known weak keys and therefore does not support the *IsWeakKey* method.

The Rijndael cipher is the fastest and supports the largest key size of all the .NET Framework ciphers.

Figure 4.6 Rijndael Encryption: C#

```
private void rijndael()
{
    string plainText = "This is a secret for Rijndael";
    Response.Write("plainText: " + plainText + "<br>");
    byte[] buffer = ASCIIEncoding.ASCII.GetBytes(plainText);
    RijndaelManaged rijndael = new RijndaelManaged();
    rijndael.GenerateKey();
    rijndael.GenerateIV();

    string encryptedString = Convert.ToBase64String(
        rijndael.CreateEncryptor().TransformFinalBlock(
        buffer, 0, buffer.Length));
```

Continued

Figure 4.6 Rijndael Encryption: C#

```
Response.Write("Encrypted string: " + encryptedString + "<br>");


buffer = Convert.FromBase64String(encryptedString);
string decryptedString = ASCIIEncoding.ASCII.GetString(
   rijndael.CreateDecryptor().TransformFinalBlock(
   buffer, 0, buffer.Length));
Response.Write("Decrypted string: " + decryptedString + "<br>");
}
```

Figure 4.7 Rijndael Encryption: VB.NET

```
Private Function rijndaelEncryption()
   Dim plainText As String = "This is a secret for Rijndael"
   Response.Write("plainText: " + plainText + "<br>")


   Dim buffer() As Byte = ASCIIEncoding.ASCII.GetBytes(plainText)
   Dim rijndael As RijndaelManaged = New RijndaelManaged
   rijndael.GenerateKey()
   rijndael.GenerateIV()


   Dim encryptedString As String = _
       Convert.ToBase64String( _
       rijndael.CreateEncryptor().TransformFinalBlock( _
       buffer, 0, buffer.Length))
   Response.Write("encryptedString: " + encryptedString + "<br>")
   buffer = Convert.FromBase64String(encryptedString)
   Dim decryptedString As String = _
       ASCIIEncoding.ASCII.GetString( _
       rijndael.CreateDecryptor().TransformFinalBlock( _
       buffer, 0, buffer.Length))
   Response.Write("Decrypted string: " + decryptedString + "<br>")
End Function
```

RC2

RC2 is a symmetric block cipher designed by Ronald Rivest of RSA. RSA designed RC2 as a direct replacement for DES, improving on the performance and providing a variable key size. RC2 is commonly used in S/MIME secure e-mail and is said to be two to three times as fast as DES. The complete RC2 specification is available at www.ietf.org/rfc/rfc2268.txt. Figure 4.8 and Figure 4.9 show examples using RC2 encryption. Like Rijndael, RC2 does not have any known weak keys and therefore does not support the *IsWeakKey* method.

RC2 is a widely used algorithm that allows a variety of key lengths, but you should be aware that security experts consider RC2 with smaller keys to be insecure. You should always use a 128-bit key, the maximum length available.

 Figure 4.8 RC2 Encryption: C#

```
private void rc2()
{
    string plainText = "This is a secret for RC2";
    Response.Write("plainText: " + plainText + "<br>");
    byte[] buffer = ASCIIEncoding.ASCII.GetBytes(plainText);
    RC2CryptoServiceProvider rc2 = new RC2CryptoServiceProvider();
    rc2.GenerateKey();
    rc2.GenerateIV();

    string encryptedString = Convert.ToBase64String(
        rc2.CreateEncryptor().TransformFinalBlock(
        buffer, 0, buffer.Length));
    Response.Write("Encrypted string: " + encryptedString + "<br>");

    buffer = Convert.FromBase64String(encryptedString);
    string decryptedString = ASCIIEncoding.ASCII.GetString(
        rc2.CreateDecryptor().TransformFinalBlock(
        buffer, 0, buffer.Length));
    Response.Write("Decrypted string: " + decryptedString + "<br>");
}
```

Figure 4.9 RC2 Encryption: VB.NET

```
Private Function rc2Encryption()
  Dim plainText As String = "This is a secret for RC2"
  Response.Write("plainText: " + plainText + "<br>")

  Dim buffer() As Byte = ASCIIEncoding.ASCII.GetBytes(plainText)
  Dim rc2 As New RC2CryptoServiceProvider
  rc2.GenerateKey()
  rc2.GenerateIV()

  Dim encryptedString As String = _
      Convert.ToBase64String( _
      rc2.CreateEncryptor().TransformFinalBlock( _
      buffer, 0, buffer.Length))
  Response.Write("encryptedString: " + encryptedString + "<br>")
  buffer = Convert.FromBase64String(encryptedString)
  Dim decryptedString As String = _
      ASCIIEncoding.ASCII.GetString( _
      rc2.CreateDecryptor().TransformFinalBlock( _
      buffer, 0, buffer.Length))
  Response.Write("Decrypted string: " + decryptedString + "<br>")
End Function
```

Selecting an Algorithm

Selecting a symmetric encryption algorithm is essentially a matter of key length, compatibility, performance, experience, and personal preference. It is extremely difficult to prove that an encryption algorithm is the most secure, although the failure to demonstrate vulnerabilities over time is usually good enough proof. Ultimately, the strength of the algorithm is based on the size of the key, but there is no guarantee that any particular algorithm is without flaws.

SYNGRESS
syngress.com

WARNING

At the time of this writing, there are no known flaws with these algorithms, other than limitations on key length. However, we do know that some government agencies spend a great amount of money and effort looking for flaws in these algorithms. If such an agency were ever to discover (or already has discovered) a flaw, you can bet that would become one of their most closely guarded secrets. In fact, they would likely go to great lengths to give the impression that they have no clue of any flaws with the algorithms.

In a situation in which security is a much higher priority than performance, you could avoid exposure by layering multiple algorithms as shown in Figures 4.10 and 4.11. Because *CryptoStreams* allow chaining, it is a simple process to provide multiple layers of encryption.

Figure 4.10 Layering Symmetric Ciphers: C#

```
private void layeringSymmetricCiphers()
{
    string plainText = "This is a secret for Layering Ciphers";
    Response.Write("plainText: " + plainText + "<br>");
    byte[] buffer = ASCIIEncoding.ASCII.GetBytes(plainText);
    MemoryStream encryptedMemoryStream = new MemoryStream();

    RijndaelManaged rijndael = new RijndaelManaged();
    rijndael.GenerateKey();
    rijndael.GenerateIV();

    RC2CryptoServiceProvider rc2 = new RC2CryptoServiceProvider();
    rc2.GenerateKey();
    rc2.GenerateIV();

    // Chain the streams together for encryption
    CryptoStream cryptoStream = new CryptoStream(
        new CryptoStream(encryptedMemoryStream, rc2.CreateEncryptor(),
        CryptoStreamMode.Write), rijndael.CreateEncryptor(),
```

Continued

Figure 4.10 Layering Symmetric Ciphers: C#

```
                    CryptoStreamMode.Write);

    cryptoStream.Write(buffer, 0, buffer.Length);
    cryptoStream.FlushFinalBlock();
    string encryptedString = Convert.ToBase64String(
        encryptedMemoryStream.ToArray());
    Response.Write("Encrypted string: " + encryptedString + "<br>");


    // Prepare for decryption
    MemoryStream decryptedMemoryStream =
        new MemoryStream(encryptedMemoryStream.ToArray());
    buffer = new byte[decryptedMemoryStream.ToArray().Length];


    // Unchain the streams for decryption
    cryptoStream = new CryptoStream(
        new CryptoStream(decryptedMemoryStream, rc2.CreateDecryptor(),
            CryptoStreamMode.Read), rijndael.CreateDecryptor(),
            CryptoStreamMode.Read);


    cryptoStream.Read(buffer, 0, buffer.Length);
    string decryptedString = ASCIIEncoding.ASCII.GetString(buffer);
    Response.Write("Decrypted string: " + decryptedString + "<br>");
}
```

Figure 4.11 Layering Symmetric Ciphers: VB.NET

```
Private Function layeringSymmetricCiphers()
    Dim plainText As String = "This is a secret for Layering Ciphers"
    Response.Write("plainText: " + plainText + "<br>")
    Dim buffer() As Byte = ASCIIEncoding.ASCII.GetBytes(plainText)
    Dim encryptedMemoryStream As MemoryStream = New MemoryStream


    Dim rc2 As RC2CryptoServiceProvider = New RC2CryptoServiceProvider
    rc2.GenerateKey()
    rc2.GenerateIV()
```

Continued

Figure 4.11 Layering Symmetric Ciphers: VB.NET

```vb
Dim rijndael As RijndaelManaged = New RijndaelManaged
rijndael.GenerateKey()
rijndael.GenerateIV()


' Chain the streams together for encryption
Dim cryptoStream As CryptoStream = New CryptoStream( _
    New CryptoStream(encryptedMemoryStream, rc2.CreateEncryptor, _
        CryptoStreamMode.Write), rijndael.CreateEncryptor, _
        CryptoStreamMode.Write)


cryptoStream.Write(buffer, 0, buffer.Length)
cryptoStream.FlushFinalBlock()
Dim encryptedString As String = Convert.ToBase64String( _
    encryptedMemoryStream.ToArray())
Response.Write("Encrypted string: " + encryptedString + "<br>")


' Prepare for decryption
Dim decryptedMemoryStream As MemoryStream = _
    New MemoryStream(encryptedMemoryStream.ToArray())


' Unchain the streams for decryption
cryptoStream = New CryptoStream( _
New CryptoStream(decryptedMemoryStream, rc2.CreateDecryptor(), _
    CryptoStreamMode.Read), rijndael.CreateDecryptor(), _
    CryptoStreamMode.Read)


cryptoStream.Read(buffer, 0, buffer.Length)
Dim decryptedString As String = ASCIIEncoding.ASCII.GetString(buffer)
Response.Write("Decrypted string: " + decryptedString + "<br>")


End Function
```

Establishing Keys and Initialization Vectors

A number of parameters determine the outcome of the ciphertext. To decrypt the ciphertext, you must use the same algorithm and the same parameters. Two of the parameters you should intentionally change each time are the key and the initialization vector (IV). The key is the secret vital to ensuring the integrity of the data and the IV ensures randomness and uniqueness of the ciphertext blocks.

If you encrypt data with the same key each time, you will always end up with the same ciphertext. Knowing this, an attacker can eventually gain enough data to decode many messages. To prevent this, the symmetric encryption algorithms use the IV to initialize the process, ensuring a unique ciphertext message. The message recipient must know both the key and the IV to decrypt the message, but only the key must remain secret.

WARNING

When creating a key and IV, never derive one from the other, because knowing the IV could allow the attacker to determine the key. Also be sure to avoid a fixed IV for all encryption. The best solution is to use the random IV that the algorithm automatically creates when it's initialized.

There are some difficulties when it comes to exchanging keys, especially when it comes to sharing a key without any prior shared secrets. The whole reason for the encryption is that you do not trust the transmission medium. Therefore, you must somehow transmit the key over an insecure connection, but if you already have a secure connection, why would you need further encryption? Suppose, for example, that you want to send someone an encrypted message. The recipient will not be able to read your message unless you give her the proper key. It makes no sense to send the key along with the message, so you instead call the recipient on the phone to convey the key. But since you already trust the phone line enough to share the key, you might as well go ahead and share the whole message. This is a major shortcoming of symmetric cryptography but is an issue we can overcome with key exchange algorithms and by using asymmetric cryptography. For an ASP.NET application, this is not as great an issue, because you can easily use SSL to establish a secure session.

Most often you will use symmetric encryption for saving sensitive settings or user data. The problem with this is that your ASP.NET application must know the key and therefore must save the key for its own use. This is a problem because if an attacker takes over the application, the attacker will gain access to the application's keys. For example, ASP.NET uses the machine.config file to store the encryption keys for many encryption operations, such as encrypting a forms authentication ticket. If an attacker were able to read this file, that attacker could forge his own authentication tickets. To help this situation, you can use DPAPI, as explained later in this chapter. You should also design your application so that it allows you to regularly change your keys.

Sometimes you might want the user to be able to encrypt information that even you cannot access. The user provides the key and then gains access to the encrypted data. However, it normally is not practical to expect a user to memorize or type a large encryption key. If users have issues remembering a password of six or eight characters, how will they remember a 128-bit key? The solution is to allow the user to enter a password that you use to derive an appropriate key.

The *PasswordDeriveBytes.CryptDeriveKey* method can produce an appropriate key based on a password, salt, algorithm, and number of iterations. This method creates a hash of the password using the supplied salt and uses that hash to create another hash, repeating this process for as many iterations specified. The result is a long string suitable to use as a key. Figures 4.12 and 4.13 demonstrate the code to use *CryptDeriveKey,* and Figure 4.14 shows an example key derived from a user's password.

WARNING

Note that although you can use *CryptDeriveKey* to turn a short password into a strong key, keep in mind that the key is only as strong as the password itself. By using *CryptDeriveKey,* you are effectively reducing the key strength to that of the password, not the other way around. However, using a large number of iterations definitely will slow a brute-force attack because the attacker would have to perform those iterations for each password attempt. For a password-cracking tool, every millisecond makes a huge difference.

SYNGRESS syngress.com

Figure 4.12 Using CryptDeriveKey: C#

```
private void cryptDeriveKeyExample()
{
  // set initial values
  string password = "ThisIsMyPassword";
  string salt = "ThisIsMySalt";
  string algname = "RC2";
  string hashName = "MD5";
  byte[] IV = new byte[8];
  int keySize = 128;

  // Create and PasswordDeriveBytes
  PasswordDeriveBytes pdb =
    new PasswordDeriveBytes(password,
    ASCIIEncoding.ASCII.GetBytes(salt));

  // Extract Key
  byte[] key = pdb.CryptDeriveKey(algname, hashName, keySize, IV);

  Response.Write("derived key: " + Convert.ToBase64String(key) + "<br>");
 }
```

SYNGRESS syngress.com

Figure 4.13 Using CryptDeriveKey: VB.NET

```
Private Function cryptDeriveKeyExample()
  ' set initial values
  Dim password As String = "ThisIsMyPassword"
  Dim salt As String = "ThisIsMySalt"
  Dim algname As String = "RC2"
  Dim hashName As String = "MD5"
  Dim IV() As Byte = New Byte(7) {}
  Dim keySize As Integer = 128

  ' Create and PasswordDeriveBytes
  Dim pdb As PasswordDeriveBytes = _
   New PasswordDeriveBytes(password, _
```

Continued

Figure 4.13 Using CryptDeriveKey: VB.NET

```
ASCIIEncoding.ASCII.GetBytes(salt))


' Extract Key
Dim key As Byte() = pdb.CryptDeriveKey(algname, hashName, keySize, IV)


Response.Write("derived key: " + Convert.ToBase64String(key) + "<br>")
End Function
```

Figure 4.14 Example of Key Derived from a Password

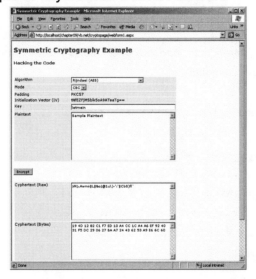

When using CBC or CFB modes, you must set an initialization vector. The IV works like a salt to further transform the data so that two plaintext messages encrypted with unique IVs will produce unique ciphertext data. This makes it more difficult to perform a dictionary attack on the ciphertext. Generally you want to use a random number for the IV, which *SymmetricAlgorithm* automatically generates when the class is created. You must read this property and store the IV so that you can later decrypt the ciphertext. If you create your own IV, you need to create one that is the same length as the key. Note that the IV is not a secret and you do not need to take special measures to protect it. Figures 4.15 and 4.16 show examples of how you can append the IV and the ciphertext so that you can store them together. They also show how you can extract the IV and decrypt the ciphertext.

Figure 4.15 Saving the IV with the Ciphertext: C#

```csharp
private void savingIVWithCipherText()
{

string plainText = "This is a secret for savingIVWithCipherText";
Response.Write("plainText: " + plainText + "<br>");
byte[] buffer = ASCIIEncoding.ASCII.GetBytes(plainText);
RijndaelManaged rijndael =
  new RijndaelManaged();
rijndael.GenerateKey();
rijndael.GenerateIV();

// Perform encryption
byte[] encryptedBytes = rijndael.CreateEncryptor().TransformFinalBlock(
  buffer, 0, buffer.Length);

// append IV to beginning of encrypted string
byte[] encryptedByteArrayWithIV =
  new byte[encryptedBytes.Length + rijndael.IV.Length];
for (int x=0; x < rijndael.IV.Length; x++)
  encryptedByteArrayWithIV[x] = rijndael.IV[x];
for (int x=0; x < encryptedBytes.Length; x++)
  encryptedByteArrayWithIV[rijndael.IV.Length + x] =
    encryptedBytes[x];

// Display ciphertext with IV appended
string encryptedStringWithIV =
  Convert.ToBase64String(encryptedByteArrayWithIV);
Response.Write("Encrypted string with IV: " +
  encryptedStringWithIV + "<br>");

// remove the IV from the beginning of the encrypted string
byte[] decryptedBytesWithIV =
  Convert.FromBase64String(encryptedStringWithIV);
byte[] decryptedIV = new byte[rijndael.IV.Length];
byte[] decryptedBytes =
  new byte[decryptedBytesWithIV.Length - rijndael.IV.Length];
```

Continued

Figure 4.15 Saving the IV with the Ciphertext: C#

```
for (int x=0; x < decryptedIV.Length; x++)
  decryptedIV[x] = decryptedBytesWithIV[x];
for (int x=0; x < decryptedBytes.Length; x++)
  decryptedBytes[x] =
   decryptedBytesWithIV[decryptedIV.Length + x];


// decrypted the ciphertext using the retrieved IV
rijndael.IV = decryptedIV;
string decryptedString = ASCIIEncoding.ASCII.GetString(
  rijndael.CreateDecryptor().TransformFinalBlock(
  decryptedBytes, 0, decryptedBytes.Length));
Response.Write("Decrypted string: " + decryptedString + "<br>");
}
```

Figure 4.16 Saving the IV with the Ciphertext: VB.NET

```
Private Function savingIVWithCipherText()
  Dim plainText As String = "This is a secret for savingIVWithCipherText"
  Response.Write("plainText: " + plainText + "<br>")


  Dim buffer() As Byte = ASCIIEncoding.ASCII.GetBytes(plainText)
  Dim rijndael As RijndaelManaged = New RijndaelManaged
  rijndael.GenerateKey()
  rijndael.GenerateIV()


  ' Perform encryption
  Dim encryptedBytes As Byte() = _
      rijndael.CreateEncryptor().TransformFinalBlock( _
      buffer, 0, buffer.Length)


  ' append IV to beginning of encrypted string
  Dim encryptedByteArrayWithIV() As Byte = _
      New Byte((encryptedBytes.Length - 1) + (rijndael.IV.Length - 1)) {}


  Dim x As Integer
```

Continued

Figure 4.16 Saving the IV with the Ciphertext: VB.NET

```vbnet
For x = 0 To rijndael.IV.Length - 1
    encryptedByteArrayWithIV(x) = rijndael.IV(x)
Next

For x = 0 To encryptedBytes.Length - 1
    encryptedByteArrayWithIV((rijndael.IV.Length - 1) + x) = _
        encryptedBytes(x)
Next


' Display ciphertext with IV appended
Dim encryptedStringWithIV As String = _
 Convert.ToBase64String(encryptedByteArrayWithIV)
Response.Write("Encrypted string with IV: " + _
    encryptedStringWithIV + "<br>")


' remove the IV from the beginning of the encrypted string
Dim decryptedBytesWithIV As Byte() = _
    Convert.FromBase64String(encryptedStringWithIV)
Dim decryptedIV As Byte() = New Byte(rijndael.IV.Length - 1) {}
Dim decryptedBytes As Byte() = _
    New Byte((decryptedBytesWithIV.Length - 1) - _
            (rijndael.IV.Length - 1)) {}
For x = 0 To decryptedIV.Length - 1
    decryptedIV(x) = decryptedBytesWithIV(x)
Next


For x = 0 To decryptedBytes.Length - 1
    decryptedBytes(x) = decryptedBytesWithIV((decryptedIV.Length - 1) + _
            x)
Next
' decrypted the ciphertext using the retrieved IV
rijndael.IV = decryptedIV
Dim decryptedString As String = ASCIIEncoding.ASCII.GetString( _
    rijndael.CreateDecryptor().TransformFinalBlock( _
    decryptedBytes, 0, decryptedBytes.Length))
Response.Write("Decrypted string: " + decryptedString + "<br>")
End Function
```

Symmetric cryptography does have its limitations and weaknesses, but it also plays an important role in protecting data. The .NET Framework provides good support for well-established symmetric ciphers, and you should always encrypt sensitive data. Establish a solid framework for encryption early in your application design.

Security Policies

- Use strong symmetric ciphers to ensure the privacy of data.

- Never rely on XOR, ROT-13, base-64 encoding, or any homegrown encryption or obfuscation algorithm.

- Avoid using DES unless absolutely necessary for backward compatibility; consider 3DES as a compatible alternative.

- Use Rijndael/AES encryption for the best security and performance.

- If using RC2 encryption, use 128-bit keys whenever possible.

- When security is a high priority and performance a low priority, consider layering encryption algorithms.

- When creating a key and IV, do not derive one from the other.

- Use *CryptDeriveKey* to create an encryption key from a user password.

Using Asymmetric Cryptography

Summary: **Asymmetric cryptography works well for public communications but is much slower than symmetric cryptography**

Threats: **Information leakage, data corruption, man-in-the-middle attacks, brute-force attacks**

Asymmetric cryptography addresses symmetric cryptography's key exchange and scalability issues by using a public and private key model. Symmetric cryptography uses only one key for all data encryption and decryption, but asymmetric cryptography uses two separate keys—one for encryption and the other for decryption. The idea is that you can freely distribute your public key, which others can use to encrypt data that only you can access with your private key.

The two keys are mathematically derived from a master key, which is then destroyed. It is mathematically infeasible to create one key from the other without this master; therefore, you can distribute your public key without compromising your private key. This solution addresses the problem of key distribution because you can freely share your public key.

TIP

Although asymmetric cryptography makes it possible to share public keys, it is vital that you protect the private key. For this reason, it is generally not a safe practice to store the private key within your Web application.

One of the problems with symmetric cryptography is that you need a different key for every person with whom you communicate, and they need a different key for everyone with whom they communicate. If you have two people exchanging encrypted messages, you need just one key. If three people want to communicate securely, they need three keys; four people need six keys; and five people need 10 keys. As you can see, the number of keys required rapidly increases, severely limiting the scalability of symmetric cryptography. Asymmetric cryptography deals with this problem by using a single public key for each user; everyone can use that key to communicate with that user while maintaining a good level of integrity.

Asymmetric cryptography is processor intensive and therefore rarely used to encrypt the entire communication. Instead, most applications use asymmetric cryptography to exchange a session key and then use a symmetric cipher to encrypt the traffic during that session.

Because asymmetric cryptography often involves code on both the client and the server, you will rarely find uses for custom implementations on most public Web applications. Nevertheless, you will find yourself using asymmetric cryptography in conjunction with other technologies such as SSL. The SSL protocol uses asymmetric cryptography to establish a symmetric session key for secure data exchange. SSL maintains the security and integrity of the Web communications and authenticates the server to the client (and optionally the client to the server). You will learn more about SSL later in this chapter.

Working with Hashing Algorithms

Summary: **Hashing algorithms are one-way functions used to verify integrity of data**

Threats: **Information leakage, data corruption, man-in-the-middle attacks, brute-force attacks**

Even though encryption is important for protecting data, sometimes it is important to be able to prove that no one has modified the data. This you can do with hashing algorithms. A *hash* is a one-way function that transforms data in such a way that, given a hash result (sometimes called a *digest*), it is computationally infeasible to produce the original message. Besides being one-way, hash functions have some other basic properties:

- They take an input of any length and produce an output of a fixed length.

- They should be efficient and fast to compute.

- They should be computationally infeasible to invert.

- They should be strongly collision free.

A hash function takes input of any length and produces a fixed-length string. That means that you can use hashes on something as small as a password or as large as an entire document. The hashing algorithms the .NET Framework provides are very efficient and fast, making them useful for many applications. The most important property of hash functions is the size of the hash. A larger hash makes it more difficult to invert the function, and it ensures that the function is collision free.

Because hash functions have a fixed output but unlimited inputs, multiple values can produce the same hash. However, because there are so many possible hash values, it is extremely difficult to find two inputs that do produce hashes that match. For that reason, hashes are like a fingerprint for the original data. If the data changes, the fingerprint will no longer match, and it is unlikely that any other useful data will produce the same fingerprint. Therefore, you can store these small fingerprints, or hashes, to later verify your data's integrity.

Another common use for a hash is for someone to demonstrate knowledge of a piece of information without actually disclosing that information. For example, to prove you know a password, you could send the actual password, or you could produce and send the hash of that password. This is useful for Web site authentication, because the server does not have to store the actual password—it needs only the hash.

The .NET Framework supports the hashing algorithms shown in Table 4.3.

Table 4.3 Hashing Algorithms Available in the .NET Framework

Name	Class	Hash Length
MD5	MD5CryptoServiceProvider	128 bits
SHA-1	SHA1CryptoServiceProvider SHA1Managed	160 bits
SHA-256	SHA256Managed	256 bits
SHA-384	SHA384Managed	384 bits
SHA-512	SHA512Managed	512 bits

The MD5 algorithm, defined in RFC 1321, is probably the most well-known and widely used hash function. It is the fastest of all the .NET hashing algorithms, but it uses a smaller 128-bit hash value, making it the most vulnerable to attack over the long term. MD5 has been shown to have some partial collisions and is not likely to be able to withstand future attacks as hardware capabilities increase. Nevertheless, for now it the most commonly used hashing algorithm.

SHA is an algorithm designed by the National Security Agency (NSA) and published by NIST as FIPS PUB 180. Designed for use with the Digital Signature Standard (DSS), SHA produces a 160-bit hash value.

The original SHA specification published in 1993 was shortly withdrawn by the NSA and superceded by the revised FIPS PUB 180-1, commonly referred to as SHA-1. The NSA's reason for withdrawing the original specification was to correct a flaw in the original algorithm that reduced its cryptographic security. However, the NSA never gave details of this flaw, prompting researchers to closely examine both algorithms. Because of this close scrutiny, SHA-1 is widely considered to be quite secure.

The NIST has since published three variants of SHA-1 that produce larger hashes: SHA-256, SHA-384, and SHA-512. Although with the larger hash sizes these algorithms should be more secure, they have not undergone as much analysis as SHA-1. Nevertheless, the hash length is important to protect from brute-force and birthday attacks.

Hacking the Code...

About Birthday Attacks

Birthday attacks are based on a unique problem with hashing algorithms based on a concept called the Birthday Paradox. This puzzle is based on the fact that in a room of 183 people, there would be a 50 percent chance of one of them sharing your birthday. However, if you wanted a 50 percent chance of finding any two people who had matching birthdays, you would surprisingly only need 23 people in the room. For hashing functions, this means that it is much easier to find any two matches if you don't care which two they are. It is possible to precompute hashes for a given password length to determine if any collisions occur.

Verifying Integrity

You can use hashes to verify integrity, but many developers use them incorrectly, undoing their effectiveness. For example, many Web sites allow you to download a file as well as the MD5 checksum for that file. They do this so that you can verify the integrity of the file, but you are downloading the checksum from the same location and over the same connection as the file itself. If you don't trust the file enough to actually need to verify the hash, how can you trust the hash that came from the same location? If someone is able to modify the file, they could just as easily compute and save a new hash.

TIP

To verify the integrity of file downloads, many Web sites provide an MD5 sum as well as a PGP signature of the sum. The MD5 sum verifies integrity, and the PGP signature proves that the MD5 sum is authentic.

Hashes are useful if you keep them private to verify data such as a cookie. For example, suppose you write a cookie to the client's browser and store the hash of that cookie in your database. When the client returns that cookie at a later time, you can compute the hash and compare that to the one stored in the database to verify that it has not changed. Since ASP.NET stores session and authentication tokens entirely in the cookie and not on the server, it computes a hash of the cookie data and encrypts both the data and the hash. This encrypted result is encoded and saved in a cookie on the client side. When the client returns the cookie data, the server decrypts the string and verifies the hash. In this way, ASP.NET protects the hash and protects the privacy of the data.

Another way to make hashes more secure is to use a *keyed hash* algorithm. Keyed hashes are similar to regular hashes except that the hash is based on a secret key. To verify the hash or to create a fake hash, you need to know that key. The .NET Framework provides two keyed hashing algorithms:

- **HMACSHA1** This function produces a hash-based message authentication code based on the SHA-1 hashing algorithm. HMACSHA1 combines the original message and the secret key and uses SHA-1 to create a hash. It then combines that hash again with the secret key and creates a second SHA-1 hash. Like SHA-1, the HMACSHA1 algorithm produces a 160-bit hash.

- **MACTripleDES** This algorithm uses *TripleDES* to encrypt the message, discarding all but the final 64 bits of the ciphertext.

With keyed hashing algorithms, you can send the hash with the data, but you must keep the key secret. Note that this method does have limitations similar to the key exchange issues of symmetric cryptography. Figures 4.17 and 4.18 demonstrate using the HMACSHA1 function.

Figure 4.17 Keyed Hashing Using HMACSHA1: C#

```
private void HMACSHA1Example()
{
    // Setup
    string plainText = "This is a secret for HMACSHA1Example";
    Response.Write("plainText: " + plainText + "<br>");
    byte[] key = ASCIIEncoding.ASCII.GetBytes("SecretKey");
    byte[] data = ASCIIEncoding.ASCII.GetBytes(plainText);

    // Perform Hash
    HMACSHA1 hmac = new HMACSHA1(key);
```

Continued

Figure 4.17 Keyed Hashing Using HMACSHA1: C#

```
byte[] result = hmac.ComputeHash(data);
Response.Write("HMACSHA1Example results: " +
   Convert.ToBase64String(result) + "<br>");
}
```

Figure 4.18 Keyed Hashing Using HMACSHA1: VB.NET

```
Private Sub HMACSHA1Example()
  ' Setup
  Dim plainText As String = "This is a secret for HMACSHA1Example"
  Response.Write("plainText: " + plainText + "<br>")
  Dim key() As Byte = ASCIIEncoding.ASCII.GetBytes("SecretKey")
  Dim data() As Byte = ASCIIEncoding.ASCII.GetBytes(plainText)

  ' Perform Hash
  Dim hmac As HMACSHA1 = New HMACSHA1(key)
  Dim result() As Byte = hmac.ComputeHash(data)
  Response.Write("HMACSHA1Example results: " + _
     Convert.ToBase64String(result) + "<br>")
End Sub
```

Hashing Passwords

Another important use for hashes is storing passwords. As described in Chapter 1, you should not store actual passwords in your database. Using hashing algorithms, you can store the hash and use that to authenticate the user. Because it is highly unlikely that two passwords would produce the same hash, you can compare the stored hash with a hash of the password submitted by the user. If the two match, you can be sure that the user has the correct password.

Protecting passwords with hashes has some unique problems. First, although hashes are not reversible, they are crackable using a brute-force method. You cannot produce the password from the hash, but you can create hashes of millions of passwords until you find one that matches. For this reason, the hash's strength isn't based so much on the key length of the hashing algorithm, but on the length of the password itself. And because passwords have such low entropy, are predictable, and are often too short, this usually is not a difficult task.

Another problem with hashes is that the same data will always produce the same hash. This can be a problem if someone ever obtains the hashes, because they can use a precomputed dictionary of hashes to instantly discover common passwords. To prevent this situation, we can add a salt to the password to ensure a different hash each time. The salt should be a large random number uniquely generated for that purpose. You do not need to keep the salt private, so you can save the salt with the hash itself.

When you use a salt, there are as many possible hashes for any given piece of data as there are bits in the salt. Of course, if the intruder has access to the hashes, they also have access to the salts, but the key here is to force the attacker to compute each hash individually and not gain any benefit from passwords he or she has already cracked. Figures 4.19 and 4.20 show hashing algorithms that include salts.

Figure 4.19 Hashing with a Salt: C#

```
private void hashExample()
{
    string plainText = "This is a secret for hashExample";
    Response.Write("plainText: " + plainText + "<br>");

    // Create strong random byte values
    byte[] saltBytes = new byte[8];
    RNGCryptoServiceProvider rng = new RNGCryptoServiceProvider();
    rng.GetNonZeroBytes(saltBytes);

    // Create an array to hold plain text and salt
    byte[] plainTextBytes = ASCIIEncoding.ASCII.GetBytes(plainText);
    byte[] plainTextAndSaltBytes =
        new byte[plainTextBytes.Length + saltBytes.Length];

    // Append salt value and create byte array for hash
    for (int x=0; x < saltBytes.Length; x++)
        plainTextAndSaltBytes[x] = saltBytes[x];
    for (int x=0; x < plainTextBytes.Length; x++)
        plainTextAndSaltBytes[saltBytes.Length + x] =
        plainTextBytes[x];
```

Continued

Figure 4.19 Hashing with a Salt: C#

```
// Perform hash using SHA1

HashAlgorithm hash = new SHA1Managed();

byte[] hashBytes = hash.ComputeHash(plainTextAndSaltBytes);

Response.Write("Hashed string with salt: " +

    Convert.ToBase64String(hashBytes) + "<br>");

}
```

Figure 4.20 Hashing with a Salt: VB.NET

```
Private Function hashExample()

    Dim plainText As String = "This is a secret for hashExample"

    Response.Write("plainText: " + plainText + "<br>")


    ' Create strong random byte values

    Dim saltBytes() As Byte = New Byte(8) {}


    Dim rng As RNGCryptoServiceProvider = New RNGCryptoServiceProvider

    rng.GetNonZeroBytes(saltBytes)


    ' Create an array to hold plain text and salt

    Dim plainTextBytes As Byte() = ASCIIEncoding.ASCII.GetBytes(plainText)

    Dim plainTextAndSaltBytes As Byte() = _

        New Byte(plainTextBytes.Length + saltBytes.Length) {}


    ' Append salt value and create byte array for hash

    Dim x As Integer

    For x = 0 To saltBytes.Length - 1 Step x + 1

        plainTextAndSaltBytes(x) = saltBytes(x)

    Next


    For x = 0 To plainTextBytes.Length - 1 Step x + 1

        plainTextAndSaltBytes(saltBytes.Length + x) = plainTextBytes(x)

    Next


    ' Perform hash using SHA1

    Dim hash As HashAlgorithm = New SHA1Managed
```

Continued

Figure 4.20 Hashing with a Salt: VB.NET

```
Dim hashBytes As Byte() = hash.ComputeHash(plainTextAndSaltBytes)
Response.Write("Hashed string with salt: " + _
      Convert.ToBase64String(hashBytes) + "<br>")
End Function
```

You might think that a salt is similar to an IV. In fact, it is essentially the same technique that accomplishes the same purpose. Note that it is also similar in function to a keyed hash algorithm, and a keyed function such as HMACSHA1 is an excellent replacement for the code in Figure 4.20. To use a keyed hash, simply use the salt in place of the key, and otherwise follow the sample code in Figure 4.19.

Security Policy

- Use hashing algorithms to verify integrity and store passwords.

- For data verification, you can allow others to view a hash, but you must protect it from being modified.

- Use keyed hashing algorithms to protect the hash from being modified.

- For password authentication, keep the hashes secret to prevent brute-force attacks.

- Add salt to a hash to ensure randomness.

Working with .NET Encryption Features

Now that you understand the basics of .NET encryption, we need to examine some topics related to using these features. In this section, we will cover:

- Creating random numbers

- Keeping memory clean

- Protecting secrets

- Protecting communications with SSL

Creating Random Numbers

Summary: Random numbers are a key part of cryptography, but it is nearly impossible for a computer to be completely random on its own

Threats: Information leakage, data corruption, man-in-the-middle attacks, brute-force attacks

Random numbers are a key element of most forms of cryptography. At some point, the strength of the system is based on the ability to produce a random, unpredictable number. Without this randomness, an attacker might be able to predict the cryptographic calculations. For example, Netscape's SSL encryption was cracked in 1995 because it used a weak random-number generator.

Because computers have difficulty with true randomness, they use what are called pseudorandom-number generators (PRNGs). To be used with cryptography, a PRNG should have good *entropy*. Entropy is the measure of randomness that refers to the unpredictability and the uniform distribution of a random number. A strong random-number generator is one that, given a list of numbers already generated, could not predict the next number in the sequence.

The .NET Framework uses the *RNGCryptoServiceProvider* to generate random numbers, which is a wrapper for the *CryptGenRandom* function in CrytpoAPI. This PRNG is considered random enough for all but the most extreme security requirements. If you want to implement even stronger random-number generators, check out www.schneier.com/yarrow.html and www.irisa.fr/caps/projects/hipsor/HAVEGE.html. Note that CryptoAPI gets its entropy from a surprisingly large number of system factors, but if you want to add further entropy, you can pass a string or byte array of entropy when creating the class.

WARNING

When you're using random numbers for cryptographic purposes, always use *RNGCryptoServiceProvider*, not the *System.Random* class. *System.Random* is based on a predictable function and is not considered a strong random-number generator.

Security Policy

- Use only *RNGCryptoServiceProvider* to generate strong random numbers; avoid using *System.Random*.

- Use external sources of entropy to further increase randomness of the PRNG.

Keeping Memory Clean

Summary: **You must carefully plan your code to prevent leaving secrets exposed in memory**

Threats: **Information leakage**

When working with sensitive data, you should always make sure you clean up after yourself; you don't want unencrypted data left around in memory. To limit the possibility of leaving sensitive data in memory, you should use as few variables as possible, avoid caching plaintext, and explicitly clean up after cryptographic operations.

Normally the .NET Framework garbage collector will take care of reclaiming objects no longer used. But it is not predictable when garbage collection will occur, and when it does, the system does not actually clear the memory; it just marks it as available for reuse. Because that memory may contain important information, it is important to always clean up any cryptographic objects and variables. To do this, the .NET Framework provides a *Clear()* method for all cryptographic objects.

When you are finished with any cryptography-related variables, you should clear their contents. This includes not only ciphertext and plaintext variables but also crypto objects, keys, salt, and IV variables. Figures 4.21 and 4.22 show examples of how to do this.

Figure 4.21 Clearing Crypto-Related Objects: C#

```
private void cleaningExample()
{
  // Setup
  byte[] buffer = ASCIIEncoding.ASCII.GetBytes(
    "This is a secret for cleaningExample");
  RijndaelManaged rijndael = new RijndaelManaged();
```

Continued

Figure 4.21 Clearing Crypto-Related Objects: C#

```csharp
rijndael.GenerateKey();
rijndael.GenerateIV();

// Perform encryption
string encryptedString = Convert.ToBase64String(
    rijndael.CreateEncryptor().TransformFinalBlock(
    buffer, 0, buffer.Length));

// Perform decryption
buffer = Convert.FromBase64String(encryptedString);
string decryptedString = ASCIIEncoding.ASCII.GetString(
    rijndael.CreateDecryptor().TransformFinalBlock(
    buffer, 0, buffer.Length));

// Clean up
rijndael.Clear();
encryptedString = decryptedString = String.Empty;
buffer = null;
}
```

Figure 4.22 Clearing Crypto-Related Objects: VB.NET

```vbnet
Private Sub cleaningExample()
    ' Setup
    Dim buffer() As Byte = ASCIIEncoding.ASCII.GetBytes( _
        "This is a secret for cleaningExample")
    Dim rijndael As RijndaelManaged = New RijndaelManaged
    rijndael.GenerateKey()
    rijndael.GenerateIV()

    ' Perform encryption
    Dim encryptedString As String = Convert.ToBase64String( _
        rijndael.CreateEncryptor().TransformFinalBlock( _
        buffer, 0, buffer.Length))

    ' Perform decryption
```

Continued

Figure 4.22 Clearing Crypto-Related Objects: VB.NET

```
buffer = Convert.FromBase64String(encryptedString)
Dim decryptedString As String = ASCIIEncoding.ASCII.GetString( _
 rijndael.CreateDecryptor().TransformFinalBlock( _
 buffer, 0, buffer.Length))

' Clean up
rijndael.Clear()
encryptedString = decryptedString = String.Empty
buffer = Nothing
End Sub
```

Note that some variables do not have *Clear()* methods, so we explicitly zero those out. Be sure to watch all subroutines you call to clear any variables used in those.

Security Policies

- Clear out all variables used with cryptographic operations, including those for plaintext, ciphertext, keys, salts, IVs, and random numbers.

- Use the *Clear()* method to clear out any sensitive data.

- Use the *Dispose()* method to immediately free memory resources.

- Explicitly zero out any variables that do not provide a *Clear()* method.

Protecting Secrets

Summary: **Secrets are a key part of a security system, but it is very difficult to completely protect all secrets**

Threats: **Information leakage, data corruption, man-in-the-middle attacks, brute-force attacks**

One of the most difficult aspects of secure programming is the process of keeping secrets, even if the code itself is compromised. It's easy to store a secret in server-side code, but you cannot always be sure that your code is safe. Many ASP developers have been burned by storing database passwords in the Global.asa file, which should be secure, but a history of IIS exploits has left it and the passwords exposed.

Even the best solutions we have for protecting secret data are not perfect and are still vulnerable if someone gains full access to the Web server.

You might use encryption to protect your data, but at some point your application must store the key used to encrypt that data. You want your application to have access to that key, but you must protect it so that others do not have access. Ultimately, it is impossible to protect this data from misuse, because an attacker could use the application itself to gain access. The best we can accomplish is to limit the ability to access these secrets. In addition to encryption keys, other important secrets to protect are:

- Passwords to access other systems
- Database connection strings
- IP addresses of private servers
- File paths to sensitive data files

There are many ways to gain unauthorized access to a Web server, some giving the attacker full control over the server and others giving only partial access. Here are some examples of the type of access attackers have gained in the past through various Windows, IIS, and other application exploits:

- The ability to view a directory listing of the Web content directories
- The ability to view the contents of any file within the Web content directories
- The ability to view any file on the same partition as the Web content directories
- The ability to write files to the Web content directory
- The ability to execute any program on the same partition as the Web content directories
- The ability to run a command prompt under the context of the anonymous user
- The ability to run a command prompt under the context of the SYSTEM account
- The ability to run commands and access the registry under the context of the SQL Server or other database account
- The ability to view unencrypted traffic as it crosses the network

The important lesson here is that Web content is not always safe. On the other hand, the attacker might not always have full access to your server. The key to protecting secrets is to use a variety of protection techniques so that your application will be more resilient to an attacker who has partial access.

Some of the methods you can use to protect secrets are:

- Storing secret data in a file

- Storing secret data in the registry

- Storing secret data in a database

- Using the Data Protection API (DPAPI) to access the operating system's protected store

Storing Secrets in a File

When using the file system to store secrets, be sure to use a file located outside the Web root and preferably on a separate partition. Use strict file permissions to limit read and write access to this file. Rather than hard-coding the file path, refer to it using environment variables. Although "security through obscurity" is not the best way to protect a file, you should avoid giving the file an overly obvious name such as passwords.txt.

The .NET Framework provides a storage system called *isolated storage* that provides a simple method for storing secrets to a file. The benefits of isolated storage are that you can restrict access to the store by user, assembly, or application domain and that the .NET Framework handles the details of managing file access. To the application, the isolated storage works like a file system. The storage appears as a root container to the application and where it can create files and directories. But the isolated storage system prevents the application from stepping outside the bounds of this storage container. Isolated storage works particularly well when you have multiple semitrusted applications on the same server. Although isolated storage does provide some mechanisms to secure the data, it was not designed to protect secrets, so you should not rely on it alone. Figures 4.23 and 4.24 show examples of how to store and retrieve data from isolated storage.

Figure 4.23 Storing and Retrieving Data from Isolated Storage: C#

```csharp
private void isolatedStorageExample()
{
  // using System.IO.IsolatedStorage;
  string data = "dataForIsolatedStorage";

  // prepare isolated storage for writing
  IsolatedStorageFileStream isolatedStorage =
    new IsolatedStorageFileStream("isolatedStorageExample.txt",
    FileMode.OpenOrCreate, FileAccess.Write);

  // write to isolated storage
  StreamWriter sw = new StreamWriter(isolatedStorage);
  sw.WriteLine(data);
  sw.Close();
  isolatedStorage.Close();

  // prepare isolated storage for reading
  isolatedStorage =
    new IsolatedStorageFileStream("isolatedStorageExample.txt",
    FileMode.Open, FileAccess.Read);

  // read from isolated storage
  StreamReader sr = new StreamReader(isolatedStorage);
  Response.Write("Read from isolated storage: " +
    sr.ReadLine() + "<br>");
  sr.Close();
}
```

Figure 4.24 Storing and Retrieving Data from Isolated Storage: VB.NET

```vbnet
Private Sub isolatedStorageExample()
  ' using System.IO.IsolatedStorage;
  Dim data As String = "dataForIsolatedStorage"

  ' prepare isolated storage for writing
```

Continued

Figure 4.24 Storing and Retrieving Data from Isolated Storage: VB.NET

```
Dim isolatedStorage As IsolatedStorageFileStream = _
   New IsolatedStorageFileStream("isolatedStorageExample.txt", _
   FileMode.OpenOrCreate, FileAccess.Write)


' write to isolated storage
Dim sw As StreamWriter = New StreamWriter(isolatedStorage)
sw.WriteLine(data)
sw.Close()
isolatedStorage.Close()


' prepare isolated storage for reading
isolatedStorage = New IsolatedStorageFileStream( _
   "isolatedStorageExample.txt", FileMode.Open, FileAccess.Read)


' read from isolated storage
Dim sr As StreamReader = New StreamReader(isolatedStorage)
Response.Write("Read from isolated storage: " + _
   sr.ReadLine() + "<br>")


sr.Close()
End Sub
```

Storing Secrets in the Registry

The registry has traditionally been a better mechanism for storing secrets in a Web application, because an attacker usually needs a higher level of access to be able to read the registry than one would ascertain from an anonymous account. For example, an attacker might be able to access the file system through FTP or a file share, but to read the registry usually requires running some code on the server. When storing secrets in the registry, be sure to set strict ACLs on the appropriate registry keys to limit access to those keys. Just as with files, obscurity is not full protection, but you should avoid using overly obvious key names.

Storing Secrets in the Database

Storing secrets in the database can be a good method, especially if you use a trusted connection to your database. Of course, the database connection string itself is a secret, so there are limits to this strategy. One benefit of using the database is that you can easily share the secrets across multiple servers in a Web farm.

Storing Secrets Using DPAPI

DPAPI is probably the most secure method for storing data using the operating system to manage encryption keys, but it does have some limitations. First, there are two choices where to store the data: the machine store and the user store. The machine store is less secure because it is accessible by anyone on the server, but a user store requires a loaded profile that ASP.NET does not provide. User stores can also get more complicated when impersonating multiple users in your Web application. The easiest method is to use the machine store but using extra entropy to help protect the data from others. Of course, you must store this entropy somewhere that your Web application can access.

To use DPAPI, you must wrap the P/Invoke calls to Crypt32.dll. For an example of using DPAPI, see http://msdn.microsoft.com/architecture/application/default.aspx?pull=/library/en-us/dnnetsec/html/SecNetHT08.asp.

Ultimately, the best strategy for storing secrets is to use a combination of the previously described techniques. For example, you could use a registry key to store the entropy for DPAPI access and store the DPAPI encrypted data using isolated storage. The actual techniques you use depend on how you prioritize security and performance and on the rights you have available on the hosting server.

In the end, you still will not have perfect protection of secrets, and your only real protection is to follow security best practices to keep your server secure.

Security Policies

- Avoid storing secrets in code, even if it is compiled.
- Never store any secret in plaintext.
- Use a combination of file, registry, database, or DPAPI to store secrets.
- Use obscurity, but only sparingly as an additional layer of protection in addition to proper encryption and access control.

Protecting Communications with SSL

Summary: SSL provides easy-to-use encryption for HTTP communications

Threats: Information leakage, data corruption, man-in-the-middle attacks, brute-force attacks

SSL is a protocol that involves many of the cryptographic techniques described in this chapter, yet it is simple enough to use that most users are completely unaware of the underlying technologies and know it only as the small lock icon in their browser. SSL provides basic encryption and authentication for all HTTP traffic.

A client and server establish an SSL session by the client requesting a certificate from the server. The server responds by sending its certificate and its cipher preferences. The client then generates a master key, which it encrypts with the server's public key, and transmits that key to the server. The server authenticates itself to the client by returning a message authenticated with the master key. All data is now encrypted and authenticated with keys derived from this master key. The process can optionally include a similar method for authenticating the client. SSL is a crucial piece of any Web application's security process. It does not protect against all types of attacks, but it provides the basis for many of the other techniques described in this book.

> ## WARNING
>
> Despite best efforts by some companies to market SSL as the solution for server security, it is important to note that SSL does nothing to make the server itself secure. SSL authenticates the server to the client and ensures the privacy of the communications between the server and client. It is the digital equivalent of a security envelope.

Because the encryption process requires more CPU cycles, SSL does put an extra load on the server, especially on slower processors. For this reason, many Web site operators choose not to use SSL, even for sensitive traffic. It is difficult to justify sacrificing the security benefits of SSL, however, so you might want to consider some of these techniques to improve performance:

- Upgrading hardware or load balancing across multiple servers
- Using hardware SSL accelerators
- Optimizing Web content for minimal traffic

Even inexpensive hardware upgrades or SSL accelerators can make up for the extra load required for the SSL traffic. Note that most of the additional processing comes from the initial handshake that involves the much slower asymmetric cryptography used to exchange the session key. Once the key is established, the rest of the traffic is encrypted with symmetric cryptography using that key. Since most symmetric algorithms are quite efficient, there is a much smaller overhead once the session is established.

TIP

Some Web sites, in an effort to avoid the overhead of SSL, use it only for the initial authentication process and then switch back to a normal HTTP connection. However, most of the processing overhead is for the initial session handshake that involves asymmetric cryptography. So, if you go through the process of initiating an SSL session, you might as well keep the SSL connection for the rest of the traffic.

SSL is always important, but in some scenarios you should *always* use SSL:

- When transferring sensitive information
- When using forms authentication
- When using basic authentication

One mistake that many programmers make is not keeping an SSL session once a user authenticates using basic authentication. With basic authentication, the browser automatically sends user credentials with every request. Not only should you keep the SSL connection, but you should be careful that all page elements, such as images, style sheets, and scripts, are also sent over the SSL connection. One way to avoid this mistake is to use a unique host name for your SSL traffic, such as *secure.example.com*.

SSL is based on a well-established public certificate infrastructure, but technology cannot make up for human shortcomings. A user's browser may show a lock icon, but few users will actually open the site's certificate to make sure it is valid. Even if they do, it might be possible to produce fake information that looks authentic. Even if the browser warns the user of an invalid certificate, many users are trusting enough to continue browsing the site anyway. The only way to prevent this type of attack is to provide detailed information on your certificate and educate users about SSL and SSL certificates.

Security Policies

- Always use SSL for protecting sensitive HTTP traffic.
- Upgrade hardware or use an SSL accelerator to handle the processing overhead of SSL.
- Once the session is established, keep using SSL as much as possible.
- Be careful to use SSL for all included page elements.
- Educate users about SSL and SSL certificates.

Coding Standards Fast Track

Using Cryptography in ASP.NET

Employing Symmetric Cryptography

- ☑ Never rely on XOR, ROT-13, base-64 encoding, or any homegrown encryption/obfuscation algorithm.

- ☑ Avoid using DES unless absolutely necessary for backward compatibility; consider 3DES as a compatible alternative.

- ☑ Use Rijndael/AES encryption for the best security and performance.

- ☑ If using RC2 encryption, use 128-bit keys whenever possible.

- ☑ When security is a high priority and performance a low priority, consider layering encryption algorithms using *CryptoStreams*.

- ☑ When creating a key and IV, do not derive one from the other. Use the random key and IV generated when the class is initialized.

- ☑ Use *CryptDeriveKey* to create an encryption key from a user password.

Working with Hashing Algorithms

- ☑ Use hashing algorithms to verify integrity of data and to store and verify passwords.

- ☑ For data verification, store the hashes in a secure location so they cannot be modified.

- ☑ Use keyed hashing algorithms such as HMACCHA1 to protect the hashes.

- ☑ For password authentication, keep the hashes secret to prevent brute-force attacks.

- ☑ Add salt to a hash manually or using a keyed hashing algorithm to ensure randomness.

Working with .NET Encryption Features

Creating Random Numbers

- ☑ Use only the *RNGCryptoServiceProvider* to generate strong random numbers; avoid using *System.Random*.

- ☑ Use external sources of entropy to further increase randomness of the PRNG.

Keeping Memory Clean

- ☑ Use the *Clear()* method to clear out any sensitive data on cryptographic objects.

- ☑ Use the *Dispose()* method to immediately free memory resources.

- ☑ Explicitly zero out any variables that do not provide a *Clear()* method.

Protecting Secrets

- ☑ Avoid storing secrets in code, even if it is compiled into binary.

- ☑ Never store any secret in plaintext.

- ☑ Use a combination of file, registry, database, or DPAPI to store secrets.

- ☑ Use obscurity, but only sparingly as an additional layer of protection.

Protecting Communications with SSL

- ☑ Always use SSL for protecting sensitive HTTP traffic.

- ☑ Upgrade hardware or use an SSL accelerator to handle the processing overhead of SSL.

- ☑ Once the session is established, keep using SSL as much as possible.

- ☑ Be careful to use SSL for all included page elements.

Code Audit Fast Track

Using Cryptography in ASP.NET

Employing Symmetric Cryptography

- ☑ Does the application use only well-established encryption algorithms, avoiding weak encryption methods and encoding techniques?

- ☑ Does the application use DES when 3DES would work as a compatible replacement?

- ☑ If using RC2 encryption, does the application use 128-bit keys whenever possible?

- ☑ Does the application derive the key from the IV or the IV from the key rather than using a strong random-number generator?

- ☑ Does the application avoid hard-coded values for the IV?

Working with Hashing Algorithms

- ☑ Does the application use hashing algorithms where appropriate to ensure data integrity?

- ☑ Does the application store hashes rather than actual passwords in the database?

- ☑ Does the application store hashes in a secure location?

- ☑ Does the application use keyed hashing algorithms whenever possible?

- ☑ Does the application add salt to all hashes?

Working with .NET Encryption Features

Creating Random Numbers

- ☑ Does the application only use the *RNGCryptoServiceProvider* to generate strong random numbers, avoiding *System.Random*?

- ☑ Does the system require further entropy than what the CryptoAPI provides?

Keeping Memory Clean

☑ Does the application clear out all variables used with cryptographic operations, including those for plaintext, ciphertext, keys, salts, IVs, and random numbers?

☑ Does the application explicitly call the *Clear()* method for all cryptographic objects?

☑ Does the application explicitly call the *Dispose()* method for all cryptographic objects?

☑ Does the application explicitly zero out any variables that do not provide a *Clear()* method?

Protecting Secrets

☑ Does the application avoid storing hard-coded secrets?

☑ Does the application use a combination of secure methods, such as the file system, the registry, a database, and using DPAPI to store secrets?

☑ Does the application use obscurity sparingly but where appropriate as an additional layer of protection?

Protecting Communications with SSL

☑ Does the application always use SSL for protecting sensitive HTTP traffic?

☑ Does the application use SSL for all included page elements, including images, style sheets, and client-side scripts?

Frequently Asked Questions

The following Frequently Asked Questions, answered by the authors of this book, are designed to both measure your understanding of the concepts presented in this chapter and to assist you with real-life implementation of these concepts. To have your questions about this chapter answered by the author, browse to **www.syngress.com/solutions** and click on the **"Ask the Author"** form. You will also gain access to thousands of other FAQs at ITFAQnet.com.

Q: Should I use the encryption algorithms based on the *CryptoAPI* or the managed versions of these algorithms?

A: The answer to this question depends on your particular requirements. You may prefer always using managed code, but the *CryptoAPI* functions are slightly faster and are FIPS 140-1 certified.

Q: Can I use the *GetHashCode* method of an object rather than bothering with creating MS5 or SHA-1 hashes?

A: The *GetHashCode* method produces a hash key that is useful with structures such as hash tables. The hash it produces does not have the secure characteristics required for cryptographic use.

Q: How can I access some of the other features of *CrytpoAPI* that the .NET Framework doesn't expose?

A: The *CryptoAPI* provides many advanced features for which the .NET Framework does not provide wrappers. Read the article "Extending .NET Cryptography with CAPICOM and P/Invoke" at http://msdn.microsoft.com/security/securecode/dotnet/default.aspx?pull=/library/en-us/dncapi/html/netcryptoapi.asp for more information.

Q: When creating hashes, should I always use the largest hash size available, SHA-512?

A: The larger hash may be useful in some scenarios, but consider what you are hashing. It doesn't make much sense to use SHA-512 to hash an eight-character password, because the attacker would just perform a brute-force attack on the password, not the hash itself.

Q: I am using *CryptDeriveKey* to produce a key from a password. I know that a password will reduce the effective strength of the key, but what would be the equivalent key length of an eight-character password?

A: It is generally accepted that due to the limited keyspace and repetitive nature of the English language, there are 1.3 bits of entropy for each 8-bit character. To achieve the equivalent of a 128-bit key, the user would need a 98-character password, and an eight-character password would be roughly equivalent to using a 10-bit encryption key. However, if you use a password with random letters, numbers, and characters, you can achieve a little more than 6 bits of entropy per character, so an eight-character random password would be roughly equivalent to 50-bit encryption.

Q: To reduce the processing overhead of SSL, should I use 40-bit encryption instead of 128-bit encryption?

A: Most of the processing overhead comes from the initial handshake process. Once the session is established, you will see little performance gain by using the much weaker 40-bit encryption.

Chapter 5

Filtering User Input

Solutions in this Chapter:

Introduction

Throughout this book we discuss a wide variety of threats and security risks. But none of these threats is as serious as when an attacker goes straight for the heart and directly attacks your application code. Many developers have faced the somber reality that their code is insecure; that some hacker broke in using nothing other than a flaw found in the Web application itself. By manipulating program input, attackers can often trick the server into revealing customer data, or allowing access to unauthorized files or execution of program code on the server itself. Indeed, insecure code is the source of countless intrusions.

The risks of insecure code are great for several reasons:

- There are so many different ways to exploit insecure code.

- There is no need to obtain a password because the code is already running in the context of an authenticated user.

- The attacker gains access to anything that the Web application can access, which usually includes sensitive user data.

- Most Web applications are not properly configured to detect and prevent these types of attacks.

Every week, security researchers flood mailing lists such as BugTraq and VulnWatch with discoveries of security flaws in commercial or widely available Web-based applications. While many programmers are finally learning the skills to avoid insecure code, there seems to be a never-ending supply of programmers who put users at risk because they don't filter the input coming into their application.

Here are some common threats caused by poor input filtering:

- **SQL injection** Manipulating user input to construct SQL statements that execute on the database server

- **Directory traversal** Accessing files outside the bounds of the Web application by manipulating input with directory traversal characters. This is also known as the *double dot attack*.

- **Server-side code access** Revealing the content of server-side code or configuration files by manipulating input to disguise the true file extension

- **File system access** Manipulating input to read, write, or delete protected files on disk

- **Denial of service** Causing the application to consume system resources excessively or to stop functioning altogether

- **Information leakage** Intentionally sending invalid input to produce error messages with information that may facilitate an attack

- **Cross site scripting** Injecting HTML or script commands, causing the Web application to attack other users

- **Command injection** Injecting special shell metacharacters or otherwise manipulating input to cause the server to run code of the attacker's choice

- **Buffer overflows** Overwriting a buffer by sending more data than a buffer can handle, resulting in the application crashing or executing code of the attacker's choice

Despite the wide variety of input injection attacks, Web developers have one great advantage: these attacks are completely preventable through careful input filtering and smart coding practices.

Handling Malicious Input

Before an attacker can exploit your application with malicious input, the attacker has to get the input to your code. And that is where Web developers have the advantage. By carefully identifying and controlling input, you can prevent the attacks before they ever get to the sensitive code.

The input handling strategies we will address here are:

- Identifying Input Sources
- Programming Defensively

Identifying Input Sources

Summary: **Sometimes the hidden sources of user input are the most dangerous.**
Threats: **Malicious input**

Half the challenge of stopping malicious input is identifying the numerous ways your application accepts input. All attacks on the application itself are based on some form of manipulating the permitted user input. If you handle form input properly, you can eliminate most, if not all, of these vulnerabilities. Not only should you handle form input and query strings, but you must also consider any other data that an attacker can modify. Often overlooked are indirect sources of input and data that you might think an attacker cannot access.

With an ASP.NET application the most obvious place to look for input is any place you use the *Request* object. Classic ASP provided the *Request* object as a property of the *Server* object. To maintain compatibility with existing ASP code, ASP.NET provides the *HttpRequest* class through the *Request* property of the *Page* class. The *HttpRequest* class exposes elements of the HTTP request through its various properties. Table 5.1 shows some of these properties and how they relate to different elements of the HTTP request.

Table 5.1 *HttpRequest* Class and HTTP Elements

Property	Source
Browser	Guessed based on the client-provided *User-Agent* header
ClientCertificate	Based on client certificate headers
Cookies	*Set-Cookie* header from client
Form	Post data from the client
Headers	All HTTP headers
Path	Parsed from the URL
PathInfo	Parsed from the URL
QueryString	Parsed from the URL
ServerVariables	Combination of client and server data
UrlReferrer	*Referer* header from the client
UserAgent	*User-Agent* header from the client
UserHostName	May be controlled by user if user controls the DNS server

An easy way to identify potential flaws in your code is to search for all references to the *Request* object to make sure that you handle user input properly. As described later in this chapter, you should always filter data coming from the *Request* object, and you should never concatenate the *Request* object directly to a string. For example, consider this code:

```
[C#]
Response.Write("Welcome " + Request.QueryString["Username"]);
```

```
[VB.NET]
Response.Write("Welcome " & Request("UserName"))
```

In this example, the code directly outputs the contents of the *UserName* variable without validating or filtering its contents. This is a common, but definitely not a safe, practice. A better solution is to filter the input before acting on the data, as shown here:

```
[C#]
string userNameSafe=FilterInput(Request.QueryString["UserName"]);
Response.Write("Welcome " + userNameSafe);
[VB.NET]
userNameSafe=FilterInput(Request("UserName"))
Response.Write("Welcome " & userNameSafe)
```

In this example, the code calls a custom function *FilterInput* that you create to perform whatever filtering is necessary for the type of data.

Other Sources of Input

The *Request* object is the most common source of input, but it is possible for a user to inject input indirectly or through less obvious sources. A user may input data directly into your database or manipulate HTTP headers sent to your server. For example, consider the ASP code shown in Figure 5.1. This code is from an ASP error handler page (found by default at C:\WINNT\Help\iisHelp\common\500-100.asp) that IIS 5 uses to handle server-side errors. The intended behavior is that if an error occurs it will show the details only if the request is going to "LocalHost" based on checking the contents of the *SERVER_NAME* server variable.

Figure 5.1 ASP Source From 500-100.ASP

```
' Only show the Source if it is available and the request is from the same
' machine as IIS
  If objASPError.Source > "" Then
    strServername = LCase(Request.ServerVariables("SERVER_NAME"))
```

Continued

Figure 5.1 ASP Source From 500-100.ASP

```
strServerIP = Request.ServerVariables("LOCAL_ADDR")

strRemoteIP =  Request.ServerVariables("REMOTE_ADDR")

If (strServername = "localhost" Or strServerIP = strRemoteIP) And_
objASPError.File <> "?" Then

   Response.Write Server.HTMLEncode(objASPError.File)

   If objASPError.Line > 0 Then Response.Write ", line " &_
   objASPError.Line

   If objASPError.Column > 0 Then Response.Write ", column " &
   objASPError.Column

   Response.Write "<br>"

   Response.Write "<font style=""COLOR:000000;_

   FONT: 8pt/11pt courier new""><b>"

   Response.Write Server.HTMLEncode(objASPError.Source) & "<br>"

   If objASPError.Column > 0 Then Response.Write_
   String((objASPError.Column - 1), "-") & "^<br>"

   Response.Write "</b></font>"

   blnErrorWritten = True

  End If

End If
```

The problem is that the server derives the *SERVER_NAME* variable from the Host header provided by the client. This Host header comes from the client based on what IP address resolves to the name "LocalHost." Normally, this IP address always points to loopback, 127.0.0.1, but anyone can edit their HOSTS file to point it to any IP address. So if an attacker were to enter your Web site IP address as the LocalHost IP address in their HOSTS file, they could browse to LocalHost and hit your Web site instead. Furthermore, the client's Host header will now return LocalHost and the server will therefore show all the error details. With IIS 6, Microsoft fixed this by removing the check for LocalHost, and showing error details only if the server IP address matches the remote IP address.

NOTE

Editing the HOSTS file is just one way to accomplish this type of attack. An attacker could also use a tool or a script to build a custom HTTP request with any of the headers he wants.

Another example of unexpected user input is the DNS host name for the client. If an attacker controls the reverse DNS entries for his IP address, he could potentially use that hostname to inject malicious input or fool access control restrictions that rely merely upon the hostname.

It is important to consider all sources of input, including input that comes from your internal network or from internal users. Rather than attack your server directly, an attacker may find it easier to go in the back way and inject malicious code where you'd least expect it—from a trusted resource.

Security Policy

- Identify all instances of the *Request* object to be sure you properly filtered this input.

- Search for and filter other forms of indirect input, including input from the application itself.

Programming Defensively

Summary: Preventing application vulnerabilities requires smart coding practices.

Threats: Malicious input

Of all the different types of application attacks brought to the world's attention in recent years, none required anything more than reasonable and foreseeable defensive coding practices. Unfortunately, until recently, few Web developers had the time, motivation, or training to build this extra code into their applications. But the never-ending discovery of application vulnerabilities painfully emphasizes the need for defensive coding practices. Although defensive coding may not always be your highest priority, it doesn't take much effort to follow some simple best practices for improving code security.

Controlling Variables

Because all user input at some point is connected to a variable (or a property or method result of an object variable), if you control variables, then you control user input. The Perl programming language has a feature called *Taint Mode* that treats all user-supplied input as tainted, and therefore unsafe. Furthermore, any variable derived from a tainted variable also becomes tainted. You cannot perform certain operations with tainted variables until you *untaint* or filter them with a regular expression.

ASP.NET has no equivalent taint feature, but Web developers can write code using the same approach. To do this, simply make sure you always assign user input to a variable, first running the input through a filtering function to make sure the input is safe to use. Next, make sure you work only with the untainted variables, and never raw user input.

TIP

To help you keep track of variable taintedness, it might be helpful to append a suffix to variable names after you check the data for safety, for example: `userName_safe=FilterString(Request.Form("UserName")`.
Now, just make sure you never act on a variable unless it contains the _safe suffix.

Classic ASP allows Web developers to use variables without first defining them. There is an *Option Explicit* directive you can use to enforce variable declaration, but this is not enabled by default. Explicit variable declaration is always a good practice, but it also has some security benefits. By declaring variables in your code you have a list of all data that you will use in your code—an excellent way to identify sources of user input. By declaring your variables, you are controlling them. Fortunately, VB.NET enables Option Explicit by default; just make sure it always stays that way. It's critical to note that C# requires variable declaration, so this does not apply.

Classic ASP has another weakness: there is no way to define a variable type; all variables are Variants. Fortunately, the CLR provides a strong type system, but VB.NET does not enforce this by default. It is important to strongly type your variables because this helps to enforce data validity and limit exposure to attacks. By defining the variable type you are limiting the type of data that variable can hold. For example, if you are passing numeric input into an SQL query, you can prevent SQL injection because a numeric variable will not accept the string data required to inject SQL commands. With classic ASP, the variant type would automatically adjust to accommodate the string data.

Because VB.NET does not enforce strict data typing, you must enable this option. In Visual Studio .NET 2003 you can enable this by selecting Tools |

Options to bring up the dialog box shown in Figure 5.2. Select the Projects folder, and then click on VB Defaults. From there, set Option Strict to On. As with variable declaration, C# automatically requires variable typing so this issue does not apply.

Figure 5.2 Enabling Option Strict for VB.NET

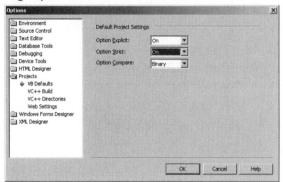

Centralizing Code

Controlling variables at some point involves filtering or sanitizing the data in those variables. Rather than writing code for each time you accept user input, it is a good practice to centralize your filtering code. As you build your ASP.NET application, use centralized filtering functions on every source of user input. Centralizing your code has several security benefits:

- It organizes your code and reduces complexity.
- It reduces the attack surface by reducing the amount of code.
- It allows you to make quick fixes to deal with future attacks as they surface.

Complexity is the enemy of security. By keeping your code organized and under control, you reduce the likelihood of application vulnerabilities. In general, reducing the code volume reduces bugs, while keeping your code simple and reusing code decreases the number of attack vectors in your code. Most of all, having centralized code allows you to easily adjust your filtering functions to address new attacks as security knowledge and research evolves.

Another benefit of using centralized code is that it is easy to identify user input that you have not properly filtered because it is not wrapped in a filtering function. For example, if you have a filtering function named *FilterInput*, you should never refer to the *Request* Object without running it through the *FilterInput* function this way: safeInput = FilterInput(Request.QueryString ("Username")). If you follow this practice, you can easily search for all references to the *Request* object not inside a *FilteringInput* function using a tool such as *Grep*.

TIP

You can download a native Win32 port of Grep and other Unix utilities from http://unxutils.sourceforge.net/

Testing and Auditing

Due to the complexity and variety of application-level attacks, it is easy to overlook simple mistakes. You should always test your security code to verify that it in fact does what you expect. For example, one commercial Web application uses a regular expression to restrict access to certain administration pages so that only users on the local system could browse those pages. To do this, it checked the client's IP address against the regular expression "127.*." Since any IP address that begins with 127 refers to the local host, the programmer expected that this expression would properly restrict access. However, because the programmer did not use the ^ anchor to force matching from the beginning of the string, and because the .* portion of the expression means zero or more occurrences of any character, the regular expression in fact matches any IP address that contains 127 in any position, such as 192.168.1.127. It would not be difficult for an attacker to find an IP address with a 127 and completely bypass this restriction.

By building a proper audit plan and testing with different IP addresses, the programmer could have prevented this flaw.

Using Explicit References

Many programming languages allow programmers to take shortcuts to save typing by allowing certain implicit defaults. For example, if you do not provide a fully qualified path when accessing a file, the system assumes that the file is in the current working directory.

This is important when it comes to filtering user input because ASP.NET allows you to reference items in the *Request* object without explicitly naming a specific collection. For example, *Request("Password")* is the same as *Request.Form("Password")*. When you refer to the generic *Request* object, ASP.NET searches the *QueryString*, *Form*, *Cookies*, *ClientCertificate*, and *ServerVariables* collections, in that order, to find a match. Therefore, by not explicitly stating the collection, you could inadvertently take input from the wrong source. The problem here is that *QueryString* is the first collection searched.

Now consider the code in Figures 5.3 (C#) and 5.4 (VB.NET). This is a simple ASP.NET page that restricts access to LocalHost by checking the IP address of the client using the *REMOTE_ADDR* variable. The server itself provides this value, so it is a reliable method for checking the IP address as shown in Figure 5.5.

Figure 5.3 Using Generic Request References [C#]

```
<html>
<body>
<%
  if (Request.QueryString["REMOTE_ADDR"]== "127.0.0.1")
    Response.Write("Access is <b>allowed</b>");
  else
    Response.Write("Access is <b>not allowed</b> from " +
      Request.QueryString["REMOTE_ADDR"]);
%>
</body>
</html>
```

Figure 5.4 Using Generic Request References [VB.NET]

```
<html>
<body>
<%
  If Request("REMOTE_ADDR")="127.0.0.1" Then
    Response.Write("Access is <b>allowed</b>")
  Else
    Response.Write("Access is <b>not allowed</b> from " & _
      Request("REMOTE_ADDR"))
  End If
```

Continued

Figure 5.4 Using Generic Request References [VB.NET]

```
%>
</body>
</html>
```

Figure 5.5 IP Address Blocked

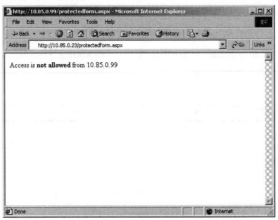

The problem with this code is that the programmer failed to specify the specific collection to use so ASP.NET will search the *QueryString*, *Form*, *Cookies*, and *ClientCertificate* collections before it tries the *ServerVariables* collection. Knowing this, an attacker could populate any of these collections with an item matching the server variable name and bypass the protection. For example, adding a query string variable named *REMOTE_ADDR* using the IP address 127.0.0.1 will fool the application's IP restriction as shown in Figure 5.6.

Figure 5.6 IP Address Allowed with *REMOTE_ADDR* in *QueryString*

In a similar manner, an attacker could trick another user by passing variables on the URL that override form, cookie, or certificate values. The solution for this is simple: always explicitly name the collection from which you expect to pull the variable. This is illustrated in Figures 5.7 (C#) and 5.8 (VB.NET) as explicitly referring to the *Request.ServerVariables* object. By avoiding implied references, you can prevent attackers from exploiting ambiguities in your code.

Figure 5.7 Using Generic Request References [C#]

```
<html>
<body>
<%

  if (Request.ServerVariables["REMOTE_ADDR"]== "127.0.0.1")
    Response.Write("Access is <b>allowed</b>");
  else
    Response.Write("Access is <b>not allowed</b> from " +
      Request.ServerVariables["REMOTE_ADDR"]);
%>
</body>
</html>
```

Figure 5.8 Using Generic Request References [VB.NET]

```
<html>
<body>
<%
  If Request.ServerVariables("REMOTE_ADDR")="127.0.0.1" Then
    Response.Write("Access is <b>allowed</b>")
  Else
    Response.Write("Access is <b>not allowed</b> from " & _
      Request("REMOTE_ADDR"))
  End If
%>
</body>
</html>
```

Security Policy

- Always assign filtered user input to variables to distinguish it from the raw data.

- When using VB.NET, always use Option Explicit and Option Strict.

- Use centralized filtering functions on all user input.

- Never use the generic *Request* collection.

Constraining Input

The key to protecting your application from malicious data is to validate all user input. There are numerous actions in your code that user input may affect, and therefore many different techniques for validating this input. Examples of actions that user input might have an effect on are:

- Accessing a database

- Reading the file system

- Allowing users to upload or save files

- Running a shell command

- Sending an e-mail

- Sending HTML output to the client

- Setting an object property

- Processing a shopping cart purchase

Each of these actions is vulnerable to one or more of the threats mentioned at the beginning of this chapter. To counter these threats, I have established the following techniques, which I will describe in more detail throughout this section:

- **Bounds checking** Checking input values for appropriate data type, string length, format, characters, and range

- **Pattern matching** Using regular expressions to match and allow known good input or match and block known bad characters or strings

- **Data reflecting** Passing data to the system, reading back the system's interpretation of the data, and then comparing it to the original data

- **Encoding** Transforming string characters to a specific format for safe handling

- **Encapsulating** Deriving a digest from user input that contains a known set of characters, making it safe to use.

- **Parameterizing** Taking user input as a parameter to fix its scope, for example, appending a file extension or prefixing a directory path

- **Double decoding** Decoding data twice to ensure that both instances match

- **Escaping** Quoting or escaping special characters so the target treats them as literal characters

- **Syntax checking** Checking a finished string to make sure the syntax is appropriate for the target

- **Exception handling** Checking for errors and performing sanity checks to ensure that results are returned as expected

- **Honey drops** Small pieces of data that work as a honey pot to help detect intrusions.

The following are examples of how to use these techniques with various programming tasks.

Bounds Checking

Summary: **Check input data to make sure it is appropriate for its purpose.**

Threats: **Malicious input**

Bounds checking is a quick and easy way to prevent many application-level attacks. Check input values to be sure they comply with the expected data type, string length, string format, set of characters, and range of values. ASP.NET provides several easy methods to check input data:

- Validator Controls

- Type Conversion

- SqlParameters

Validator Controls

ASP.NET provides a set of controls to validate all form data entered by a user. By attaching a validator control to a form control and setting a few properties, you can have ASP.NET automatically check user input values. Table 5.2 summarizes the validator controls available with ASP.NET.

Table 5.2 ASP.NET Validator Controls

Control	Description
CompareValidator	Compares a control's value to a fixed value or to the value of another control. Also performs data-type checks.
CustomValidator	Runs a user-defined validation function
RangeValidator	Checks to make sure numeric values fall between minimum and maximum values
RegularExpressionValidator	Matches a control's value against a regular expression pattern
RequiredFieldValidator	Ensures that a control is not left empty
ValidationSummary	Summarizes all validation errors on a page

To use a validator control, set the *ControlToValidate* property and then set any other properties to define the validation to perform. Figure 5.9 (C#) demonstrate how to use a validator control to check a numeric input field.

Figure 5.9 Validating Numeric Input (C#)

```
<html>
<body>
 <form runat="server">
 Enter you age:
 <br />
 <asp:TextBox id="tbox1" runat="server"/>
 <br /><br />
 <asp:Button Text="Submit" runat="server" />
 <br /><br />
 <asp:RangeValidator
   ControlToValidate="tbox1"
   MinimumValue="13"
   MaximumValue="120"
```

Continued

Figure 5.9 Validating Numeric Input (C#)

```
      Type="Integer "
      EnableClientScript="false"
      Text="Invalid age."
      runat="server"/>
   </form>
</body>
</html>
```

The most powerful of these validators is the *RegularExpressionValidator*, which allows complex pattern matching to ensure that input falls within very specific parameters.

But it is important to note that although validator controls are powerful, they do have some limitations:

- You can use them only to validate form controls.

- You can validate form controls only when the page posts back to itself, not to another page.

- They work only with server-side controls.

- ASP.NET does not perform any validation with validator controls before it fires the *Page_Load* event.

- They tend to decentralize validation code, moving it to individual pages rather than having a centralized mechanism for input filtering.

Because validator controls focus exclusively on form input, it is easy to neglect filtering other forms of user input. To deal with these limitations, you will need to develop custom functions for validating other input. Nevertheless, because of their automated error messages and the addition of client-side code, you should still always use validator controls for form input.

> **WARNING**
>
> The client-side validation features of validation controls speed up valida-
> tion for the client and prevent extra load on your server from continual
> post backs, but they are not reliable as a security measure. An attacker
> can easily disable client-side scripting, or use a custom tool to post
> forms that bypass client-side validation.

Security Policy

- Use validator controls to validate form input if a page posts back to itself.
- Never rely on client-side validation for security.

Pattern Matching

Summary: **Pattern matching is an effective technique for filtering
malicious input.**
Threats: **Malicious input**

The most common and effective method for addressing malicious input is to
apply pattern matching through regular expressions. With pattern matching you
block input that contains specific malicious characters or permit only input that
contains a set of known safe characters. Under most circumstances, the latter is
the preferred method for checking input.

Because it is difficult to anticipate the numerous ways one could exploit your
application, it is usually best to establish which characters you will allow and then
block everything else. Figures 5.10 (C#) and 5.11 (VB.NET) show how to use
regular expressions to allow only specific characters. Using this method, however,
does require some forethought. Users will quickly get frustrated if you do not
allow certain characters, such as an apostrophes or hyphens, in a last name field.

Figure 5.10 Allowing Known Good Characters (C#)

```
// Pattern match for known good characters and check length
        // Only allow 1-260 letters, numbers, spaces,
        // periods, and/or back slashes
    Regex knownGood = new Regex(@"^[a-z0-9\s\.\\]{1,260}$",
      RegexOptions.IgnoreCase);
```

Figure 5.10 Allowing Known Good Characters (C#)

```
if (!knownGood.IsMatch(decodedPath1))
  TextBoxResults.Text += "Step 2: Pattern match for " +
    "known good failed\n";
else
  TextBoxResults.Text += "Step 2: Pattern match for " +
    "known good passed\n";
```

Figure 5.12 Allowing Known Good Characters (VB.NET)

```
'Pattern match for known good characters and check length
'Only allow 1-260 letters, numbers, spaces, periods, and/or back slashes
Dim knownGood As Regex = New Regex("^[a-z0-9\s\.\\]{1,260}$", _
  RegexOptions.IgnoreCase)
If Not knownGood.IsMatch(decodedPath1) Then
  TextBoxResults.Text += "Step 2: Pattern match for " & _
    "known good failed" & vbCrLf
Else
  TextBoxResults.Text += "Step 2: Pattern match for " & _
    "know good passed" & vbCrLf
End If
```

But pattern matching is more than blocking and allowing individual characters. Some attacks might use no invalid characters but still be malicious. For example, consider a Web application that saves data to a file, and selects the filename based on user input. To prevent directory traversal or file access attacks, you might allow users to input only alphanumeric data, which you can enforce with a regular expression. But what happens if the user selects a filename using a reserved DOS device name such as COM1, PRN, or NUL? Although these device names do not contain anything other than alphabetic characters, accessing these devices might cause a denial of service or facilitate some other kind of attack. For some types of input you should allow only known good data and then perform a follow-up check to make sure that input does not contain known bad data. Figures 5.12 (C#) and 5.13 (VB.NET) show how to use a regular expression to check for these patterns.

Figure 5.12 Matching Known Bad Input (C#)

```
// Pattern match for known bad characters and strings
Regex knownBad = new Regex(@"(?:AUX|CO(?:M\d|N\.\.)" +
  @"|LPT\d|NUL|PRN|\n|\r|progra(?:\~1|m\sfiles)|system32" +
  @"|winnt|[\?\*\<\>\|\""\:\%\&])", RegexOptions.IgnoreCase);
if (knownBad.IsMatch(decodedPath1))
  TextBoxResults.Text += "Step 3: Pattern match for " +
    "known bad failed\n";
else
  TextBoxResults.Text += "Step 3: Pattern match for " +
    "know bad passed\n";
```

Figure 5.13 Matching Known Bad Input (VB.NET)

```
'Pattern match for known bad characters and strings
Dim knownBad As Regex = New Regex("(?:AUX|CO(?:M\d|N\.\.)" & _
  "|LPT\d|NUL|PRN|\n|\r|progra(?:\~1|m\sfiles)|system32" & _
  "|winnt|[\?\*\<\>\|\""\:\%\&])", RegexOptions.IgnoreCase)
If knownBad.IsMatch(decodedPath1) Then
  TextBoxResults.Text += "Step 3: Pattern match for " & _
    "known bad failed" & vbCrLf
Else
  TextBoxResults.Text += "Step 3: Pattern match for " & _
    "know bad passed" & vbCrLf
End If
```

Table 5.3 shows some common input scenarios and examples of regular expression patterns you might use to identify malicious input. Sometimes you will allow only known good data and other times you might filter out known bad data, but usually you should perform both checks. Note that the patterns in this table do not address every possible exploit, and you should customize them for your particular application.

Table 5.3 Regular Expression Patterns for Filtering Input

Action	Regex for matching known bad input
File system access	(?:AUX|CO(?:M\d|N\.\.)|LPT\d|NUL|PRN|\n|\r| progra(?:\\~1|m\sfiles)|system32|winnt| [\?*\\<\>\\\|\\"\:\%\&])
Database access	(?:\;\-\-|d(?:elete\sfrom|rop\stable)|insert\sinto |s(?:elect\s*|p_)|union\sselect|xp_)
Sending e-mail	(?:rcpt\sto|[\\\<\>\;])
Formatting HTML	(?:\<(?:applet|img\ssrc|object|s(?:cript|tyle)| a)|javascript|onmouseover|vbscript)

TIP

Matching with regular expressions can be complex, and the examples in Table 5.14 may or may not be sufficient for your needs. See www.ex-parrot.com/~pdw/Mail-RFC822-Address.html for an example of the complexity of validating something as simple as an e-mail address.

Escaping Data

Sometimes you want users to be able to enter special characters without restrictions. But allowing these characters might expose your application to attacks such as SQL injection. You might, for example, want to allow users to enter an apostrophe in their last name to allow for names such as O'Brien, but this character has special meaning in an SQL statement. Allowing this character might make the application vulnerable to SQL injection. But the fix is easy: replace every single quote with two single quotes. This allows you to build SQL statements without having to worry about users passing in single quotes. By escaping (or quoting) the single quote character, it no longer has any special meaning to the SQL interpreter.

Here are some common types of data that would require escaping:

- Shell commands
- SQL statements

- Regular expression patterns
- HTML

Security Policy

- Use regular expressions to either block known bad data or allow only known good data.
- Use regular expressions to identify malicious keywords or other patterns.
- Escape all special characters from user input.

Data Reflecting

Summary: **Data reflection verifies path or other information using trusted system functions.**

Threats: **Directory traversal**

When Microsoft first released Windows 2000, security was a long-neglected issue that rapidly gained attention. Security researchers found numerous holes in the operating system, particularly in Microsoft's Internet Information Services (IIS). Some of the most serious flaws allowed the viewing of protected files and traversing the file system to access files outside the Web content directories. Security researchers found ways to fool IIS into thinking it was retrieving a file with a different extension or a file in the same directory when it was in fact pulling a file from a parent directory. While these techniques fooled IIS, the operating system itself used a different mechanism to access files and therefore accessed them correctly. By discovering subtle differences between how IIS interpreted file paths and how the OS interpreted file paths, researchers exposed some serious vulnerabilities.

Unauthorized File Access

One of the early vulnerabilities discovered in IIS 5 was the ability to view portions of server-side source code by simply appending the string "+.htr" to any URL. Instead of processing the server-side script normally, IIS would return the source code of the file itself, often revealing sensitive information such as database connection strings and passwords. To exploit this vulnerability, an attacker could enter a URL such as this:

```
www.example.com/global.asa+.htr
```

Normally IIS does not allow requests for files with .ASP or .ASA extensions, but adding the extra characters fooled IIS into thinking it was accessing a file with the .HTR extension. However, the ISAPI filter that handled .HTR extensions discarded the extra data and returned the contents of the file itself.

Microsoft quickly released a hotfix to address this vulnerability but another researcher found that you could still fool IIS by simply adjusting the string to "%3F+.htr" like this:

```
www.example.com/global.asa%3F+.htr
```

Once again, the server returned the source code for global.asa rather than blocking the request. Although Microsoft fixed the specific known vulnerability the first time around, they failed to address the underlying weakness that made it possible to fool IIS in the first place.

IIS was also vulnerable to various directory traversal vulnerabilities. In these, an attacker requests files outside the bounds of the Web application. Normally, IIS will not allow requests outside the Web root, but by disguising the double dots ("..") through encoding and other techniques, researchers found ways to trick IIS into thinking it was accessing a file within the Web root when it was in fact accessing a file in a parent directory. These turned out to be very serious vulnerabilities because they usually allowed attackers to execute commands and quickly gain control of the server. Furthermore, many internet worms such as Code Red and Nimda exploited these vulnerabilities to propagate themselves from server to server.

Reflecting the Data

To prevent Directory Traversal and Server-Side Code Access, developers usually check file extensions and watch for paths that contain double dots. However, this is not always effective because there are techniques, such as encoding, that attackers use to disguise these characters. Rather than attempting to anticipate every way an attacker can fool your code, a more effective technique is data reflection. With this technique, you take the user input and pass it to a trusted system function. You then read back the system interpretation of that data and compare it to the user input. The steps you would take to reflect a file path are:

1. Decode the path and expand any environment variables.

2. Use the *System.IO.Path.GetFullPath()* method to reflect back a normalized path.

3. Compare the directory of user input to the directory of the reflected path.

4. Make sure this path falls within the constraints of the application.

5. Use only the reflected path from that point on in your code.
    The code in Figures 5.14 (C#) and 5.15 (VB.NET) demonstrate these steps.

Figure 5.14 Reflecting Data (C#)

```csharp
// Parameterizing and Data Reflecting
string rootPath = @"e:\inetpub\wwwroot\files\";
string fileExt = ".txt";
string expandedPath =
 System.Environment.ExpandEnvironmentVariables(decodedPath1);
string scopedPath =
 string.Concat(rootPath, expandedPath, fileExt);
string absolutePath = "";

try
{
 absolutePath = Path.GetFullPath(scopedPath);
 // Double-check to see if still within parameters
 if (!absolutePath.StartsWith(rootPath) ||
   !absolutePath.EndsWith(fileExt))
   TextBoxResults.Text += "Step 4: Data reflection failed\n";
 else
   TextBoxResults.Text += "Step 4: Data reflection passed\n";
}
catch (Exception ex)
{
 TextBoxResults.Text += "Step 4: Reflection failed " +
   "with an Exception: " + ex.ToString() + "\n";
}
```

Figure 5.15 Reflecting Data (VB.NET)

```
'Parameterizing and Data Reflecting
Dim rootPath As String = "e:\inetpub\wwwroot\files\"
Dim fileExt As String = ".txt"
Dim expandedPath = System.Environment. _
 ExpandEnvironmentVariables(decodedPath1)
Dim scopedPath = String.Concat(rootPath, _
 expandedPath, fileExt)
Dim absolutePath
Try
 absolutePath = Path.GetFullPath(scopedPath)

 'Double-check to see if still within parameters
 If Not absolutePath.StartsWith(rootPath) Or _
  Not absolutePath.EndsWith(fileExt) Then
  TextBoxResults.Text += "Step 4: Data reflection failed" & vbCrLf
 Else
  TextBoxResults.Text += "Step 4: Data reflection passed" & vbCrLf
 End If
Catch ex As Exception
 TextBoxResults.Text += "Step 4: Parameterizing failed " & _
  "with an Exception: " & ex.ToString() & vbCrLf
End Try
```

The advantage of this technique is that because the operating system will ultimately decide which file to access, you have the system tell you which file it intends to access based on the given user input. You validate the path and use that same path when actually accessing the file.

Security Policy

- Reflect data using trusted system functions to prevent attacks such as directory traversal.
- Always work with the reflected path in subsequent operations.

Encoding Data

Summary: **Data encoding neutralizes malicious HTML content.**
Threats: **Cross-site scripting**

Sometimes hackers are not trying to break into your Web site but instead want to exploit your Web application to target other users or glean user data. For example, an attacker may want to gain access to another user's online bank account or personal e-mail. Using a technique called *cross-site scripting* (sometimes referred to as XSS), an attacker injects active HTML content into a Web page to exploit other users. This content may contain malicious HTML markup, including:

- Deceptive links
- HTML form tags
- Client-side script
- ActiveX components

At the heart of this attack is the abuse of trust that results from the malicious content running on a trusted Web site. Attackers can exploit cross-site scripting vulnerabilities to carry out a large number of attacks, such as:

- Stealing client cookies
- Bypassing policy restrictions
- Accessing restricted Web content
- Gathering Web-user IP addresses
- Modifying the behavior of links or forms
- Redirecting users to an untrusted Web site

Indeed, many developers underestimate the seriousness of cross-site scripting attacks.

Cross-Site Scripting vulnerabilities occur when a Web application dynamically displays HTML output to one user based on input from another user, such as displaying the unfiltered results of a guestbook or feedback system. Attackers can exploit this by injecting HTML tags that modify the behavior of the Web page. For example, an attacker might inject JavaScript code that redirects a user to another site or steals a cookie that contains authentication information. Web-based e-mail services such as Hotmail have long been a target of cross-site scripting attacks because they display HTML content in e-mail messages. An attacker simply has to send the target a specially crafted e-mail to execute the attack.

For cross-site scripting to work, the attacker must send HTML markup through some form of input. This might include an HTML form, a cookie, a *QueryString* parameter, or even an HTTP header. For example, there are many login pages that pass error messages back to the user like this:

```
www.example.com/login.aspx?err=Invalid+username+or+password
```

The page checks the Err parameter and if it exists, displays the contents back to the user as an error message. If the page does not filter this input, an attacker might be able to inject malicious code.

Fortunately, ASP.NET will automatically block any user input that appears to contain HTML code. Figure 5.16 shows how ASP.NET blocks a request for the URL:

```
http://localhost/input.aspx?text=<a href=""></a>.
```

Figure 5.16 Built-In ASP.NET HTML Blocking

This method is limited, because it is easy to overlook all the different character sets and encoding methods that ASP.NET or the client browser supports. Some character sets allow for multi-byte or other encoded representations of special char-acters. Character sequences that may seem benign in one character set could in fact represent malicious code in another. While you can often filter out special charac-ters, you cannot completely rely upon this method for total security.

Encoding is a technique that neutralizes special characters by modifying the representation of those characters. HTML encoding in particular is a technique that replaces special characters with character-entity equivalents that prevent the browser from interpreting the characters as active HTML. Table 5.5 shows the HTML-encoded representations of some common characters. If a browser encounters any of these HTML-encoded characters, it displays the character itself rather than treating it as a special character.

Table 5.5 Example HTML Character Entity Encoding

Name	Character	Decimal Code	Entity
Quotation Mark	"	&#34;	&quot;
Ampersand	&	&#38;	&amp;
Less Than	<	&#60;	&lt;
Greater Than	>	&#62;	&gt;

Using the Table 5.5, if we had this HTML markup:

```
<a href="www.asp.net">ASP.NET</a>
```

We would encode it as follows:

```
&lt;a href=&quot;www.asp.net&quot;&gt;ASP.NET&lt;/a&gt;
```

The first example would show up as an active link, whereas the second example would display the HTML markup itself.

The .NET Framework provides methods in the *Server* object, an *HttpServerUtility* class, to encode strings that could potentially be dangerous if left unencoded. These methods are:

- **HtmlEncode** Encodes an HTML string to safely output to a client browser

- **UrlEncode** Encodes a string to safely pass it as a URL

- **UrlPathEncode** Encodes a string to safely pass it as the path portion of a URL

Figures 5.17 (C#) and 5.18 (VB.NET) demonstrate how to use the *HtmlEncode* method

Figure 5.17 Using *HtmlEncode* (C#)

```
private void Button1_Click(object sender, System.EventArgs e)
{
  Label1.Text = Server.HtmlEncode(TextBox1.Text);
  Label2.Text =
    Server.HtmlEncode(Orders.Customers[0].Name);
}
```

Figure 5.18 Using *HtmlEncode* (VB.NET)

```
Private Sub Button1_Click(ByVal sender As System.Object, ByVal e _
     As System.EventArgs) Handles Button1.Click
  Label1.Text = Server.HtmlEncode(TextBox1.Text)
  Label2.Text = _
     Server.HtmlEncode(Orders.Customers[0].Name)
End Sub
```

Another type of encoding is URL encoding for URLs and query strings embedded in HTML. You should use *UrlEncode* and *UrlPathEncode* anywhere you reference a URL or query string in an HTML document. This includes the *A, APPLET, AREA, BASE, BGSOUND, BODY, EMBED, FORM, FRAME, IFRAME, ILAYER, IMG, ISINDEX, INPUT, LAYER, LINK, OBJECT, SCRIPT, SOUND, TABLE, TD, TH,* and *TR* HTML elements. Use *UrlEncode* on full URLs and *UrlPathEncode* to encode a path only. The difference is that *UrlPathEncode* encodes spaces as %20, rather than the plus sign ("+") that *UrlEncode* uses. Furthermore, *UrlPathEncode* does not encode all punctuation characters as *UrlEncode* does.

Security Policy

■ Use *HtmlEncode* to encode a string for browser output.

■ Use *UrlEncode* to encode a URL string for output.

■ Use *UrlPathEncode* to encode the path portion of a URL for output.

Encapsulating

Summary: **Hashing encapsulates data for safe handling.**
Threats: **Malicious input**

Sometimes you need to act on user input but you may not care about the actual value of the input. For example, you might want a unique identifier based on user input or want to store a value such as a password for later comparison. You can use a hash to encapsulate the data in a safe string format while still maintaining a link to the original data.

Good hashing functions have some properties that make them useful for encapsulating data:

■ They produce long, random digests that make use of the entire key space.

■ They produce few collisions; it would be extremely rare for two input strings to generate the same hash.

■ They always produce digest strings of the same length.

■ Given a hash you cannot derive the original data.

With a hash you can neutralize any malicious content because the hash mangles the string into a safe format. You can then format the hash as a hex string for safe handling.

If you hash a password before saving it, you never need to bother with checking it for invalid characters because the hash will not contain malicious content. This allows users to enter characters they want in a password without you having to worry about the impact of special characters in the string.

Another example is when you must create a file based on user input. Because any file operation based on user input could be dangerous, you might want to first convert the input to a safe hash string. This specific technique is described in more detail in Chapter 6.

Hashes are also effective at disguising data to make it less vulnerable to guessing attacks. One e-commerce application used temporary XML files for its shopping cart. The filenames were based on the user ID and the current date. However, a flaw in the application often left the files orphaned so they were not deleted at the end of the session, leaving a directory full of temporary files containing private user information that included customer credit card details. An attacker needed simply to employ smart guessing tactics to gain access to this information. Instead, using a filename based on a hash would make it unpredictable and would use a large enough key space to prevent guessing.

Security Policy

- Use hashes to encapsulate data for safe handling.
- Convert hashes to hex values to create safe alphanumeric strings.

Parameterizing

Summary: **Parameterizing allows you to fix the context of user input.**

Threats: **Directory traversal, file system access, SQL injection, command injection**

Parameterizing is a technique in which you take user input and place it within a fixed context so that you can control the scope of access. Consider a Web application in which you access files based on a selected link. A link may take you to a URL such as this:

```
www.example.org/articles.aspx?xml=/articles/a0318.xml
```

This first problem with this URL is that it is immediately apparent to attackers that you are accessing the file system, perhaps prompting them to experiment to find ways to break the application: what happens if you pass a filename with a different extension? Or what if you add additional path information?

To prevent abuse of your Web application, accept only the minimal amount of information required and insert this as a parameter to a full path. If the path and filename are fixed, a better version of the URL may be this:

```
www.example.org/articles.aspx?article=a0318
```

Now take the /articles path and append the article parameter, followed by the .xml extension. Now, no matter what the user enters, it will start in the /articles path and have an .xml extension.

WARNING

Be careful not to rely on parameterizing alone to guarantee scope. Microsoft made this mistake with the showcode.asp sample included with early versions of IIS (see www.securityfocus.com/bid/167). The programmer checked to see if the final path string contained a specific directory, but did not check for double-dots ("..") that allowed attackers to request files from a parent directory. The best way to handle this is to combine parameterizing with data reflecting, pattern matching, and other techniques described in this chapter.

Parameterizing is not just for file access; it is an effective technique for limiting many types of attacks. Chapter 6 shows how to use parameters to prevent SQL injection.

Security Policy

- Use parameterizing to fix the context and scope of user data.

- Combine parameterization with other techniques to prevent directory traversal.

Double Decoding

Summary: **Double decoding helps detect multiple layers of encoding.**
Threats: **Directory traversal, file system access, server-side code access**

Double decoding is a technique specifically designed to counter a type of encoding attack called *double encoding*. Vulnerability to this type of attack occurs because your application may decode an encoded string more than once from different areas of the application. Attackers can take advantage of this by creating multiple layers of encoded strings, usually in a path or query string. In other words, you encode a string, and then encode that string again. This might allow an attacker to bypass pattern matching or other security checks in your application code.

IIS 5 was vulnerable to this type of attack. In May of 2001, Microsoft issued a cumulative security patch for IIS (see www.microsoft.com/technet/security/bulletin/MS01-026.aspx) that included a fix for a double decoding vulnerability. IIS decodes incoming requests to render the path in a canonical form. It then performs the necessary security checks on this path to be sure that the user is requesting a file within a web content directory. After this check, IIS performed a second superfluous decoding pass. An attacker could take advantage of this by encoding the path twice. The first decoding pass will remove the first layer of encoding but because the path still has another layer of encoding it got past the IIS security checks. In the second decoding pass, IIS decoded the second layer of encoding and produced the final path. The end result is that an attacker could bypass IIS security checks to access files outside of the web root.

Because it is difficult to anticipate a string being decoded twice in your application, a more effective strategy is to initially check user input for multiple layers of encoding. By decoding a string twice, you can detect multiple layers of encoding, but what happens if someone uses more than two levels of decoding? How do you know how many times to decode to get to the final layer? Could someone cause a denial of service by encoding a string a hundred times? The solution is that you only decode the string twice, comparing the first result with the second result. If these do not match, then you know that the string contains two or more levels of encoding and is likely not a valid request. If you encounter this, simply reject the request and return an error to the client. Figures 5.19 (C#) and 5.20 (VB.NET) demonstrate the double decoding technique.

Figure 5.19 Double Decoding (C#)

```
// Double decode
string decodedPath1 = Server.HtmlDecode(inputFilePath);
string decodedPath2 = Server.HtmlDecode(decodedPath1);
if (!decodedPath1.Equals(decodedPath2))
  TextBoxResults.Text += "Step 1: Double decode failed\n";
else
  TextBoxResults.Text += "Step 1: Double decode passed\n";
```

Figure 5.20 Double Decoding (VB.NET)

```
'Double decode
Dim decodedPath1 As String = Server.HtmlDecode(inputFilePath)
Dim decodedPath2 As String = Server.HtmlDecode(decodedPath1)
If Not decodedPath1.Equals(decodedPath2) Then
  TextBoxResults.Text += "Step 1: Double decode failed" & vbCrLf
Else
  TextBoxResults.Text += "Step 1: Double decode passed" & vbCrLf
End If
```

Security Policy

- Use double decoding to detect multiple layers of encoding.
- Reject all requests that contain more than one layer of encoding.

Syntax Checking

Summary: **Syntax checking is a last line of defense against those attacks that get past other filters.**

Threats: **Malicious input**

After accepting user input and applying one or more of the techniques described in this chapter, you will eventually need to do something with the data. You may, for instance, build an SQL statement to look up account information based on a given username. You might use one or more techniques in this chapter to check user input, but before executing that SQL statement on the server, you might want to perform a final check to be sure that the SQL syntax follows the format you expect. For example, you don't want to send an SQL statement with multiple verbs such as two *SELECT* statements or a *SELECT* and a *DELETE*. Passing the final string through a pattern-matching function can be extremely effective in stopping attacks, albeit at the cost of some additional processing overhead.

Syntax checking serves as a last line of defense against those attacks that get past all your other filters. Examples of syntax checking are:

- Ensuring that a shelled command does not contain piping, redirection, command-concatenation characters, or carriage returns
- Ensuring that e-mail address strings contain only a single address
- Ensuring that file paths are relative to a Web content directory and do not contain drive designators, UNC paths, directory traversal characters, or reserved DOS device names

Security Policy

■ When appropriate, check the final syntax of any string that is based on user input.

Exception Handling

Summary: **Exception handling can catch errors before hackers exploit them.**

Threats: **Malicious input**

Hackers don't exploit normal operations of your Web application; they usually go after the exceptions that you failed to anticipate. Properly handling exceptions is a powerful defense in stopping a large percentage of Web application vulnerabilities. Although your code might fail to catch malicious user input, an exception handler might catch an error before an attacker can exploit it.

Exception handling is a long-standing best practice, but limited error handling capabilities in classic ASP has resulted in many programmers failing to properly deal with exceptions. ASP.NET provides a much more robust error handling system that you should take advantage of.

Exception handling is much more than handling errors. Some components do not raise an error but provide error information through events or properties. Furthermore, sometimes an error never occurs, but the results are not what you would expect. For example, if you perform a database query to look up a particular user's record, you would expect only that record to be returned. If it returns more than one record, you have reason to be suspicious. You should always check results to be sure they are as you would expect them to be.

Other exceptions to consider are:

- Return codes from shelled DOS commands
- Return codes from mail servers
- The size, length, or data type of returned data
- Operation timeouts

TIP

Sometimes the nature of the error is not as important as its frequency. For higher security you might want to consider adding code to check for multiple errors from the same client within a given period of time. Because many attacks depend on exploiting errors, encountering too many errors from one user might be a strong indicator of an attack.

Security Policy

- Take advantage of the robust error handling features in ASP.NET.
- Check return results to be sure they are consistent with what you expected.

Honey Drops

Summary: **Honey drops work as mini intrusion detectors.**
Threats: **Server-side code access, file system access, command execution, SQL injection**

Many people are familiar with the concept of a *honey pot*, which is a system designed to lure and ensnare hackers, giving an administrator time to gather evidence and track down the intruder. Sometimes you can't anticipate all possible attacks, but you'll at least want to detect and log intrusions. Honey pots, if carefully managed, can prove to be effective intrusion detection systems. You can integrate this same concept into your Web application by using small honey pots, or *honey drops*. This is how it works:

1. Place unique strings throughout your application or data that you can use as honey drops. For example, create fake database records, fields, tables, or even complete databases, depending on the type of intrusion you want to monitor.

2. Configure your application so that it will never normally access this data. For example, if you created a fake database field, never use a wild-card select statement (such as "*SELECT ★ FROM*"), but instead list the specific fields you require.

3. Configure your application or an external packet sniffer (or both) to watch for these strings leaving your database or Web server.

Suppose that you have an e-commerce Web site that accepts credit card transactions and want to use honey drops to detect any unauthorized access to your data. To do this, create a single fake record in your database using a unique credit card number that you would not otherwise encounter, perhaps one containing all zeros. Make sure that you structure any SQL queries so that this record would not appear under normal circumstances so that if it ever does appear in a query, there is a good chance it is an intrusion, such as a hacker using SQL injection to access your database.

There are several ways for you to watch for this string. One method is to write code to check every query result to see if it contains that record, although this might add a considerable amount of processing overhead. Another method is to use an intrusion detection system (IDS), such as Snort (www. snort.org), to sniff the network link between the Web server and the database, and also between the Web server and the Internet. Finally, configure the sniffer to look for the fake record you created and alert you anytime this value travels from the database to the Web server or from your Web server to the Internet. Note that encrypted network connections prevent sniffing, so you might need to adjust your strategy based on your particular configuration.

Honey drops are not just for databases. You can also use them to detect access to files, directories, or even commands. Here are some more ideas:

- Place a conspicuous, blank text file with a unique filename within your Web content directories. Then, configure your IDS to watch for this filename string leaving the network.

- Place server-side comments with a unique string in your source code to detect access to server-side scripts.

- Change the prompt variable in your command prompt to a unique string to detect remote command access.

Honey drops are not appropriate for all applications, but they can provide an extra layer of protection by allowing early detection of application attacks.

Security Policy

- Use honey drops in your database to detect SQL injection attacks.
- Use honey drops in your file system to detect file system access.
- Use honey drops in your source code to detect server-side code access.

Limiting Exposure to Malicious Input

Application attacks are widespread and varied, but we have yet to discover all the possible ways a hacker could exploit your Web application. It is also improbable that every developer will write secure code 100% of the time. Security flaws are bugs, and no amount of developer training or funds can guarantee bug-free code. So while you should take every opportunity to secure your code, you must also take measures to limit exposure to attacks and make your application more resilient to hackers. In this section we will cover:

- Reducing the attack surface
- Limiting attack scope
- Hardening server applications

Reducing the Attack Surface

Summary: **Reduce the attack surface of your application to provide fewer opportunities to hackers.**

Threats: **Malicious input**

All code has a certain probability of containing flaws. The more code you have, the higher the probability your application will have flaws. The more flaws you have, the greater the attack surface of your application. Attack surface represents your application's exposure to attack, but not necessarily its vulnerability to attack. Consider a bank, for example: the outer walls and roof of the building are its attack surface. Some areas, such as windows and doors, are more vulnerable to attack than other areas, such as brick walls. And although brick walls are exposed and are part of the attack surface, they are likely not going to be vulnerable to attack. Nevertheless, a bank robber could drive a tank through a bank wall, so therefore it is part of the attack surface.

Vulnerability depends greatly on other factors, such as how easily a bank robber could get his hands on a tank, his willingness to rob the bank, or how much money is in the bank itself. It also depends on how quickly the robber could execute the plan without getting caught. Despite all these factors, the bank's attack surface remains the same. In fact, the bigger the bank, the bigger the attack surface. And if a bank has multiple branches, each one increases the overall attack surface for the bank as a whole.

A Web application also has an attack surface. This attack surface is made up of every dynamic Web page, every open TCP/IP port, every system account, and every running application or service, among a list of other factors. Many security efforts address the need to reduce an application's attack surface. A firewall, for example, limits the number of accessible TCP/IP ports. There are also a number of techniques for limiting attack surface within your application itself.

The attack surface consists of any component of your application that meets these requirements:

- The component is visible or discoverable by the attacker.
- The component is accessible to the attacker.
- The component is potentially exploitable, even though actual vulnerability might not be foreseeable or likely.

Note that addressing any of these items will reduce your application's attack surface. With this in mind, there are many creative strategies you could use to reduce exposure to attack.

Unused Code

As your Web application matures and grows in features, you might find yourself adding more and more functionality to key modules. Sometimes a central module expands to handle much of the functionality of the application. Consider, for example, this URL from Microsoft's search engine application that contains nine parameters:

http://search.microsoft.com/search/results.aspx?na=81&st=a&View=enus&qu=a sp.net&qp=&qa= &qn=&c=2&s=0

Notice that this particular search does not even make use of all the parameters, so therefore their values are empty. While this is not a vulnerability, it increases the attack surface because it offers the hacker a variety of potential attack vectors. If you are not using a parameter, don't even show the parameter. The less the hacker can see, the less there is to exploit. Although this does not increase the actual attack surface of the application, it has the same effect because it limits the attacker's ability to discover all the available parameters.

WARNING

Hiding parameters does not mean that you need not secure the code that handles them. Obscurity does not replace security, but it does enhance other security measures you might have in place. If fewer people see the parameters, fewer will attack them; therefore it has the effect of reducing the attack surface.

Even though you should hide unused parameters, you must also consider parameters that should not even be there in the first place. You might, for instance, have code that handles parameters that should not exist in the production application. Carefully review each module to identify any debugging, testing, or dead code. Never rely on obscurity to hide this type of parameter.

TIP

Software developers do need to test and debug code, and you will inevitably end up with code that someone forgot to remove. To help prevent this, establish a coding policy to always use the same naming scheme with testing or other temporary variables. This makes it easy to quickly search for any leftover code that should not go into the production environment.

Limiting Access to Code

The most obvious way to limit attack surface is to limit the code in your application. A single static HTML page is much more secure than a fully functional e-commerce application. The less code you have, the less there is to attack. While this is not a realistic strategy, you can accomplish the same effect by limiting access to components of you application.

Carefully consider how you allow access to these features:

- **Online demos** You might want to showcase the features of your application with an online demo, but this gives everyone access to all of your code. Instead, consider providing static HTML demos that only simulate the features of the full application. Doing this doesn't fix any vulnerabilities you might have, but it does have the effect of reducing the attack surface, limiting access only to customers or registered users.

- **Administration or content-management modules** Your administration pages might require authentication to gain access, but the authentication page itself might be vulnerable. Limit access to administration modules by enforcing IP restrictions, using obscure ports, using client certificates, and moving administration modules to a separate Web site.

- **Intranet or extranet modules** Restrict access to intranet or extranet modules using the same strategies as with administration modules.

- **Sample code and applications** Many Web servers or applications come with sample or default code, or programs that should always be removed when migrating to a production environment.

- **Third-party applications** Many organizations opt to buy rather than build certain features in their Web application. There are thousands of widely available search engines, shopping carts, guest books, user management, and content management systems. Running one of these might not make you vulnerable, but consider that just about anyone can gain access to the source code. Wide code availability has the effect of increasing the attack surface, especially if it is a popular component used on many different Web sites. Some hackers will find a vulnerability in these components and then use a search engine to discover which sites use this component. If you do use third-party components, try obscuring their identities, and always review and test the code carefully.

Security Policy

- Reduce the attack surface of the application to limit exposure to hackers.

- Don't show query string parameters if you do not use them in a particular context.

- Remove testing, debug, and dead code from production applications.

- If possible, use static content in application demos.

- Limit access to administration or other private modules.

- Remove sample code and programs from production servers.

- Avoid or carefully audit third-party components.

Limiting Attack Scope

Summary: **Use security permissions to limit the scope of attacks.**
Threats: **Malicious input**

It might be impossible to build a bullet-proof application that is impervious to all current and future application-level attacks. You can filter input and reduce your attack surface, but you must also consider that someone might eventually find a way to exploit your code. Build your application so that exploiting your code does not provide much information for the attacker.

Least Privilege

An important strategy is to always follow the principle of *least privilege*. Consider the security context of the Web application user and evaluate this user's access to the following:

- The file system
- Registry keys
- Executables
- COM components
- WMI classes
- TCP/IP ports

- Databases
- Other Web sites on the same server

Plan the security context of your Web application to properly limit access to these items. Careful attention to user security will contain and separate the Web application from the rest of the operating system.

Server-Side Code

A common mistake Web developers make is assuming that server-side code is protected from intruders. Although it is meant to be protected, experience has shown us that this is not always the case. You should work with the assumption that this code is not safe, and therefore take appropriate precautions with what you include in these files. Server-side code is not an appropriate place to store secrets such as passwords, database connection strings, or other sensitive information. Sometimes something as simple as a comment could reveal vital information for an intruder to further an attack. Look at your server-side code from the perspective of a hacker to see what information might be a security risk.

Security Policy

- Use the principle of least privilege to limit the access of Web users.
- Avoid storing passwords, private comments, or other sensitive information in server-side code.

Hardening Server Applications

Summary: **Many Web applications have settings to protect from various types of attacks.**

Threats: **Malicious input**

Writing secure code is an important way to defend yourself from attack, but ASP.NET and IIS both help in this effort by providing settings to prevent or mitigate application-level attacks. Some settings you can use to harden your Web server against attack are as follows:

Request Length

Some attacks rely upon being able to send data beyond expected limits. A buffer overflow, for example, might require sending a very large string as part of the Web request. IIS 6.0 allows you to limit the size of the entity body of a request with the *MaxRequestEntityAllowed* and *AspMaxRequestEntityAllowed* metabase settings. Both of these settings let you set the maximum size, in bytes, for the entity body of a request, as specified by the HTTP content-length header. In other words, the content-length header of a request cannot exceed the limits imposed by these settings. *MaxRequestEntityAllowed* can be set at any level of the metabase, such as for the server, a specific site, a virtual directory, or even for a single file. The *AspMaxRequestEntityAllowed* setting is similar, but applies only to ASP files.

IIS 6 also provides registry settings for specific control over the length of various parts of a request. Table 5.6 summarizes these settings.

Table 5.6 IIS 6 Registry Settings to Limit Request Length

Registry Key: HKLM/CurrentControlSet/Services/HTTP/Parameters			
Value	**Range**	**Default Value**	**Description**
MaxFieldLength	64 to 65,534 (bytes)	16k	Maximum length of any individual header
MaxRequestBytes	256 to 16,777,216 (bytes)	16k	Maximum length of the request URI and any headers
UrlSegment MaxLength	0 to 32,766 (characters)	260	Maximum length of any single URL segment (that is, a single directory in a full path)
UrlSegment MaxCount	0 to 16,383 (segments)	255	Maximum number of URL segments in a request

Allowed Characters

To limit exposure to directory traversal and encoding attacks, IIS 6 provides several registry settings to limit which characters users can send in a request. These two settings are shown in table 5.7.

Table 5.7 IIS 6 Registry Settings to Restrict Characters

Registry Key: HKLM/CurrentControlSet/Services/HTTP/Parameters

Value	Range	Default Value	Recommended Value	Description
AllowRestrictedChars	0 or 1	0	0	If set to 0, accepts hex-escaped chars in request URLs that decode to U+0000 to U+001F and U+007F to U+009F ranges
EnableNonUTF8	0 or 1	1	0	If set to 1, the server allows requests that contain ANSI or DBCS characters.
PercentUAllowed	0 or 1	1	0	If set to 1, allows requests that contains characters encoded in the %UNNNN format

The first of these settings, *EnableNonUTF8*, allows you to limit requests so that they contain only UTF-8 encoded characters. This helps prevent ambiguity with various character encodings.

The second setting, *PercentUAllowed*, allows users to send request URLs using the format %UNNNN, where NNNN is the Unicode value of the character you want to submit. Again, allowing this might cause ambiguity, so it is best not to allow this unless you have a specific use for it.

Security Policy

■ Use the *MaxRequestEntityAllowed* and *AspMaxRequestEntityAllowed* metabase settings to limit the overall length of a request.

■ Use the *MaxFieldLength*, *MaxRequestBytes*, *UrlSegmentMaxLength*, and *UrlSegmentMaxCount* registry settings to limit the length of specific parts of a request.

■ Use the *EnableNonUTF8* and *PercentUAllowed* registry keys to limit valid characters in a request.

Coding Standards Fast Track

Handling Malicious Input

Identifying Input Sources

- ☑ Always identify any source of user input, including all references to the *Request* object.
- ☑ Carefully identify other indirect or less obvious sources of input.

Programming Defensively

- ☑ Always assign filtered user input to variables to distinguish it from the raw data.
- ☑ When using VB.NET, use Option Explicit and Option Strict.
- ☑ Use centralized filtering functions on all user input.
- ☑ Never use the generic *Request* collection when gathering user input.

Constraining Input

Bounds Checking

- ☑ Use validator controls to validate form input if a page posts back to itself.
- ☑ Never rely on client-side validation for security.

Pattern Matching

- ☑ Use regular expressions either to block known bad data or allow only known good data.
- ☑ Use regular expressions to identify malicious keywords or other patterns.

Data Reflecting

☑ Reflect data using trusted system functions to prevent attacks such as directory traversal.

☑ Always work with the reflected path in subsequent operations.

Encoding Data

☑ Use *HtmlEncode* to encode a string for browser output.

☑ Use *UrlEncode* to encode a URL string for output.

☑ Use *UrlPathEncode* to encode the path portion of a URL for output.

Encapsulating

☑ Use hashes to encapsulate data for safe handling.

☑ Convert hashes to hex values to create safe alphanumeric strings.

Parameterizing

☑ Use parameterizing to fix the context and scope of user data.

☑ Combine parameterization with other techniques to prevent directory traversal.

Double Decoding

☑ Use double decoding to detect multiple layers of encoding.

☑ Reject all requests that contain more than one layer of encoding.

Syntax Checking

☑ Check the final syntax of any string that is based on user input to be sure it matches the expected format.

Exception Handling

☑ Take advantage of the robust error handling features in ASP.NET.

☑ Check return results to be sure they are consistent with what you expected.

Honey Drops

☑ Use honey drops in your database to detect SQL injection attacks.

☑ Use honey drops in your file system to detect file system access.

☑ Use honey drops in your source code to detect server-side code access.

Limiting Exposure to Malicious Input

Reducing the Attack Surface

☑ Reduce the attack surface of the application to limit exposure to hackers.

☑ Don't show query string parameters if you do not use them in a particular context.

☑ Remove testing, debug, and dead code from production applications.

☑ If possible, use static content in application demos.

☑ Limit access to administration or other private modules.

☑ Remove sample code and programs from production servers.

☑ Avoid or carefully audit third-party components.

Limiting Attack Scope

☑ Use the principle of least privilege to limit the access of Web users.

☑ Avoid storing passwords, private comments, or other sensitive information in server-side code.

Hardening Server Applications

- ☑ Use the *MaxRequestEntityAllowed* and *AspMaxRequestEntityAllowed* metabase settings to limit overall length of a request.

- ☑ Use the *MaxFieldLength*, *MaxRequestBytes*, *UrlSegmentMaxLength*, and *UrlSegmentMaxCount* registry settings to limit the length of specific parts of a request.

- ☑ Use the *EnableNonUTF8* and *PercentUAllowed* registry keys to limit valid characters in a request.

Code Audit Fast Track

Handling Malicious Input

Identifying Input Sources

- ☑ Does the application properly identify all possible sources of user input, including less obvious and secondary input sources?

Programming Defensively

- ☑ Does the application assign filtered user input to variables to distinguish it from the raw data?

- ☑ When using VB.NET, does the application use Option Explicit and Option Strict?

- ☑ Does the application use centralized filtering functions on all user input?

- ☑ Does the application avoid using the generic *Request* collection when gathering user input?

Constraining Input

Bounds Checking

- ☑ Does the application use validator controls to validate form input if a page posts back to itself?

☑ Does the application avoid enforcing security through client-side validation?

Pattern Matching

☑ Does the application use regular expressions to either block known bad data or allow only known good data?

☑ Does the application use regular expressions to identify malicious keywords or other patterns?

Data Reflecting

☑ Does the application reflect data using trusted system functions to prevent attacks such as directory traversal?

☑ Does the application always work with the reflected path in subsequent operations?

Encoding Data

☑ Does the application use *HtmlEncode* to encode all strings for browser output?

☑ Does the application use *UrlEncode* to encode all URL strings for output?

☑ Does the application use *UrlPathEncode* to encode the path portion of all URLs for output?

Encapsulating

☑ Does the application use hashes to encapsulate data for safe handling?

☑ Does the application convert hashes to hex values to create a safe alphanumeric string?

Parameterizing

☑ Does the application use parameterizing to fix the context and scope of user data?

☑ Does the application combine parameterization with other filtering techniques to prevent directory traversal?

Double Decoding

☑ Does the application use double decoding to detect multiple layers of encoding?

☑ Does the application reject all requests that contain more than one layer of encoding?

Syntax Checking

☑ Does the application check the final syntax of any string that is based on user input?

Exception Handling

☑ Does the application take advantage of the robust error handling features in ASP.NET?

☑ Does the application check return results to be sure they are consistent with what is expected?

Honey Drops

☑ Does the application use honey drops in the database to detect SQL injection attacks?

☑ Does the application use honey drops in the file system to detect file system access?

☑ Does the application use honey drops in your source code to detect server-side code access?

Limiting Exposure to Malicious Input

Reducing the Attack Surface

☑ Does the application reduce the attack surface of the application to limit exposure to hackers?

☑ Does the application avoid showing unused query string parameters?

☑ Is the code devoid of any testing, debug, or other dead code?

☑ Does the application use static content in application demos?

☑ Does the application limit access to administration or other private modules?

☑ Is the production server devoid of sample code?

☑ Did any third party components undergo a thorough security audit?

Limiting Attack Scope

☑ Does the application use the principle of least privilege to limit the access of Web users?

☑ Does the application avoid storing passwords, private comments, or other sensitive information in server-side code?

Hardening Server Applications

☑ Does the application use the *MaxRequestEntityAllowed* and *AspMaxRequestEntityAllowed* metabase settings to limit overall length of a request?

☑ Does the application use the *MaxFieldLength, MaxRequestBytes, UrlSegmentMaxLength*, and *UrlSegmentMaxCount* registry settings to limit the length of specific parts of a request?

☑ Does the application use the *EnableNonUTF8* and *PercentUAllowed* registry keys to limit valid characters in a request?

Frequently Asked Questions

The following Frequently Asked Questions, answered by the authors of this book, are designed to both measure your understanding of the concepts presented in this chapter and to assist you with real-life implementation of these concepts. To have your questions about this chapter answered by the author, browse to **www.syngress.com/solutions** and click on the **"Ask the Author"** form. You will also gain access to thousands of other FAQs at ITFAQnet.com.

Q: I want to allow users to enter some HTML tags such as <b> and <i> but the built-in validation feature will not allow it. How do I configure ASP.NET to allow this and how do I allow these tags without exposing other users to cross-site scripting attacks?

A: To allow users to send HTML markup from a form field, query string, or cookie, you must first disable the built-in validation feature. This setting is an attribute of the <pages> element in machine.config. You can also disable it on a per-page basis with this tag on the page itself:

```
<% @ Page validateRequest="True" %>
```

Once you disable this feature, you must manually encode user input to make sure that it does not contain any HTML markup. Next, search for the encoded tags you want to allow and change them back to their original form. For example, to allow bold markup, search for the string <b> and replace it with <b>. Repeat this for each allowed tag. Likewise, replace all occurrences of </b> with </b>.

Note that since you have disabled the built-in validation you must be very careful to always check user input for HTML markup.

Q: Is ASP.NET vulnerable to buffer overflow attacks?

A: Managed code is generally not vulnerable to buffer overflow attacks, but that does not mean you are completely safe. Because fully trusted code has the capability of calling unmanaged code such as external components or Windows API calls, buffer overflows are still a risk. Always use caution to check string lengths when calling unmanaged code. Also, be sure to run code with a low privilege account, and use strong NTFS permissions to limit access to the file system. For example, Web users should not have access to files outside the Web content directories.

Q: Can I configure IIS to stop or at least minimize source-code viewing and file access attacks?

A: You can often minimize the effects of file system attacks with how you configure IIS and the file system. Here are some tips:

- In the Internet Services Manager, remove Read permissions for all scripts and executables. Neither scripts nor executables need read permissions to run.

- Set strong NTFS permissions on Web content files and directories to prevent Web users from modifying or creating files. If you need Web users to be able to create and modify data files, consider placing these files outside the Web root. If you must allow users to create or modify files in a Web content directory, use specific NTFS permissions to allow access only to those particular files, rather than the entire directory.

- Use the file system to set the read-only attribute on Web content files and directories to prevent easy modification of these files.

Q: Microsoft states that you don't need URLScan with IIS 6. Is there any benefit for using URLScan to stop application-level attacks?

A: IIS 6 has many security features that for the most part make URLScan irrelevant. However, there are still some features that can reduce the attack surface and help limit application level attacks. For example, you can use URLScan to block requests that contain certain strings and you can limit the length of specific HTTP headers. See www.microsoft.com/technet/security/tools/urlscan.mspx for more information on using URLScan with IIS 6.

Chapter 6

Accessing Data

Solutions in this Chapter:

- Introduction
- Securing Databases
- Writing Secure Data Access Code
- Coding Standards Fast Track
- Code Audit Fast Track

Introduction

Depending on a hacker's goal, an application's data may be his or her primary target. In general, the back end of the application is where all the personal, sensitive, and often desirable data is stored—from credit card numbers to medical information. Most Web application use some kind of data storage. This chapter describes how easy it is to compromise a database and demonstrates the problems that plague many current Web applications. However, after you read the solutions in this chapter, your own Web application will not have to be one of them.

To secure your database, we will take a bottom-up approach by first discussing how to secure drivers that an application uses to communicate with a database. Next, we'll examine how to secure the database as a whole by tightening the default installation and using policies such as least privileges. We will cover firewalls and other means to protect your application as well as monitor intrusion attempts. Finally, we'll have an in-depth discussion of how to write secure code that safely connects to your database. This discussion will include specific details of the ways attackers crack systems using SQL injections and the multiple layers of security you can use to protect your application.

The threats discussed in this chapter are:

- **Data compromise** An attacker gains access to read or modify private data.

- **Database compromise** An attacker gains access to modify the database structure itself.

- **SQL injection** Manipulating user input to construct SQL statements that execute on the database server.

- **Buffer overflows** Overwriting a buffer by sending more data than a buffer can handle, resulting in the application crashing or executing code of the attacker's choice.

- **Privilege escalation** Accessing system resources or executing code within the security context of a privileged user account.

- **Information leakage** Revealing sensitive information or private user data.

Securing Databases

Your data access code's security depends greatly on your entire database infrastructure. Security vulnerabilities may occur due to bugs in the database or its drivers, unsafe database location, or poor database configuration. Before writing any data access code in your Web application, you should first consider the security of the database itself.

Securing the Database Location

Summary: **Carefully design your database's location with regard to firewalling technologies**

Threats: **Database compromise, bypassing security measures**

An important first step in securing your database is to properly control access to the database itself. You should be careful to configure your firewall to restrict access so that only the Web application itself can directly access database ports. Where you physically place the database server on your network can also have an impact on database security.

For an example, let's say that we have a .NET Web application named *myApplication* that uses a database called *myApplication Database*. Figure 6.1 shows a common firewall layout for this scenario.

Figure 6.1 Firewall Layout #1

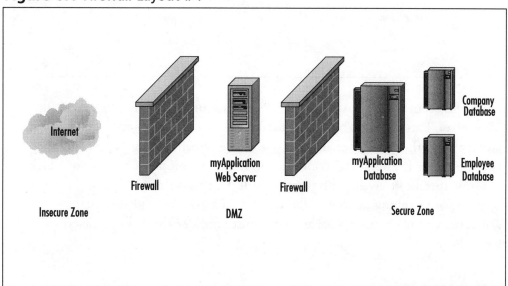

Notice that a firewall separates the myApplication Web server from the Internet, and another firewall separates the myApplication Web server from the myApplication database. The area in which the Web server resides is called a *demilitarized zone (DMZ)*. Behind the second firewall reside the database and often the internal company network.

This scenario is common because many administrators believe it provides a second layer of protection for the database in case an attacker compromises the Web server or another server in the DMZ. However, this may not be the most secure configuration. If an attacker obtains access to the database itself, perhaps through SQL injection or a buffer overflow, the attacker gains a direct line to the internal network, completely sidestepping the protections of the firewall. Consider an alternative network layout, presented in Figure 6.2.

Figure 6.2 Firewall Layout #2

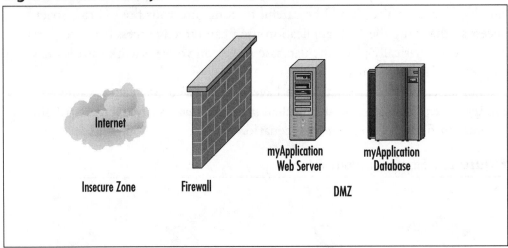

In this scenario, we have placed the database in the DMZ, along with the Web server. This scenario treats the database server as a high-risk server and isolates it from other databases and the rest of the internal network. Placing the database server in the DMZ contains and limits the scope of a database attack.

Your specific firewall configuration will depend on the needs of the applications you are running as well as the type of data you store in the database. Wherever you place your database, you must consider the risks involved.

Security Policy

- Review your network topology and security needs to design a firewall layout best suited for your environment.

- Assume worst-case scenarios when designing your firewall layout.

A *database driver* is the software interface that communicates with a database. Because drivers are essential for database communication, they are a popular point of attack. The single most important thing you can do to protect your database drivers is to keep them up to date. As with most popular enterprise software, drivers are frequently updated because vulnerabilities in them can have such dire effects on a system. Many recent viruses, worms, and Internet exploits could have been prevented if the compromised systems had updated drivers and software.

In addition to keeping your drivers up to date, other good security practices you can follow include limiting the areas of your system an attacker can compromise and understanding and preventing buffer overflow attacks. We will also examine logging and tracing methods to determine when and how attackers may have invaded, or attempted to invade, your system.

Limiting the Attack Surface

Summary: **Remove unused drivers from your database to reduce the number of attack vectors**

Threats: **Database compromise**

Software companies build databases to accommodate a huge variety of Web site needs. Chances are, your application doesn't use every feature available with a default database installation. Every database feature is a potential attack vector; therefore, unused features do nothing more than increase the attack surface for a hacker. Decrease this attack surface by removing any unused database drivers.

By default, a Windows 2000 installation comes with various Open Database Connectivity (ODBC) drivers. You can safely remove the ODBC drivers if you are not using them. You need to manually remove the ODBC drivers from the registry. Using *regedit*, remove any unused drivers from the following keys:

- HKLM\SOFTWARE\ODBC\ODBCINST.INI

- HKLM\SOFTWARE\ODBC\ODBC.INI

Figure 6.3 shows how to use *regedit* to remove these keys.

Figure 6.3 Removing an ODBC Driver from the Registry

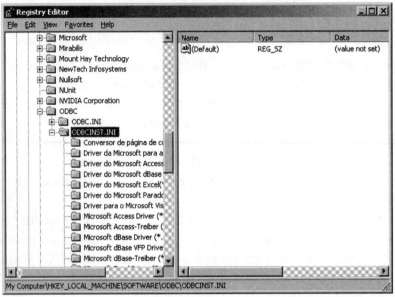

If you are not using the Jet drivers, you can safely remove them as well. Delete the unused Jet engines and Index Sequential Access Method (ISAM) formats that you find below the HKEY_LOCAL_MACHINE\SOFTWARE\ Microsoft\Jet registry key.

Finally, some Windows applications install User, System, or File data source names (DSNs). Generally, the applications do not even notify you that they installed these DSNs. If you don't use these DSNs, you should delete them. Use the User Data Sources (ODBC) Administrative Tool and click **Remove** for each unused driver, as shown in Figure 6.4. Alternatively, you can remove the DSNs by deleting the entries under the HKEY_LOCAL_MACHINE\SOFTWARE\ ODBC\ODBCI.INI registry key.

Figure 6.4 Removing DSNs

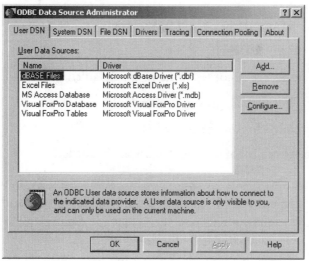

> **TIP**
>
> Some updates or patches may replace the registry entries you removed.
> Check your registry and remove any restored entries after you install
> updates.

Securing Specific Drivers

After removing unused database drivers, you should further reduce the attack
surface by securing the remaining drivers. Most database drivers provide settings
to limit functionality or restrict driver usage. Here we discuss some example settings for various common drivers.

SQL Server

Keeping a record of who is trying to log in to your database is a valuable practice
from many standpoints. If you see multiple attempts and failures with different
usernames and/or passwords, you can surmise that an attacker is trying to use
brute force to access your database. Likewise, if you notice successful logins at
strange times, you may need to contact the user who logged in to make sure
there was a valid reason for his or her use of the database.

By default, SQL Server does not audit logins and login attempts. You can record login attempts by setting a value in the registry key located at HKEY_LOCAL_MACHINE\SOFTWARE\Microsoft\MSSQLServer\AuditLevel. The possible values are:

- **0** No logins are recorded (this is the default).
- **1** Only successful logins are recorded.
- **2** Only failed logins are recorded.
- **3** Both successful and failed logins are recorded.

Alternatively, you can set the recording level using SQL Server's Enterprise Management tool. Right-click the database group and select **Properties**. A new window will pop up. Select the **Security** tab from the top. You should see a window similar to Figure 6.5.

The Audit level area lets you set the logging level. Whether you use the registry setting or the GUI, set the audit level to record all login attempts. SQL

Figure 6.5 Setting the Maximum Logging Level

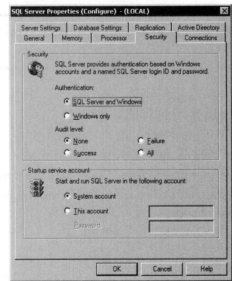

Server's default location to write the logs in C:\Program Files\Microsoft SQL Server\MSSQL\LOG.

IIS with ODBC

You can configure IIS to automatically log details to an ODBC source. You can log data such as the client's IP address, the request the client performed, parameters passed, page requested, and many other properties of the connected user's communication. With this data stored in a database, you can search for and respond to attacks and abnormal activity.

To set up IIS for ODBC logging, right-click your Web site, shown in the IIS Administration window. Select **Properties**, and you will see a window similar to Figure 6.6.

Figure 6.6 Setting IIS for ODBC Logging

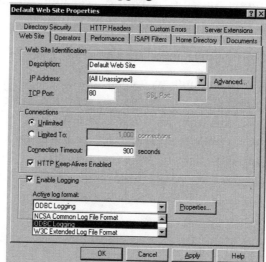

From this window, you can select **ODBC Logging** from the bottom area labeled "Active log format." After selecting ODBC Logging, you need to click the **Properties** button to the right to configure the ODBC DSN, the table to log to, and your user credentials to connect to the data source. You can find a list of the table structure appropriate for logging, as well as a script to create the table for you, in Microsoft's Knowledge Base Article 245243, at http://support.microsoft.com/default.aspx?scid=kb;en-us;Q245243.

Jet and ISAM

If you are using Jet or ISAM, you should use certain settings to improve your security. Jet drivers can and should run in Sandbox mode. You may have heard the term *sandbox* applied to Java applets. The idea with Jet drivers is the same. A sandbox is a protected portion of memory in which an application or drivers can run without the risk of causing damage to other applications running. The Jet Sandbox mode prevents users from embedding sensitive commands such as Shell in SQL queries.

You should change the registry entries at HKEY_LOCAL_MACHINE\ Software\Microsoft\Jet\3.5\engines\SandboxMode and HKEY_LOCAL_ MACHINE\Software\Microsoft\Jet\4.0\engines\SandboxMode to run at the value of 3, which is the most secure Sandbox mode. The possible modes are:

- **0** Sandbox mode is disabled.
- **1** Sandbox mode is used only with Access applications.
- **2** Sandbox mode is used only with non-Access applications.
- **3** Sandbox mode is used on all applications.

Another setting you can tighten to increase security deals with the text ISAM. By default, the text ISAM allows you to read and write any text file. The registry key that controls this feature is located at HKEY_LOCAL_MACHINE\ Software\Microsoft\Jet\4.0\Engines\Text\DisabledExtensions and contains the default values of *!txt,csv,tab,asc,tmp,htm,html*. Increase the restrictions on which files can be read and written by replacing the *txt* entry with whatever text extensions you are using.

Security Policy

- Remove or disable unused drivers from your database.
- Periodically check for and remove any new unused drivers, especially after updates or patches.
- Configure your database drivers to maximum security.
- Configure your database drivers to log access activity.

Ensuring Least Privilege

Summary: **Restrict access and permissions to your database to the smallest set of permissions that still retains functionality**

Threats: **Information leakage, database compromise, elevated permissions**

Software engineers by nature are concerned with meeting their deadlines and producing their deliverables. When a programmer needs to connect to a database, he or she often writes code that uses the quickest and easiest way to connect and get the data needed. This generally involves using SQL Server's *sa*, or System Administrator, account, which has superuser access and won't give the developer any hassles about permissions or authorization. "I'll go back and lock the system down once I get time," the programmer often thinks.

Experience shows that with the approaching deadlines and last-minute bugs, the programmer forgets or does not have time to go back and tighten the database's security. This is how software can end up in a production environment with elevated permissions. It's also why an attacker can leverage one system running with unnecessarily high permissions to gain access to every other machine in the company.

The rule of least privilege states that any user, application, or process should have the bare minimum of access to do what it needs to complete its function. Do not give or allow access based on the idea that the user might need the access later or that it's easier than figuring out what the minimum allowed access should be. Grant only the minimum required privileges to a user. If, in the future, the user needs more access, grant it then and not before.

SQL Server has various mechanisms to help you apply the rule of least privilege, including roles, groups, and access control lists (ACLs). We've already mentioned the first and most obvious (but often neglected) thing you should do: Never use the sa account for data access. The sa account has rights to do all kind of things your application likely doesn't need to do, such as deleting an entire database. Instead, create a user account on the SQL Server that only has rights to do specifically what your code requires, whether reading a table, executing a stored procedure, or the like. You can set permission rights as specific as an individual column of a table or an individual stored procedure. As you find you need more access, add the explicit right you need. Locking down your access on a database this way obviously limits the actions a user can perform. This is fantastic from a security point of view. If an attacker is able breach your database, the attacker will find himself restricted by the same rights the application had. This could potentially minimize both the data the attacker can steal and the damage he can cause.

A firewall is another method of applying least privilege. By giving permission only to the ports your database uses to go through the firewall, you are further restricting unexpected or unauthorized communication. SQL Server, by default, communicates through port 1433 for TCP/IP access. You can change this setting, but be aware that a port change will cause complexity for traffic profiling and other monitoring that relies on SQL Server using port 1433.

Internet Protocol Security (IPSec) and Secure Sockets Layer (SSL) are two additional methods you can use to restrict who can connect to your database. IPSec uses policies that consist of filters, filter actions, and rules. With IPSec, you explicitly specify, by IP address, which computers may connect to your database. SSL uses certificates to restrict who can connect. A client computer must have a known and trusted certificate to successfully connect to the database. An advantage of SSL over IPSec is that configuration changes are not required if the client's IP address changes.

Use the rule of least privilege throughout the design and implementation of your application in many different ways. It is part of a solid foundation of good security. We will continue to mention this policy and recommend more ways to use it in other areas of your application.

Security Policy

- Always grant the minimum of required access and permission.
- Use firewalls to restrict inappropriate access.
- Use IPSec or SSL to restrict who can connect to your database.

Securing the Database

Summary: **Remove unused features and restrict default settings on your database to prevent successful attacks**

Threats: **Database compromise**

As we've mentioned before, databases include many features to appeal to the widest market and range of uses as possible. You will probably not need the majority of these features and can safely reduce your attack surface by disabling or removing these unused features. Furthermore, databases often have weak default settings. The following is a list of features you can remove, as well as default settings you should strengthen:

- Keep your service packs, drivers, updates, hotfixes, and patches current. Review your database vendor's Web site often to find what service patches are available.

- Use strong passwords for all accounts. This is especially important for the sa account, which is present by default in SQL Server. Strong passwords decrease an attacker's ability to successfully guess, brute-force, dictionary attack, or otherwise discover an account's password. Always use long and complex passwords for database accounts.

- Remove sample code, sample databases, and sample stored procedures. By default, SQL Server comes with the Northwind and Pubs databases and associated stored procedures. There is no reason for these databases to be present in a production environment.

- Remove unused network libraries. SQL Server can communicate with applications in a variety of ways. Network libraries, or *netlibs*, are the modules that determine the method of communication SQL Server can use. TCP/IP is the most popular method of communication, but you can also use Shared Memory, Named Pipes, Banyan Vines, AppleTalk, or VIA GigaNet SAN, as well as others. While you are deciding which communication method to use, disable all the netlibs to prevent access to your database. When you have decided which netlib(s) to use, disable the unused netlibs to limit your attack surface.

- Remove extended stored procedures. By default, SQL Server comes with over 60 stored procedures that you might not need. These stored procedures are primarily for convenience and provide the functionality of certain graphical user interface (GUI) tools, such as the SQL Server Enterprise Manager. By removing these stored procedures, you will limit tools and methods an attacker can use to gain access and compromise your database.

The process for securing a database is complex and unique for each platform and database application; the tips mentioned here are only an introduction. Take time to learn the specific security measures for your particular environment.

Security Policy

- Keep your database software up to date.

- Disable or remove unused features of your database.

- Strengthen weak default passwords and permissions.

Writing Secure Data Access Code

We have covered how to secure the database drivers and the database itself, and you've seen the various settings you can use to lock down functionality and access. However, this is only the half the solution to securing data access. If your code does not properly filter user input, an attacker might be able to leverage your Web application to execute SQL statements on the database.

In this section, you will learn how to prevent an attacker from gaining access to your database. Here we will cover:

- Connecting to a data source

- Preventing SQL injection

- Writing secure data access code

- Reading and writing to data files

Connecting to the Data Source

Summary: **Connecting to the data source can potentially expose sensitive information**

Threats: **Information leakage, data corruption, data destruction**

Authentication and authorization are critical elements when using a data source. Before your application can use your data source, the data source should authenticate your application to connect and authorize the activities your application attempts to perform. The lack of either of these steps suggests a database with weak security. A data source that does not authenticate allows anyone and everyone to connect, from the most trusted user to the most dangerous hacker. A data source that does not authorize regards every connected user as a superadministrator, with rights to read all stored data and perform any kind of data source change. SQL Server has multiple options for both authentication and authorization, which we explore in this section.

Authentication

Authentication is the process by which your application connects to the database. An attacker would have a difficult time gaining access to a database to which he cannot connect.

Your application can authenticate to an SQL Server database in two different ways. We recommend the more secure method, called Windows Authentication. With Windows Authentication, Windows manages credentials for you, so there is no need to transmit them over the network. For this reason, there is no need for usernames or passwords to be stored in the connection string. You have various options as to how you use Windows Authentication when connecting to an SQL Server from an ASP.NET application. These options include using the ASP.NET process identity, using fixed identities within ASP.NET, using serviced components, using the LogonUser API to impersonate a specific identity, using the original caller's identity, and using the anonymous Internet User account.

We recommend using the ASP.NET process identity, because it is one of the simplest and most secure methods of connection. To use ASP.NET, you need to change the local ASP.NET process identity's password value on the Web server and create a mirrored account on the database server by creating a local user with the same name and password. Outlined here are the necessary steps in this process:

1. Change the ASPNET account on the Web server to a known strong password value containing upper- and lowercase letters, numbers, and specials characters such as !, @, #, or %. For example, *wh!t3Rabitt..hop..hop.*

2. Change the password in Machine.config (usually found at C:\Windows\Microsoft.NET\Framework\<Framework version>\CONFIG) at the *processModel* element to match. Example:

```
<processModel userName="machine"
  password="wh!t3Rabitt..hop..hop">
```

3. Protect the machine.config file from unauthorized access by using ACLs.

4. Create this same account (a mirrored account) on the database server.

5. On the database server, create a server login for the local ASPNET account and map the login to a user account within the appropriate

database. Create a database user role, add the database user to the role, and configure the appropriate database permissions for the role.

After completing these steps, you will be able to connect to the SQL Server using Windows Authentication. Figure 6.7 (C#) and Figure 6.8 (VB.NET) show example connection strings using Windows Authentication.

Figure 6.7 Windows Authentication [C#]

```
SqlConnection sqlConnection = new SqlConnection("server=apollo;" +
    "database= EmployeePersonalInformation;" +
    "Integrated Security=SSPI;");
```

Figure 6.8 Windows Authentication [VB.NET]

```
Dim sqlConnection = New SqlConnection( _
    "server=apollo; database=EmployeePersonalInformation; " + _
    "Integrated Security=SSPI;")
```

Windows Authentication is not always a possibility, however. The second and less secure method for an application to connect to a SQL Server database is SQL Authentication. Consider SQL Authentication only if:

- Your database doesn't support Windows Authentication.
- Your application cannot use Windows Authentication because of a firewall.
- Your application must connect to the database using multiple identities and you are not using impersonation in your ASP.NET application.

SQL Authentication can be dangerous because credentials must be stored and passed to the database. You must protect the credentials on the application server as well as in transit to the SQL Server. One method is to install a server certificate on the SQL Server database to automatically encrypt credentials sent over the network. You could also use an IPSec encrypted channel to protect communication between the application and SQL Server. Encrypt the database connection string your application uses as well, in case an attacker finds a way to read your file system. The next section discusses methods for encrypting the database connection string. Figure 6.9 (C#) and Figure 6.10 (VB.NET) show example connection strings for SQL Authentication.

Figure 6.9 SQL Authentication Connection String [C#]

```
string SqlConnectionString = "Server=apollo;" +
    "Database=EmployeePersonalInformation;" +
    "uid=colsen;pwd=g0ld3n.GREMlin;";
```

Figure 6.10 SQL Authentication Connection String [VB.NET]

```
Dim SqlConnectionString = New String("Server=apollo;" + _
    "Database=EmployeePersonalInformation;" + _
    "uid=colsen;pwd=g0ld3n.GREMlin;")
```

With either method, it is imperative that you connect to the database using a least privileged account. ASP.NET Web applications, by default, use the ASPNET account. Create the appropriate account on the SQL Server and give the minimum appropriate permissions for the application to access and use the desired database. Again, we are applying the rule of least privilege.

Protecting Connection Strings

Protecting your connection strings is particularly important if you are using SQL Authentication, because the connection string will contain a username and password. You should never store connection information in the Web application code itself. Even if you are using Windows Authentication, the connection string still contains the server and database to which you are connecting. The less information your application server exposes in case of a compromise, the better. The following methods are better alternatives to protect your connection string.

DPAPI

Data Protection Application Programming Interface (DPAPI) is one of the most secure methods for storing your connection strings, although it is a bit complicated to use. DPAPI is part of Windows 2000 and later Windows operating systems. Use DPAPI for encrypting and decrypting data. The advantage of DPAPI is that the operating system manages the encryption key, instead of the application. DPAPI also leverages the login of the account calling the DPAPI code to derive the encryption key. See http://msdn.microsoft.com/library/en-us/dnnetsec/html/SecNetHT08.asp for more information on using DPAPI from ASP.NET.

UDL Files

If you are using the OLE DB .NET data provider, using UDL files is an option. Take care to store the UDL outside the Web application's virtual directory, and protect the files with the proper NTFS permissions. Always use a fully qualified path for UDL files to be sure that you are using the correct UDL file. Note that UDL files do not use encryption to store connection information.

COM+ Component

If your application includes service components, you can use COM+ to store connection strings. Store the connection strings as constructor strings, and administer them using the Components Service tool. For more information on using COM+ for storing connection strings, see http://support.microsoft.com/default.aspx?scid=kb;en-us;Q271284.

Registry

A connection string can be stored in the HKEY_LOCAL_MACHINE or HKEY_CURRENT_USER registry hive. Use proper ACLs and encryption to protect any information stored in the registry.

Text Files

Text files are an insecure method of storing connection strings. If you must use text files, make sure you encrypt the files, store them outside the Web application's virtual directory, and protect them with proper NTFS permissions.

WARNING

Never use the sa or db_owner accounts for application data access. Attackers will always first try using these built-in default accounts. Make sure these accounts have very strong passwords and that you use them only for administration.

Authorization

Authorization is the process by which the database determines whether your connected application has sufficient rights for the operations it is trying to perform.

In other words, does the connected application have permission to read this table or modify this column? SQL Server provides a role-based approach for authorization. Roles can grant and restrict read and write access to databases, tables, columns, roles, and stored procedures. Three categories of role are supported:

- **User-defined database roles** These roles are used to group users who have the same access rights on the database. For example, the administrator can make a role named Human Resources and specify that this role can only view the EmployeePersonalInformation databases. All other databases on the server, such as CustomerInformation, will refuse access to a user in the Human Resource role. Finally, the administrator needs to assign specific users to the role. In this example, the database admin would assign the login for Martha from Human Resources to the Human Resource role.

- **Application roles** These are roles used to grant specific applications access rights on the database. An application uses a built-in stored procedure to activate the rights.

- **Fixed database roles** These are fixed roles the SQL Server database comes with out of the box. These general-use roles are for common activities such as the db_backup role that has access to back up the database.

Security Policy

- Use roles to apply the least privileged accounts.
- Use Windows Authentication whenever possible.
- Keep database connection strings secure.
- Set strong passwords for the sa and db_accounts. Do not use these accounts in your applications!

Preventing SQL Injection

Summary: **An attacker can run malicious SQL code against your database**

Threats: **Information leakage, data corruption, data destruction**

SQL injection attacks are among the most dangerous and commonly used Web-based attacks today. The basis for an SQL injection attack involves a malicious user causing a database to run destructive and compromising SQL commands. We will give specific examples of how attackers use SQL injection attacks, the information the attacker can gather, and the damage an attacker can perform. We will then cover several methods for preventing these attacks.

SQL Injection Examples

Virtually every Web site reads information entered by users, from login information to search criteria. When a user purposely inserts SQL code into data that the database is going to process, a SQL injection occurs. For example, a Web site may read in the username and password of a user during login and check the database to see if this is valid login information. A common and insecure SQL query string may look like the strings shown in Figure 6.11 (C#) or Figure 6.12 (VB.NET).

Figure 6.11 Common Query String [C#]

```
string queryString = "select * from Accounts where username = '" +
    Request.QueryString["username"] + "' and password='" +
    Request.QueryString["password"] + "'";
```

Figure 6.12 Common Query String [VB.NET]

```
Dim queryString = New String("select * from Accounts " + _
    "where username = '" + Request.QueryString["username"] + _
    "' and password='" + Request.QueryString["password"] + "'")
```

The intention is that users enter their information, and the following query would run against the database:

```
select * from Accounts where username = 'chris',
  password='Gob.stop.er.112'
```

The code uses the result set returned from this query to determine whether or not to grant access. However, for a username, a malicious user might enter:

```
hahaha
```

and for a password:

```
'; drop table Accounts
```

This means that the following query runs against the database:

```
select * from Accounts where username = 'hahaha',
  password=''; drop table Accounts
```

Two statements run. The first performs a useless lookup on the user *hahaha*; the second statement destroys your accounts database table. This is the crux of SQL injections: Malicious code runs against your database when user input is not cleaned, validated, and secured.

Some basic SQL notation will help explain these attacks:

- ‘ Opens and closes a database string.

- ; Ends a statement.

- -- Creates a comment. Anything after the -- is ignored.

The following list shows some of the attacks a malicious user can use to compromise and destroy data. The attacks use our original query string shown in Figure 6.9.

- **Retrieve database structure information** For an attacker to mount a successful attack, he or she needs to learn which tables and columns are available. The default behavior of SQL Server is to return informational error messages when incorrect queries run. For example, if for the username the attacker entered:

```
' having 1=1
```

the database will return an error message containing the table name as well as the first column in the code's query, as shown in Figure 6.13.

Figure 6.13 Table Name Exposed in Error Message

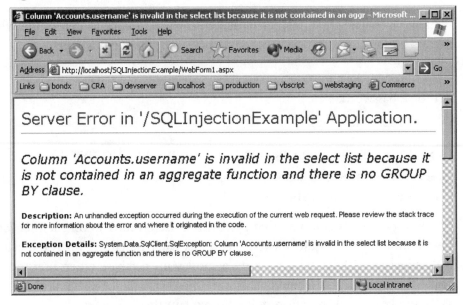

You can see that the error message contains the table "Accounts" and the first column of the query "username." The *group by* statement can ascertain further columns in the query, as shown here:

```
' group by Accounts.username having 1=1--
```

The database will return the next column in the query, as shown in Figure 6.14.

Figure 6.14 Next Column in Query Is Exposed in Error Message

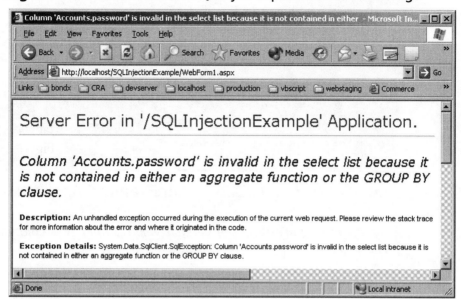

You can see that the error message contains the next column in the query, "password." An attacker can continue to append *group by* statements until he stops receiving error messages. In our example query string, the attacker will stop getting error messages when he enters:

```
' group by Accounts.username,Accounts.password having a=a--
```

The error messages stop because all the columns in the table "Accounts" are present in the *group by* statement. The attacker now knows the columns in the Accounts table and can insert a record to gain access.

- **Retrieve database content information** An attacker can retrieve the data stored in the database by taking advantage of a conversion error message. When a query tries to perform an illegal conversion, SQL Server returns the actual data that could not be converted. For example, if for a username the attacker enters:

```
' union select min(username),1 from Accounts where
  username > 1 --
```

the database returns the first username in the Accounts table—in this case, "admin," as shown in Figure 6.15.

Figure 6.15 Username Value Exposed in Error Message

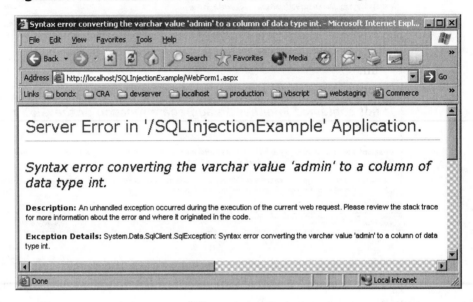

An attacker could use the same SQL injection and substitute *password* for username to learn the admin account's password, and so forth for every table or record in the database.

- **Compromise database integrity** This attack aborts a query by closing the original statement appropriately, often by a closing quotation mark and/or a semi-colon, and then appends a destructive or corruptive SQL statement. Here are some examples of destructive input that could be entered as a password:

```
'; delete from Accounts
```

or

```
'; insert into Accounts (username, password) values
('hahaha', '0wn3d')
```

These queries result in the intended query running with a blank password and an unintended, destructive query running second.

- **Compromise a query** An attacker may shorten a query and circumvent the authentication process. In this example, the user name entered was:

```
admin'--
```

Using the example query shown previously in Figure 6.1, this query causes the SQL query to prematurely end after specifying the using "admin." Assuming an account named "admin" exists, the attacker circumvented knowing the admin password, and the code permits the attack to log in as "admin" with the appropriate password.

Logical statements can also corrupt a query. If for a username, the attacker entered:

```
' or a=a--
```

the attacker will be logged in as the first user in the database table. This works because the SQL Server will match the logically always true statement of a=a with the first account in the table.

These are some of the more common methods used for SQL injection. Most attacks use one or more of these methods. This is not, however, an exhaustive list of all the different permutations. Hackers are developing new SQL injection techniques all the time. Thankfully, code and operating policies can protect you from most, if not all, attacks.

Many Web sites will tell you that all you need to do to prevent SQL injections is to filter out or escape certain characters used in SQL injection attacks, such as ', --, and ;. Filtering and escaping is not enough. The following are some solutions you can use to prevent SQL injections. Ideally, you should use more than one of these techniques.

Filtering or Escaping Dangerous Characters

Filtering or escaping dangerous characters is the most common and easiest to break method of preventing SQL injections. The idea behind the technique is to either remove (filter) dangerous characters from user input or cause the database to treat a dangerous character as a literal (escape).

Filtering can be a bad idea because the "dangerous" character might be a valid part of the user's input. For example, removing a single quote (') from the company's name or a user's password could cause problems. You can, however, raise an error in the presence of "known bad" data. Known-bad data is characters that generally have no place outside an SQL statement, such as — or ; characters. If these characters are inappropriate for the specific field—for example, a user-name field or a password field that doesn't allow punctuation characters—instead of trying to filter or escape the characters, present an error to the user that says these characters are not allowed.

Escaping characters generally involves duplicating the dangerous character so that the code treats the character as a literal instead of the close of a string, in the case of the ' character. Figure 6.16 (C#) and Figure 6.17 (VB.NET) show example code to escape the ' character.

Figure 6.16 Escaping the ' Character [C#]

```
private string escapeQuoteCharacter(string stringToEscape)
{
    return stringToEscape.Replace("'", "''");
}
```

Figure 6.17 Escaping the ' Character [VB.NET]

```
Private Function escapeQuoteCharacter(ByVal stringToEscape As String) _
  As String
    Return stringToEscape.Replace("'", "''")
End Function
```

Merely escaping dangerous characters is not sufficient protection, because an attacker could still insert malicious data into your database that your database accidentally activates later. For example, consider an attacker entering the following as a username:

```
Timebomb'; drop table account--
```

The *escapeQuoteCharacter* method escapes the string, The new string reads:

```
Timebomb''; drop table Accounts--
```

Since the double " marks means the literal ', the code safely inserts into the database:

```
Timebomb'; drop table Accounts--
```

No damage has been caused at this point, since the ' character was treated as a literal; the user just has a strange username. For this example, assume that the Accounts table contains an e-mail column. Consider what happens when the Web site tries to send all users in the system an e-mail. Code would typically create a dataset containing the username of all the users to whom the application will send an e-mail. Here is the code that will run when the application uses the username data to retrieve the e-mail of the user with the malicious username:

```
select email from emailAddress where username='Timebomb'; drop table
    Accounts--'
```

The ' character in the username closes the select statement, the drop clause is appended, and the final quotation mark is commented out. The database interprets the username and drops the Accounts table. To prevent attacks such as this, escape the data contained in the results of all database queries. If the application had run the *escapeQuoteCharacter* method on each username in the result set before querying for the e-mail, the attack would have failed.

Another reason escaping characters is not sufficient protection is that an attacker could use ASCII hexadecimal characters and other character sets to bypass the checks. The database and code can interpret these hexadecimal characters correctly as the ' character, but if your escape code sees the value 0x2C instead of the ' character, it won't escape it.

Using *SqlParameters*

The .NET framework has a collection type called *SqlParameter* that can provide type and length checking as well as automatically escaping user input. Figure 6.18 (C#) and Figure 6.19 (VB.NET) show examples of how to use the *SqlParameter* collection to assign variables when you're building an SQL statement.

Figure 6.18 Using SqlParameters in Building SQL Statements (C#)

```
SqlDataAdapter command =
    new SqlDataAdapter("select password from Accounts " +
    "where password=@password", conn);
SqlParameter sqlParameter =
    command.SelectCommand.Parameters.Add("@password",
    SqlDbType.VarChar, 8);
sqlParameter.Value = Request.Form["username"];
```

Figure 6.19 Using SqlParameters in Building SQL Statements (VB.NET)

```
Dim command = New SqlDataAdapter("select password " + _
    "from Accounts where password=@password", conn)
Dim sqlParameter = command.SelectCommand.Parameters.Add( _
    "@password", SqlDbType.VarChar, 8)
sqlParameter.Value = Request.Form["username"]
```

Use this same technique when calling stored procedures. See Figure 6.20 (C#) and Figure 6.21 (VB.NET) for an example of how to use the *SqlParameter* when calling a stored procedure.

Figure 6.20 Using SqlParameters in Calling Stored Procedures (C#)

```
SqlDataAdapter command = new SqlDataAdapter("AccountInsert", conn);
command.SelectCommand.CommandType = CommandType.StoredProcedure;
SqlParameter sqlParameter =
    command.SelectCommand.Parameters.Add("@username",
    SqlDbType.DateTime, 8);
sqlParameter.Value = Request.Form["username"];
```

Figure 6.21 Using SqlParameters in Calling Stored Procedures (VB.NET)

```
Dim command = New SqlDataAdapter("AccountInsert", conn)
command.SelectCommand.CommandType = CommandType.StoredProcedure
Dim sqlParameter = _
    command.SelectCommand.Parameters.Add("@username", _
    SqlDbType.DateTime, 8)
sqlParameter.Value = Request.Form["username"];
```

The database regards input assigned to the *parm.Value* as a literal, so there is no need to escape the user input. Notice *SqlParameter* also enforces types and type length. If the user input values don't conform to the described type and size, the code throws an exception. Whenever possible, constrain user data by the type and length it must be to benefit from type and length checking.

Constraining Data Types and Length

If you are collecting a date from a user, store it as a date in the database. If you are collecting an ID number, store it as a number in the database. If you are collecting an eight-character password, store it as a *varchar* of 8 characters maximum. If you combine the use of *SqlParameter* and data constraints, your code can reject data that doesn't belong. For example, if an attacker to tries to inject a new user account on the end of the password field:

```
'; insert into Accounts (username, password) values
   ('hahaha', 'Own3d')
```

our SqlParameter code will detect that the password is more than 8 characters long, and it will throw an exception. Alternatively, if an attacker tries to perform the same attack on a numeric field, the *SqlParameter* code will refuse it because the attack includes nonnumeric characters.

Using Least Privileges

Restrict the database user to the bare minimum of actions. If your application only needs to read data from the database, there is no reason to allow the database user to drop tables, insert records, or anything other than reading data. If hostile code does make it to the database, lack of permission will minimize the damage.

Rejecting Known Attack Signatures

Depending on what your application does, you might be able to reject a query based on bad data that could be dangerous. Another way to look at this idea is to apply the principle of least privilege through code. Consider filtering user input keywords for dangerous SQL commands, such as *drop* or *delete*. Figure 6.22 (C#) and Figure 6.23 (VB.NET) show an example of filtering potentially dangerous SQL commands.

Figure 6.22 Filtering Dangerous SQL Commands (C#)

```
private bool containsBadData(string stringToCheck)
{
    string[] badData = new string[]
       { "drop", "delete", "insert", "update" };
    for (int x=0; x < badData.Length; x++)
    {
```

Continued

Figure 6.22 Filtering Dangerous SQL Commands (C#)

```csharp
        if (stringToCheck.IndexOf(badData[x]) > -1)
            return true;

    }
    return false;
}
```

Figure 6.23 Filtering Dangerous SQL Commands (VB.NET)

```vbnet
Private Function containsBadData(_
   ByVal stringToCheck As String) As Boolean
    Dim badData = _
      New String() {"drop", "delete", "insert", "update"}

    For x As Integer = 10 To badData.Length
        If (stringToCheck.IndexOf(badData(x)) > -1) Then
            Return True
        End If
    Next

    Return False
End Function
```

If the method returns *true*, the user input contained bad data. You can take this idea further by creating regular expressions that check for an attacker trying to enter SQL syntax into a field. Take care to consider which user input fields you check with this kind of method. If you are validating a field that contains a user's comments, there may be legitimate reasons for the user to type some of the dangerous command words.

Handling Errors on the Server

As explained in the SQL injection examples, error messages can give an attacker many details about your database. Wrap database actions in *Try* and *Catch* statements and properly process errors on the server side. In your *Catch* statement, log details about the error that occurred. This will help you know that an attack was attempted and what the attack was trying to do. By processing errors on the server, you will prevent the server from passing error messages, and the sensitive details they contain, to the client. Keep in mind that a successful SQL injection attack won't necessarily cause errors. SQL injections that cause errors are often an attacker gathering information about your database as a precursor to an attack. See Chapter 7 for more details on how to properly handle errors.

Properly implemented, these solutions will greatly reduce your susceptibility to SQL injection attacks. Keep in mind, however, that preventing SQL injections is an ongoing battle. Hackers regularly find new exploits across all the different databases. Here are a few sites you can use to keep up to date with the latest SQL injection developments:

- www.nextgenss.com/papers.html
- www.governmentsecurity.org/articles/ SQLInjectionModesofAttackDefenceandWhyItMatters.php
- www.owasp.org

Security Policy

- Code a variety of protections against SQL injection, not just one method.
- Escape user input upon insertion into and retrieval from the database.
- Use *SqlParameters*.
- Process all errors on the server side.
- Enforce the rule of least privilege in the code and in the database account.

Writing Secure SQL Code

Summary: **Security-conscious code can protect your application from future attacks and code compromise**
Threats: **Information leakage, data corruption, data destruction**

An environment as hostile as the Internet will expose your application to threats that did not exist when you wrote the application. By writing security-conscious code, you can increase your application's resiliency against known attacks as well as future attacks. Here are some examples of how you can code defensively to reduce or eliminate your code's vulnerability:

- **Avoid "SELECT ★ FROM"** Use specific column names in your database queries to reduce the attack surface available. Use of the ★ wildcard is easier than enumerating all the columns you want from the database, but it gives a potential intruder or eavesdropper more data to work with. Use of the ★ wildcard also makes it easier for an attacker to manipulate the query without causing an error, since the ★ wildcard will match anything. By naming specific columns in your query, you will limit the query structure and output, making it more difficult for an attacker to construct the proper query for an attack. Always retrieve the minimum needed set of data.

- **Sanity-check query results** You can increase your code's robustness by checking that your result set makes sense. For example, say you are retrieving information about a user from the database by username, and usernames are unique. Check that your result set contains exactly one record of data, and abort your application if it doesn't. You certainly wouldn't expect your result set to contain more than one user, but this is an example of coding defensively. An attack may come out that causes your result set to contain all the users, either by code injection, or a database flaw. The cost of checking the count of your result set is well worth it to avoid the damage done by compromised user's information.

- **Use stored procedures** Stored procedures not only tend to run faster than constructed SQL, but they have security benefits as well. The fixed nature of the stored procedure deters SQL injection attacks (but does not solve them!), and it constrains the amount of information returned. Each stored procedure can have a specific security permission assigned to it. A read-only user is only able to call read-only stored procedures, which continue to support the rule of least privilege. Also, in the case of application code compromise, an attacker cannot infer the structure of your database from a stored procedure. The attacker will know you called the *CreateAccount* stored procedure with a username and password as parameters, but the attacker will not know the names of the tables or columns modified from the stored procedure.

- **Structure your code for security** The order in which your code operates can even enforce security. For an example, let's use the logon scenario again, since logging in to a system is one of the most vulnerable and logical points of attack. Common code to authenticate a user to a Web site is shown in Figure 6.24 (C#) and Figure 6.25 (VB.NET).

Figure 6.24 Common Authentication Code (C#)

```
SqlDataAdapter adapter =
  new SqlDataAdapter("select username from Accounts " +
  "where username=@username and password=@password", cn);
SqlParameter sqlParameter =
  adapter.SelectCommand.Parameters.Add("@username",
  SqlDbType.VarChar,15);
adapter.SelectCommand.Parameters["@username"].Value =
  username.Text;
sqlParameter =
  adapter.SelectCommand.Parameters.Add("@password",
  SqlDbType.VarChar,8);
adapter.SelectCommand.Parameters["@password"].Value =
  password.Text;

DataSet ds = new DataSet();
adapter.Fill(ds, "authenticate");
if (ds.Tables["authenticate"].Rows.Count == 1)
{
    authenticated();
}
else
{
    rejected();
}
```

Figure 6.25 Common Authentication Code (VB.NET)

```
Dim adapter = New SqlDataAdapter("select username " + _
  "from Accounts where username=@username and " + _
  "password=@password", cn)

Dim sqlParameter = _
  adapter.SelectCommand.Parameters.Add("@username", _
  SqlDbType.VarChar, 15)
```

Continued

Figure 6.25 Common Authentication Code (VB.NET)

```
adapter.SelectCommand.Parameters("@username").Value = _
  username.Text
sqlParameter = adapter.SelectCommand.Parameters.Add( _
  "@password", SqlDbType.VarChar, 8)

adapter.SelectCommand.Parameters("@password").Value = _
  password.Text

Dim ds = New DataSet
adapter.Fill(ds, "authenticate")
If ds.Tables("authenticate").Rows.Count = 1 Then
    authenticated()
Else
    rejected()
End If
```

The code simply takes a user's credentials (username and password) and queries to see if there is an account in the database matching those credentials. This code isn't bad, but it could be better. Consider what happens if perhaps through a new exploit, an attacker succeeds in injecting SQL into the username, so that the password isn't checked by using *admin'—* as the username. (See the "Compromise a Query" bullet point in the "Preventing SQL Injection" section for details on this attack.) The code will authenticate the user if there is an account with a username *admin* without the attacker knowing the password.

Prevent this kind of attack simply by slightly modifying the structure of the authenticating code. Retrieve the password of the user based on the given username. If the query returns a password, check the retrieved password against the user supplied password for a match. Figure 6.26 (C#) and Figure 6.27 (VB.NET) show this code.

Figure 6.26 Improved Authentication Code (C#)

```
SqlDataAdapter adapter =
    new SqlDataAdapter("select password from Accounts " +
    "where username=@username", cn);
SqlParameter sqlParameter =
```

Continued

Figure 6.26 Improved Authentication Code (C#)

```csharp
            adapter.SelectCommand.Parameters.Add("@username",
            SqlDbType.VarChar,0);
adapter.SelectCommand.Parameters["@username"].Value =
            username.Text;


DataSet ds = new DataSet();
adapter.Fill(ds, "authenticate");
if (ds.Tables["authenticate"].Rows.Count == 1 &&
            password.Text == ds.Tables["authenticate"].Rows[0]
                ["password"].ToString())
{
            authenticated();
}
else
{
            rejected();
}
```

Figure 6.27 Improved Authentication Code (VB.NET)

```vbnet
Dim adapter = New SqlDataAdapter("select password " + _
    "from Accounts where username=@username", cn)

Dim sqlParameter = _
    adapter.SelectCommand.Parameters.Add("@username", _
    SqlDbType.VarChar, 15)

adapter.SelectCommand.Parameters("@username").Value = _
    username.Text

Dim ds = New DataSet
adapter.Fill(ds, "authenticate")
If ds.Tables("authenticate").Rows.Count = 1 And _
    password.Text = ds.Tables("authenticate").Rows(0) _
    ("password").ToString() Then
```

Continued

Figure 6.27 Improved Authentication Code (VB.NET)

```
    authenticated()
Else
    rejected()
End If
```

This code is no longer vulnerable to the aforementioned SQL injection attack. For the given username, the attacker's entered password must match the returned password from the database. The code now enforces the match rather than database enforcing it.

Programming with security in mind can prevent current and future exploits. A good rule of thumb is to evaluate how exposed the area of code is to an attacker and then apply one or more of the given suggestions. We've emphasized how important it is to write secure logon code. The same security precautions may not apply to an internal module that calculates a coefficient for gravity (unless you work for NASA). But by applying secure coding principles, you can stay one step ahead of an attacker.

Security Policy

- Retrieve the minimum required data from the database.
- Check result sets for expected attributes.
- Use coding structures that emphasize security.

Reading and Writing to Data Files

Summary: **An attacker can damage or destroy your application and operating system by attacking your data files**

Threats: **Data compromise and/or destruction, application compromise and/or destruction, operating system compromise and/or destruction**

Any application that reads and writes data files can be susceptible to a number of risks. The data files might be from a file-based database, such as Access or dbase, or the data files might be files the application sends or receives from a user. Either way, since these data files generally reside on the host operating system, the application has permission to access the operating system's file system. A malicious user can take advantage of this by launching attacks that attempt to read or delete information contained in sensitive files or even critical operating system files. That attacker could also launch a DoS attack by filling up your operating system's file space.

In this section, we will review some of the most prevalent and damaging attacks and what you can do to prevent them. Any one of the solutions mentioned may prevent all the other attacks from succeeding. Our intention is not to be as secure as required but as secure as possible. There is always the possibility that a new flaw or newly discovered attack will render one of the precautions useless, validating the implementation of redundant precautions.

The first thing you should do is lock down the file system of your .NET application. If possible, place all your data files outside the Web root. If you must keep the data files within your application because of a policy or architecture constraints, make sure to place the files inside a directory that does not have IIS read or write permissions. To lock down IIS, launch the Internet Information Services administration window. Find the Web application, and expand its directory structure. Then right-click the directory that contains your data files, and select **Properties**. Figure 6.28 shows an example with a Web application named *webapp* and a file directory named *data file directory*.

Figure 6.28 Locking Down Access

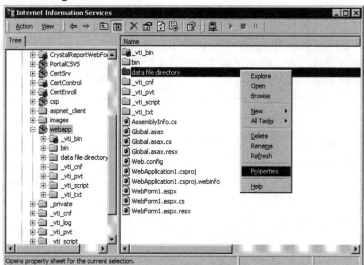

From the Properties window that appears, make sure the **Read** and **Write** options are unchecked, as shown in Figure 6.29.

Figure 6.29 Restricting Read and Write Access

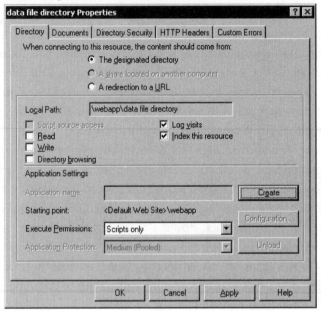

Next, you need to give the ASPNET process access to these data files through NTFS. Using Windows Explorer, browse to the directory where you have placed your data files. Right-click the directory, and select **Properties**. Select the **Security** tab at the top of the window to view the directory's security access, as shown in Figure 6.30.

Figure 6.30 Setting NTFS Permissions

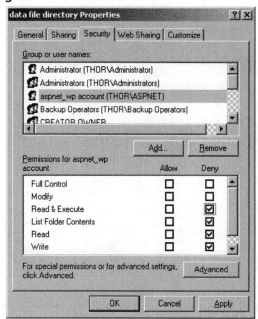

From this window, you can lock down the directory access by preventing Read & Execute, List Folder Contents, Write, and Read access. Lock down the data file directory, but relax the permission on the files your Web application uses. Now if a malicious user gains access to the directory, he or she will not be able to create files.

Another precaution is to use a specialized .dll to restrict access to specific file extensions in IIS 5. For example, if you are using Access database files, you can map all requests for files with the .mdb extension to a "404– File Not Found" page instead of returning the requested database file. You can use 404.dll, available at www.xato.net/files/404.zip, to accomplish this task. In IIS 6 you do not need to do this, because that version will not allow requests for a file extension unless it already has a MIME mapping for that type of file.

You can specify and remove file extension mappings by clicking the **Configuration** button of the Web Application properties window, as previously shown in Figure 6.29. This will bring up the Application Configurations window, with the Mappings tab selected by default, as shown in Figure 6.31.

Figure 6.31 Add and Remove Extension Mappings

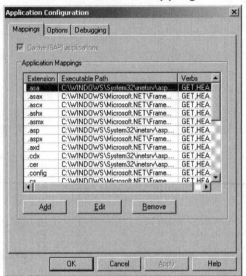

From this window, you can add mappings between file extensions you want to restrict and the 404.dll that will return the "404- Page Not Found" message. By using the 404.dll, you are not only restricting access to the file, you are also denying even the validation for the existence of the file. An attacker won't be able to tell the difference between a file that doesn't exist and file to which he cannot gain access.

Some applications, either directly or indirectly, allow a user to influence the name of the file created or accessed on the Web server's operating system. This might happen through a Web site that creates a file for the user to download based on the user's username. This is a security risk because a user can choose a username that may be unsafe for a file system. For example, what if the user chose *c:\ntdetect.com* for her username? There is a possibility that the Web application will overwrite an important operating system file when it attempts to create a file based on that username. Or maybe your application doesn't try to write a file, but it reads a file instead based on the username or some other user-controlled input. An attacker may be able to specify any file on the Web application's operating system and receive its contents through your Web page.

For these reasons, never base any file access on names that a user could influence. Instead, consider using a hash of a username or some other pseudorandom identifier that an attacker could not easily guess or manipulate.

If your Web application creates files on the operating system, take precautions to prevent a DoS attack. Evaluate the conditions that cause the Web application to create a file and what a user could do to abuse this system. For example, many banking applications allow you to download banking data for import into personal finance programs such as MS Money. In this scenario, you could ask yourself questions such as:

- What would happen if a user requests a thousand downloads every minute?

- For every request, does the application create a new file on the file system?

- Are there restrictions on how often a user can request a download?

- Does code automatically erase previous records when a user requests a new record?

- Are there restrictions on how much disk space each user can consume?

- What happens to your application—or platform, for that matter—when there is no disk space available for writing files?

Without a mechanism to prevent users from filling your file system with temporary files, an attacker could not only cause your application to fail but could bring down your entire operating system by consuming all the operating system's disk space. Solving this problem is relatively easy now that you're aware of it. First, always implement some kind of automatic notification when disk space is getting low. Second, restrict the quantity of files a user can create in an appropriate time interval. If a user tries to create more files than allowed, either remove the user's previous files or deny the request.

As we've seen, an application that uses data files on their host operating system needs to take extra precautions. Start with locking down the accessed files using both IIS and NTFS permissions. Continue by filtering requests to sensitive file types to a "404- File Not Found" page, and don't allow users to influence the names of files created on the server. Finally, protect your application and operating system against a file system-based DoS attack by restricting the number of files a user can create.

Security Policy

- Lock down your file system with both IIS and NTFS settings.
- Do not allow users to influence the name of files created on the server.
- Restrict the quantity and/or size of files users can create on the server.

Coding Standards Fast Track

Securing Database Drivers

Limiting the Attack Surface

- ☑ Remove or disable unused drivers from your database.
- ☑ Periodically check for and remove any new unused drivers, especially after updates or patches.

Securing Database Drivers

- ☑ Configure your database drivers to maximum security.
- ☑ Configure your database drivers to intelligently log access activity.

Securing Databases

Securing the Database Location

- ☑ Review your network topology and security needs to design a firewall layout best suited for your environment.
- ☑ Assume worst-case scenarios when designing your firewall layout.

Ensuring Least Privilege

- ☑ Always provide and utilize the minimum required access and permission
- ☑ Use firewalls to restrict inappropriate access.
- ☑ Use IPSec or SSL to restrict who can connect to your database.

Securing the Database

- ☑ Keep your database software up to date.
- ☑ Disable or remove unused features of your database.
- ☑ Strengthen weak default passwords and permissions.

Writing Secure Data Access Code

Connecting to the Data Source

- ☑ Use roles to apply the rule of least privileged accounts.
- ☑ Use Windows Authentication whenever possible.
- ☑ Keep database connection strings secure.
- ☑ Set strong passwords for the sa and db_ accounts. Do not use these accounts in your applications.

Preventing SQL Injection

- ☑ Code a variety of protections against SQL injection, not just one method.
- ☑ Escape user input upon insertion into and retrieval from the database.
- ☑ Use *SqlParameters* to type and length-check user input.
- ☑ Process and resolve all errors on the server side.
- ☑ Enforce the rule of least privilege in the code and in the database account.

Writing Secure SQL

- ☑ Retrieve the minimum required data from the database.
- ☑ Check result sets for expected attributes.
- ☑ Use coding structures that emphasize security.

Reading and Writing to Data Files

- ☑ Lock down your file system with both IIS and NTFS settings.
- ☑ Do not allow users to influence the name of files created on the server.
- ☑ Restrict the quantity and/or size of files users can create on the server.

Code Audit Fast Track

Securing Database Drivers

Limiting the Attack Surface

☑ Has either the software engineering or IT team removed all extraneous drivers before the database reaches a production environment?

☑ Is there a policy in place to periodically check for software security updates and patches?

Securing Database Drivers

☑ Is the database driver(s) you are using set to run in the most secure context available, such as Sandbox mode for Jet drivers?

☑ Is IIS set to record Web server activity?

☑ Are the database drivers recording login attempts?

Securing Databases

Securing the Database Location

☑ Are you using firewalls to restrict access to your application?

☑ Have you evaluated whether you should place the data source in the same environment as the Web server or separated from the Web server behind another firewall?

Ensuring Least Privilege

☑ Do the users, applications, and processes have the minimum required permissions to complete their functions?

☑ Are firewalls restricting the ports available for communication to the smallest required set?

☑ Are you using either IPSec or SSL to restrict which computers can communicate with your database?

Securing the Database

- ☑ Have you strengthened the sa account's password?

- ☑ Have you removed extended stored procedures and netlibs you are not using?

- ☑ Have you removed all sample databases, sample stored procedures, and sample code from the database before using it in a production environment?

Writing Secure Data Access Code

Connecting to the Data Source

- ☑ Have you carefully evaluated which authentication method to use and chosen Windows Authentication if feasible?

- ☑ Are your connection strings protected using encryption and ACLs where applicable?

- ☑ Have you created and applied roles, groups, and permissions to appropriately restrict the access of your database users?

Preventing SQL Injection

- ☑ Do the software engineering and programming teams understand the mechanics of an SQL injection attack?

- ☑ Are there various overlapping mechanisms in the code to prevent SQL attacks, such as escaping and filtering input, use of *SqlParameters*, and properly processing errors on the server side?

- ☑ Are there policies in place to periodically research the latest SQL injection attacks to ensure that your code is still protected from new attacks?

Writing Secure SQL

- ☑ Does query code retrieve the minimum set of required data from the database?

☑ Depending on the needed security of the module, have additional security checks been applied, such as expected result set size or content parameters?

☑ Has the software engineer written code structured to maximize security?

Reading and Writing to Data Files

☑ Has the application's file system been locked down using both NTFS and IIS permissions?

☑ If your application creates or reads files on the server, is the user prevented from influencing the name of the file created or read?

☑ If your application creates files based on user action, have precautions been implemented to prevent a user from using excessive amounts of disk space?

Frequently Asked Questions

The following Frequently Asked Questions, answered by the authors of this book, are designed to both measure your understanding of the concepts presented in this chapter and to assist you with real-life implementation of these concepts. To have your questions about this chapter answered by the author, browse to **www.syngress.com/solutions** and click on the **"Ask the Author"** form. You will also gain access to thousands of other FAQs at ITFAQnet.com.

Q: Does SQL injection affect all databases or just SQL Server? Is any database more secure than another.

A: All database servers are vulnerable to SQL injection to some extent. The actual risk depends on many factors, including server features, default configuration, complexity, documentation, etc. SQL injection is more of a code issue than a database issue. If you properly filter input and follow the best practices covered in this chapter, the capabilities or vulnerabilities of the backend database should have little consequence.

Q: Are there any quick black box tests I can run to see if my application is vulnerable to SQL injection?

A: It is much more difficult to fully identify SQL injection vulnerabilities from the outside, they usually require a thorough code review. However, there are some checks to quickly identify SQL injection vulnerabilities. Find some form of user input, such as a web form, a query string parameter, or a cookie, and try inserting invalid characters such as a single quote or a semicolon. If you see an actual database error, chances are it is vulnerable to SQL injection. Another favorite is entering the string ' or 1=1-- into a web login form. Poorly written login code will sometimes accept this and log you in as the first user listed in the database.

Q: When choosing a SQL Server authentication strategy, when should I use Windows Authentication and when should I use Windows and SQL Server Authentication (mixed)?

A: As a general rule, using Windows Authentication provides far more benefits, including a more robust authentication and authorization infrastructure, the ability to keep credentials out of connection strings, and the administrative benefits of not having to maintain a new security model (SQL Server's native authentication and authorization mechanisms). You can simply grant SQL Server access to any Windows group(s) that need access and apply permissions accordingly. A common argument for using the mixed security model is that connection pooling is defeated when users have their own security context. Connection pooling is the ability to recycle established database connections, thus increasing connection speed for newer connections. However, in Web-based applications, it is likely that all users will share a single user context anyway when performing data access. It makes no difference from a connection pooling perspective whether the account performing the data access is a single Windows account or a native SQL Server account.

Chapter 7

Developing Secure ASP.NET Applications

Solutions in this Chapter:

- Introduction
- Coding Standards Fast Track
- Code Audit Fast Track

Introduction

Although much of your security effort is focused on the mechanics of your application and code that runs on the server, you should also consider the HTML content you send to client browsers. Throughout this book we have covered topics such as managing and authenticating users, using encryption, accessing data, and filtering input. But even after following all the recommendations in this book, poor HTML coding practices can provide attackers with sensitive information and even put your users at risk. Although this might not be a big issue for some web sites, it is a serious issue for large sites with substantial community involvement such as Yahoo! or eBay.

While you have no control over the user's browser and have little influence over the decisions they make, the content you produce can limit user exposure to these threats.

Understanding the Threats

Some of the threats covered in this chapter are:

- **Cross site scripting (XXS)** Injecting HTML or script commands, causing the Web application to attack other users

- **Cross-site request forgery (CSRF)** Exploiting a site's trust of a user to perform a transaction in behalf of the user

- **Information leakage** Intentionally sending invalid input to produce error messages with information that may facilitate an attack

- **Social engineering** Using a hacker's social skills to extract information from or otherwise manipulate employees or other trusted individuals at a target organization.

- **Repudiation** The ability for a user to deny having taken an action or performed a transaction.

Writing Secure HTML

Many attacks take advantage of inherent weaknesses or security flaws in the HTML standard, or how servers or browsers interpret that standard. By following secure HTML coding practices, you can limit user exposure to these attacks. In this section we will cover:

- Constructing Safe HTML
- Preventing Information Leaks

Constructing Safe HTML

Summary: **Careful use of HTML markup will help prevent cross-site scripting and other attacks**

Threats: **Cross site scripting**

Preventing Cross-Site Scripting Attacks

In Chapter 5, we covered input filtering to prevent cross-site scripting attacks. But cross-site scripting doesn't occur until you actually write the output to the browser. Because it is easy to overlook all the different character sets and encoding methods that ASP.NET or the client browser supports, you cannot completely rely on the input filtering to prevent cross-site scripting attacks.

One solution, as mentioned in Chapter 5, is to always HTML-encode any data you send to the browser. In addition to this, you should also specify a character encoding set for your Web pages. Enforcing a specific character set limits which characters are valid for your site and eliminates the ambiguity that hackers might exploit by using other character sets.

You can specify the character set for your entire application in the web.config file:

```
<configuration>
  <system.web>
    <globalization
      requestEncoding="ISO-8859-1"
      responseEncoding="ISO-8859-1"/>
  </system.web>
</configuration>
```

You can also specify the character set on a per-page basis with the following meta-tag:

```
<meta http-equiv="Content Type" content="text/html; charset=ISO-8859-1" />
```

If you use DHTML, another technique to limit cross-site scripting attacks is to not use the *InnerHTML* property to set or read values between HTML elements. Instead, always use the *InnerText* property. If you do use *InnerHTML*, always be careful to filter input and encode output. Also use similar caution with *insertAdjacentElement* and *insertAdjacentHTML* methods as well as with *TEXTAREA* elements and *TextArea* objects.

Another method to limit the scope of cross-site scripting attacks is to set security restrictions on a *frame* or *iframe* element. You can restrict security with the *Security* attribute this way:

```
<IFRAME SECURITY='restricted' SRC='message.htm'>
```

Setting this property has the following effects:

- The source file specified by the *SRC* attribute inherits Internet Explorer's security settings for the *Restricted Sites* zone.

- All hyperlinks render in a new browser window, regardless of the *TARGET* attribute in the hyperlink element.

- Use of JavaScript, VBScript, and the About protocol is restricted.

- All nested frames inherit the same restrictions.

Related to cross-site scripting is an attack called Cross-Site Request Forgery (CSRF). *Cross site request forgery* is when an attacker causes a user to make a request, on the user's behalf, to another Web site. The attack works by getting the user to visit a URL, for instance by specifying an external URL in an *IMG* tag. Then when the client's browser requests the image from the external URL, it does so in the context of the user, including any session tokens, cookies, or saved authentication credentials of that user.

Here's an example: suppose an attacker wants to trick the user into performing some transaction, such as making a funds transfer from one account to another. The attacker somehow gets the user to view an HTML page, perhaps through an HTML-formatted e-mail. In the HTML, the attacker includes an *IMG* tag that contains the URL and any parameters required to make the transfer. The hypothetical URL might look something like this:

```
https://www.example.org/banking/transfer.aspx?from=123467&to=987655&amt=1000
```

Now suppose that this Web site doesn't follow best security practices and lets users automatically sign in based on a saved cookie. When the user views the e-mail, it will try to request the image. In doing so, it will submit the transaction and complete the transfer. The return from the server obviously will not be a single image so it will show up as a broken link in the HTML document.

This particular example is obviously oversimplified, but it certainly is feasible with many Web sites. Consider some things an attacker could accomplish with this type of attack:

- Initiate a stock trade

- Forge a post to a Web forum

- Purchase an item using stored credit card information

- Send an e-mail from a Web-based mail account

- Authenticate to a secure Web site

- Access resources on a private intranet site

- Change a user's password for an online account

- Gather information about the user or the user's environment

As you can see, this can be a very serious threat to both users and Web site operators. You cannot prevent these attacks with input filtering and they do not require client-side scripting to be enabled. The critical issue here is that CSRF attacks compromise your ability to enforce non-repudiation. If you have a Web page vulnerable to a CSRF attack, a user could argue that they did not perform a transaction, even if it originated from their own computer using their own login credentials.

Nevertheless, you can limit your exposure to CSRF attacks. Here are some tips:

- **Require POST on forms** This does not completely eliminate the threat, but it does make it more difficult to execute the attack.

- **Require multi-step transactions** Do not allow a user to complete a sensitive transaction in a single step. For example, require a second page to confirm the transaction and maybe even use a CAPTCHA (see Chapter 2) to verify that it is a human user.

- **Verify referer headers** Check HTTP referer headers to make sure form POSTs come in your own form. Although referer headers are not always reliable, it would be more difficult to forge these through a CSRF attack.

- Do not allow users to automatically log in to your application with credentials saved in a cookie.

- Follow the guidelines in Chapter 3 for securely managing user sessions.

- Do not allow users to post IMG tags to your application, such as to a forum or guestbook. Also use caution allowing users to post hyperlinks or URLs.

Security Policy

- Always encode any HTML output based on dynamic input.

- Enforce a specific character set in the web.config file or on a per-page basis.

- Use caution with the DHTML *innerHTML* property, *insertAdjacentElement* method, *insertAdjacentHTML* method *TEXTAREA* element and *TextArea* object. Use *innerText* rather than *innerHTML* whenever possible.

- Set security restrictions on *frame* and *iframe* elements with the *Security* attribute.

- Use POST on forms whenever possible.

- Require multi-step transactions with user confirmation.

- Verify referer headers on form POSTs.

- Do not allow users to save credentials in cookies.

- Use caution when allowing users to enter HTML such as IMG tags or hyperlinks.

- Use HTML syntax checking tools to verify that you have valid and properly-structured HTML content.

Preventing Information Leaks

Summary: **Your Web site content might provide a wealth of information to an attacker**

Threats: **Information leakage, social engineering**

One of the first things an attacker will do is case your Web site, looking for bits of information useful for an attack. This is generally a low-risk step for the attacker because in most cases this generates the same traffic as a typical Web user. The information gathered by doing this might help the attacker direct the attack to specific resources, discover other resources, or gather information to focus an attack.

Here are some tips to limit the information you leak to an attacker:

- Avoid hard-coded e-mail addresses and use e-mail aliases when possible. For example, instead of sending sales inquiries to your sales manager's e-mail address, create a generic sales alias that forwards to his real e-mail account.

- Use caution when listing employee names, e-mail addresses, or phone extensions. Information like this can be useful for a social engineering attack.

- Remove meta tags from HTML source that reveal what page layout, content management, source control, or other software you use.

- Avoid HTML comments that reveal information about your application, server environment, network infrastructure, or organizational structure.

Security Policy

- Use aliases for e-mail links.

- Avoid listing employee details such as e-mail addresses or phone extensions.

- Remove HTML meta tags that reveal unnecessary information.

- Avoid HTML comments in a production system.

Handling Exceptions

Before ASP.NET, error handling was never a strong suit of ASP. Despite taking great efforts to handle possible error conditions, it is not uncommon to see classic ASP applications crash and display cryptic error messages. For applications critical to a company's success, this is might be a huge embarrassment and perhaps even a security risk. You may have seen something like this quite often with classic ASP:

```
Microsoft VBScript runtime error '800a0006'

Overflow

/asp/test.asp, line 25
```

To build a secure application, you must handle exceptions. The .NET Framework provides much improved error handling mechanisms to allow proper and consistent error handling across your application. The .NET Framework provides features to:

- Detect and handle errors

- Report errors to clients

- Log error details for administrators and developers

- Generate events for external monitoring

While every programmer hopes to write bug-free programs, this may not always be a realistic goal. Bugs in programs can be incredibly frustrating, usually disrupting the programs they infect. Such errors can be classified into these four categories, which we'll discuss in the following sections:

- **Syntax Errors** Errors caused by writing code that does not follow the rules of the language. An example would be a misspelled keyword.

- **Compilation Errors** Errors that are detected during the compilation stage. An example would be assigning a big number to an integer variable, causing it to overflow.

- **Runtime Errors** Errors that happen after the codes are compiled and executed. An example would be a division-by-zero error.

- **Logic Errors** Errors due to incorrect implementations of algorithms. This is the kind of error that programmers dread most since they are the most difficult to debug.

A syntax error is one of the most common errors in programming. This is especially true if you are new to a particular language. Fortunately, syntax errors can be resolved quite easily. In Visual Studio .NET, syntax errors are underlined similar to that of misspellings typed into Microsoft Word. To know the cause of the error, simply position the mouse over the underlined word and the tool tip box will appear. You generally catch syntax errors while coding and they usually have little effect on the final security of the application.

Compilation errors occur when the compiler tries to compile the program and realizes that the program contains code that may potentially trip up a program. Since compiler errors prevent the compiling process from finishing, you usually catch these errors before your code goes into production.

Runtime errors occur during the time when the application is running and something unexpected occurs. It happens regularly in projects that have very tight deadlines. Programmers stretched to their limits are often satisfied that their program runs. They do not have the time to carefully consider all the different possible scenarios in which their programs may be used; hence the result is often a buggy and potentially vulnerable program. To ensure that an application is as robust and bug-free as possible, it is important to place emphasis on anticipating all the errors that can occur in your program. Runtime errors are a security risk because they might reveal sensitive information and facilitate attacks such as denial of service and SQL injection.

Finally, there are logic errors, which consist simply of code segments of that do not work as expected. The failure may result in the absence of certain features or providing extra unintended features. Logic errors might result in privilege escalation, account hopping, or other application attacks.

Using Structured Error Handling

Summary: **Structured error handling promotes careful forethought to exception handling**

Threats: **Information leakage**

Error handling got a big boost in the .NET Framework. With classic ASP, error handling was unstructured, done using the limited *On Error* statement. In VB.NET, error handling can both be structured and unstructured. Error handling allows you to catch, react to, and add relevancy to application errors.

Unstructured Error Handling

Unstructured error handling in VB.NET is similar to what was available in classic ASP. Consider the following code:

```
Dim shortNum As Int16
Dim intNum As Int32
intNum = 999999
shortNum = intNum ' narrowing will fail!
```

If you run this code, you should see the error as shown in Figure 7.1.

Figure 7.1 Runtime Error

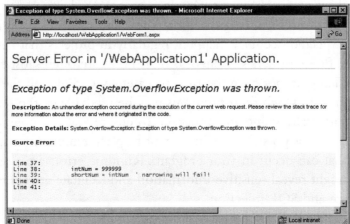

An error message such as this might reveal sensitive information about your application but it might also tip off a hacker that you do not handle errors. To prevent the error from appearing, VB.NET supports the unstructured *On Error* statement:

```
Dim shortNum As Int16
Dim intNum As Int32
On Error Resume Next
intNum = 999999
shortNum = intNum ' narrowing will fail!
If Err.Number <> 0 Then
   Response.Write(Err.Description)
End If
```

The *On Error Resume Next* statement ignores any error that happens and continues as though no error has occurred. The error information is contained within the *Err* object. If an error has occurred, the property *Number* of the *Err* object would contain a nonzero value.

In the preceding example, we examine three errors. The first error will cause the execution to jump to the *ErrorHandling* block, and after the error description has been printed, it resumes execution at the point it was interrupted. The second error will be ignored while the third error will cause the program to fail.

As you can see, unstructured error handling makes your code messy and difficult to debug, and also affects future maintenance. Hence, the recommended way to handle errors is to use structured error handling.

Structured Error Handling

Rather than placing an *On Error* statement at the beginning of a block to handle potential errors, .NET supports structured error handling using the *Try-Catch-Finally* construct to handle exceptions. The *Try-Catch-Finally* construct then allows developers to actively catch different forms of errors and respond to them appropriately. It has the following syntax:

```
Try
    ' Executable statements that may cause
    ' an exception.
Catch [optional filters]
    ' Catches the error and responds to it
Catch [optional filters]
    ' Catches the error and responds to it
[Additional Catch blocks]
Finally
' Always executed, with or without error
End Try
```

Using structured error handling, we get:

```
Dim shortNum As Int16
Dim intNum As Int32
intNum = 999999
Try
    shortNum = intNum ' narrowing will fail!
Catch anyException As Exception
    Response.Write(anyException)
End Try
```

When executed, the error message printed is:

```
System.OverflowException: Exception of type System.OverflowException was
thrown. at WebApplication1.WebForm1.Page_Load(Object sender, EventArgs
e) in C:\Documents and Settings\lwm\VSWebCache\LWM\WebApplication1\
WebForm1.aspx.vb:line 31
```

When the line in the *Try* block is executed, it generates an exception, which is then caught by the *Catch* block. The statement in the *Catch* block prints out the reason for causing that exception. The previous example doesn't really do justice to the structured error-handling construct in VB.NET. Consider the following revised example:

```
Dim shortNum As Int16
Dim intNum As Int32
intNum = 999999
Try
   shortNum = intNum ' narrowing will fail!
Catch outofMemoryException As System.OutOfMemoryException
   Response.Write("Out of memory!")
Catch overflowException As System.OverflowException
   Response.Write("Overflow!")
Catch anyException As Exception
   Response.Write("Some exception!")
End Try
```

Here we have multiple *Catch* statements. Each *Catch* statement tries to catch the different kinds of exceptions. If discovered, the exception is evaluated from top to bottom. Once a match is found, the codes within the *Catch* block are executed. If no match is found, an error message is displayed. The three exceptions in the preceding list include:

- **OutOfMemoryException** Thrown when there is not enough memory to continue the execution of a program

- **OverflowException** Thrown when an operation results in an overflow condition

- **Exception** The base class for exception. This means that all unmatched exceptions would be matched here

When the statement within the *Try* block generates an exception, the few *Catch* statements are evaluated in order. First, it compares with the initial *Catch* block and checks to see if it matches the kind of exception specified in the *Catch* statement. If it doesn't, it will compare it with the next, and so on. It stops only when a match is found. In our case, the exception is an overflow exception and hence the second *Catch* block is matched. If no match is found, an error message will be generated. Lastly, the *Finally* block allows you to perform whatever cleaning up operation codes need doing, regardless of whether the exception occurs.

```
...
Catch anyException As Exception
  'Response.Write(anyException)
  Response.Write("Some exception!")
Finally

  '---code here always executes
  '---regardless of the exception
End Try
```

There are some key points to remember when writing structured error-handling routines. First, you must be sure to structure the error handler so that when the code fails, it fails securely. Also, carefully consider the effect of using exception filters and *Finally* blocks with multiple layers of error handling. Sometimes these blocks run in an unexpected order so you must use caution when making security decisions within these blocks of code.

Security Policy

- Use structured error handling to avoid using the default ASP.NET error handler.

- Always code error handlers to fail securely.

- Carefully consider the execution order of exception filters and *Finally* blocks.

Reporting and Logging Errors

Summary: **Give users generic error details while gathering more comprehensive information for administrators and developers**

Threats: **Information leakage**

If your application encounters an exception, it must somehow handle this exception. Most often, this appears as a 500 error returned to the client along with a default error page like that shown in Figure 7.1. You will generally want to avoid the default error handler because it provides little useful information to the legitimate user, yet it might provide a wealth of information to an attacker.

If the user did something wrong, you should instruct them on how they can fix the error. For example, if they left a required form field blank, you should let them know that you require data in that field. Nonetheless, you should never reveal too much information in your error messages. If there is nothing the user can do to remedy the situation, for instance if the back-end database is down, then you should simply provide a generic message indicating that an error occurred on the server.

Generic Errors

Generic errors are the key to safe error reporting. You'll usually want to hide detailed exception information from end users. Here are some example error messages you should avoid:

- "Error accessing file c:\inetpub\wwwroot\orders\orders.mdb"
- "Error executing SQL: SELECT ★ FROM Users WHERE ID=2318"
- "Error connecting to server \\WEBDB"

Instead, you should consider error messages such as these:

- "Error opening database; please contact the administrator or try again later."
- "An error occurred looking up user information; please contact the administrator."
- "A server resource is currently unavailable; please try again later."

In ASP.NET you can provide generic HTML pages for handling various classes of errors. The following is an example of the exception settings in a web.config file:

```
<customErrors defaultredirect="/error/error.aspx" mode="on">
    <error statuscode="404" redirect="/error/404Error.htm"/>
    <error statuscode="500" redirect="/error/500error.aspx"/>
</customErrors>
```

This configuration provides a generic page named error.aspx, but also provides custom redirect pages for 404 and 500 errors. Any unhandled error will cause a redirection to one of these three pages.

NOTE

The default error handler settings in the web.config file apply only to files mapped to ASP.NET. If you want these settings to apply to other files, such as HTM or GIF files, you must either configure IIS to use these same pages or configure IIS script maps to allow ASP.NET to handle these other file extensions. See Chapter 2 for instructions on mapping non-ASP.NET resources.

ASP.NET also allows you to specify error handlers on the page or application levels. To specify a global error handler for a page, use the *Page.Error* event. For a global application error handler, use the *Application.Error* event in Global.asax.

Logging Errors

Although you do not want the end users to see detailed error messages, you certainly do need this information for correcting errors or to alert you of an attack. You can use several methods for logging errors in your ASP.NET application, examples of which are as follows:

- **IIS log file** Add custom text to the standard IIS log file using the *Response.AppendToLog* method.

- **Windows Event Log** Add events to the Windows Event Log using the *EventLog* class.

- **Custom log file** Write to a custom text file using the *FileStream* and *StreamWriter* classes.

- **Centralized database** Log errors as records in a centralized database.

- **WMI events** Raise WMI events to be captured by some other enterprise-logging mechanism.

- **Sending an E-mail** Send an e-mail via SMTP to an administrator when an exception occurs.

The method you choose for logging errors depends greatly on the particular needs and size of your application. Here are some questions to ask yourself when evaluating a logging mechanism:

- Does logging fail if the system or network undergoes a denial of service attack?

- Does the mechanism allow for detailed and comprehensive logging without much burden on the application or the network?

- Is it possible to restrict access to the log data?

- Is it possible for an attacker to modify logs or submit fake log entries?

- Will a compromise of the application or server also compromise log data?

In some cases, it might be appropriate to provide multiple logging mechanisms. This helps ensure accuracy and reinforces the non-repudiation of log data. You might, for instance, use the IIS logs to track errors but save additional error details to a separate log file. In addition, you might want to use a sniffer or intrusion detection system to log suspicious network traffic between the client and the server.

When you log exception details, you should try to anticipate which information will be most useful to you. You might, for instance, log the following details:

- Information that allows you to identify where in the application the error occurred

- Information that allows you to establish the exact time, date, and server location

- Information that allows you to reproduce an error or, if applicable, reproduce an attack

- Information that allows you to identify an attacker and to be able to correlate this information with other application logs

Information that you might not want to log includes:

- Information that reveals too much information about application code or network infrastructure

- Personal information such as user passwords or credit card numbers

- Anything else that an attacker might use against you

Security Policy

- Always provide users with generic messages that do not reveal too much information.

- Configure generic error handlers in the web.config file or create global error handlers on the application or page level.

- Do not log user passwords, credit card numbers, or other sensitive information in log files.

- Turn off debugging, tracing, and detailed error messages in production applications.

Coding Standards Fast Track

Writing Secure HTML

Constructing Safe HTML

- ☑ Always encode any HTML output based on dynamic input.
- ☑ Enforce a specific character set in the web.config file or on a per-page basis.
- ☑ Use caution with the DHTML *innerHTML* property, *insertAdjacentElement* method, *insertAdjacentHTML* method *TEXTAREA* element and *TextArea* object. Use *innerText* rather than *innerHTML* whenever possible.
- ☑ Set security restrictions on *frame* and *iframe* elements with the *Security* attribute.
- ☑ Use POST on forms whenever possible.
- ☑ Require multi-step transactions with user confirmation.
- ☑ Verify referer headers on form POSTs.
- ☑ Do not allow users to save credentials in cookies.
- ☑ Use caution when allowing users to enter HTML such as IMG tags or hyperlinks.

Preventing Information Leaks

- ☑ Use aliases for e-mail links.
- ☑ Avoid listing employee details such as e-mail addresses or phone extensions
- ☑ Remove HTML meta tags that reveal unnecessary information.
- ☑ Avoid HTML comments in a production system.

Handling Exceptions

Using Structured Error Handling

- ☑ Use structured error handling to avoid the default ASP.NET error handler.
- ☑ Always code error handlers to fail securely.
- ☑ Carefully consider the execution order of exception filters and finally blocks.

Reporting and Logging Errors

- ☑ Always provide users with generic messages that do not reveal too much information.
- ☑ Configure generic error handlers in the web.config file or create global error handlers on the application or page level.
- ☑ Do not log user passwords, credit card numbers, or other sensitive information in log files.
- ☑ Turn off debugging, tracing, and detailed error messages in production applications.

Code Audit Fast Track

Writing Secure HTML

Constructing Safe HTML

- ☑ Does the application send any dynamic output without first encoding it?
- ☑ Does the application enforce a specific character set in the web.config file or on a per-page basis?
- ☑ Does the application filter input and encode output with the DHTML *innerHTML* property, *insertAdjacentElement* method, *insertAdjacentHTML* method *TEXTAREA* element and *TextArea* object?

☑ Could the programmers use *innerText* rather than *innerHTML*?

☑ Do *frame* and *iframe* elements have the *Security* attribute set to restricted?

☑ Do forms use GET when a POST would be more appropriate?

☑ Do sensitive transactions require multiple steps, including user confirmation?

☑ Do forms check the referer headers to verify the source of input?

☑ Can users enter IMG or hyperlink tags to perform a CSRF attack?

Preventing Information Leaks

☑ Does the HTML content contain employee names, e-mail addresses, phone numbers that could be used in a social engineering attack?

☑ Do HTML meta tags reveal unnecessary information?

☑ Does the HTML content contain any unnecessary comments?

Handling Exceptions

Using Structured Error Handling

☑ Does the application use structured error handling to avoid the default ASP.NET error handler?

☑ Do error handlers always fail securely?

Reporting and Logging Errors

☑ Do errors reveal too much information?

☑ Does the application use generic error handlers rather than the built-in error handlers?

☑ Do log files contain user passwords, credit card numbers, or other sensitive information?

☑ Are all debugging, tracing, and detailed error messages turned off in production applications?

Frequently Asked Questions

The following Frequently Asked Questions, answered by the authors of this book, are designed to both measure your understanding of the concepts presented in this chapter and to assist you with real-life implementation of these concepts. To have your questions about this chapter answered by the author, browse to **www.syngress.com/solutions** and click on the **"Ask the Author"** form. You will also gain access to thousands of other FAQs at ITFAQnet.com.

Q: Is there anything we can do on the server side to prevent cross-frame and cross-windows scripting attacks?

A: Cross-frame and cross-window scripting attacks are mostly a client issue, in particular, a client visiting a server with malicious content. However, you can somewhat limit an attackers ability to use your web site in such an attack. Most important is to address any cross-site issues in your application. You might also consider some of the DHTML features and their impact on security mentioned at this URL:
http://msdn.microsoft.com/workshop/author/dhtml/sec_dhtml.asp.

Q: Is it ever okay to use GET on a form rather than POST?

A: GET requests are generally appropriate with query or lookup requests, for example an article ID or a search engine query. POST requests are preferred if the requests contains user-submitted information, sensitive information, or information that changes something on the server.

Q: Should I use an HTML encryptor or obfuscator to prevent information leaks?

A: Although these types of tools do have some small benefit, they are generally an inadequate substitution for solid HTML coding practices. Encrypting and obfuscating relies on the client and the techniques are not foolproof. At some point the browser needs to see the HTML to be able to render it so an attacker could do the same.

Chapter 8

Securing XML

Solutions in this Chapter:

- Applying XML Encryption
- Applying XML Digital Signatures

☑ Coding Standards Fast Track

☑ Code Audit Fast Track

☑ Frequently Asked Questions

Introduction

XML is a powerful technology for structuring data in a platform-independent, human-readable format. Documents in XML are easy to create and simple to parse. There are countless applications using XML in the connected, Web world as well as the offline world. Describing all the benefits of XML is beyond the scope of this chapter, but if you would like further details on XML, Amazon.com currently lists over 2,500 books on the subject.

For all of XML's useful and important benefits, until recently it has come up short in the area of security. For example, XML previously had no specification to protect the privacy or integrity of data. Data contained in XML was vulnerable to viewing and modification by external parties without detection. To solve these security problems, developers had to use external, disparate technologies to protect their XML-contained data.

The World Wide Web Consortium (W3C) addressed these concerns by leveraging the tools of encryption and digital certificates. XML now contains internal and standardized specifications to describe encrypted and signed data. You can now use encryption to protect the privacy and integrity of data contained in XML. Use the public and private keys of digital certificates to sign XML data. Signing XML data protects the integrity, authentication, and nonrepudiation of data. The XML encryption and digital signature specifications are clear and detailed about disclosing the algorithms, formats, and methods used to decrypt and validate signatures. Using these specifications, you can be confident that your data will not only be protected but also be useful to other applications that implement the specifications.

Applying XML Encryption

The goal of the XML encryption specification is to describe a digitally encrypted Web resource using XML. Following the XML encryption specification creates a document that combines the benefits of both XML and encryption to produce a human-readable, standardized document that code can parse independent of platform, at the same time containing secrets encrypted with your choice of symmetrical or asymmetrical algorithms.

The Web resource used in XML encryption can be anything from an HTML document to a GIF file or even an entire XML document. With respect to XML documents, the XML encryption specification provides for the encryption of an element, including the start and end tags, the content within an element between the start and end tags, and the entire XML document. The specification describes that the encrypted data is placed within an *EncryptedData* element. The *EncryptedData* element also contains details pertaining to encrypting and/or decrypting the information. These details include the pertinent encryption algorithm, the key used for encryption, references to external data objects, and either the encrypted data or a reference to the encrypted data.

Encrypting XML Data

Summary: **XML encryption is useful for encrypting specific elements of a document for transport across insecure networks as well as for archival purposes**

Threats: **Information leakage, data corruption, man-in-the-middle attacks**

The SSL Internet encryption protocol might seem sufficient in protecting data transferred across the Internet. However, XML encryption provides a slightly different solution than creating an encrypted data stream. XML encryption allows you to encrypt a single, specific element of an XML document instead of encrypting the entire document, as would be the case in SSL. For example, if you are sending medical information across the Internet, a patient's nonidentifying details such as height, weight, and blood test could remain unencrypted, whereas you would encrypt the patient's identity and more sensitive information such as name and Social Security number. The resource benefit of encrypting only a small amount of data instead of the entire document becomes substantial.

Another benefit of the XML encryption specification arises with stored data. SSL provides an encrypted channel only or transient data across the Internet. In contrast, XML is a data-formatting specification that you can use to archive and store data. For instance, the previously mentioned medical records could be archived without concern for exposing the patient's identity.

XML Encryption Specification

The XML encryption specification is in the recommended stage and is ready for adoption. For further details, you may review the official W3C XML Encryption Syntax and Processing specification, found at www.w3.org/TR/xmlenc-core. Figure 8.1 shows the XML encryption specification syntax.

Figure 8.1 XML Encryption Specification Syntax

```
<EncryptedData Id? Type? MimeType? Encoding?>
  <EncryptionMethod/>?
  <ds:KeyInfo>
    <EncryptedKey>?
    <AgreementMethod>?
    <ds:KeyName>?
    <ds:RetrievalMethod>?
    <ds:*>?
  </ds:KeyInfo>?
  <CipherData>
    <CipherValue>?
    <CipherReference URI?>?
  </CipherData>
  <EncryptionProperties>?
</EncryptedData>
```

You can find the entire XML encryption schema at www.w3.org/TR/xmlenc-core/xenc-schema.xsd, as well as in Figure 8.2. The elements in bold are explained following the schema.

Figure 8.2 XML Encryption Schema

```
<?xml version="1.0" encoding="utf-8"?>
<!DOCTYPE schema  PUBLIC "-//W3C//DTD XMLSchema 200102//EN"
 "http://www.w3.org/2001/XMLSchema.dtd"
 [
   <!ATTLIST schema
     xmlns:xenc CDATA #FIXED 'http://www.w3.org/2001/04/xmlenc#'
     xmlns:ds CDATA #FIXED 'http://www.w3.org/2000/09/xmldsig#'>
   <!ENTITY xenc 'http://www.w3.org/2001/04/xmlenc#'>
   <!ENTITY % p ''>
   <!ENTITY % s ''>
 ]>

<schema xmlns='http://www.w3.org/2001/XMLSchema' version='1.0'
        xmlns:xenc='http://www.w3.org/2001/04/xmlenc#'
```

Continued

Figure 8.2 XML Encryption Schema

```
        xmlns:ds='http://www.w3.org/2000/09/xmldsig#'
        targetNamespace='http://www.w3.org/2001/04/xmlenc#'
        elementFormDefault='qualified'>


<import namespace='http://www.w3.org/2000/09/xmldsig#'
        schemaLocation='http://www.w3.org/TR/2002/REC-xmldsig-core-
        20020212/xmldsig-core-schema.xsd'/>


<complexType name='EncryptedType' abstract='true'>
  <sequence>
    <element name='EncryptionMethod' type='xenc:EncryptionMethodType'
     minOccurs='0'/>
    <element ref='ds:KeyInfo' minOccurs='0'/>
    <element ref='xenc:CipherData'/>
    <element ref='xenc:EncryptionProperties' minOccurs='0'/>
  </sequence>
  <attribute name='Id' type='ID' use='optional'/>
  <attribute name='Type' type='anyURI' use='optional'/>
  <attribute name='MimeType' type='string' use='optional'/>
  <attribute name='Encoding' type='anyURI' use='optional'/>
</complexType>


<complexType name='EncryptionMethodType' mixed='true'>
  <sequence>
    <element name='KeySize' minOccurs='0' type='xenc:KeySizeType'/>
    <element name='OAEPparams' minOccurs='0' type='base64Binary'/>
    <any namespace='##other' minOccurs='0' maxOccurs='unbounded'/>
  </sequence>
  <attribute name='Algorithm' type='anyURI' use='required'/>
</complexType>


  <simpleType name='KeySizeType'>
    <restriction base="integer"/>
  </simpleType>
```

Continued

Figure 8.2 XML Encryption Schema

```xml
<element name='CipherData' type='xenc:CipherDataType'/>
<complexType name='CipherDataType'>
   <choice>
     <element name='CipherValue' type='base64Binary'/>
     <element ref='xenc:CipherReference'/>
   </choice>
  </complexType>


 <element name='CipherReference' type='xenc:CipherReferenceType'/>
 <complexType name='CipherReferenceType'>
     <choice>
       <element name='Transforms' type='xenc:TransformsType'
         minOccurs='0'/>
     </choice>
     <attribute name='URI' type='anyURI' use='required'/>
 </complexType>


   <complexType name='TransformsType'>
     <sequence>
       <element ref='ds:Transform' maxOccurs='unbounded'/>
     </sequence>
   </complexType>



<element name='EncryptedData' type='xenc:EncryptedDataType'/>
<complexType name='EncryptedDataType'>
  <complexContent>
    <extension base='xenc:EncryptedType'>
    </extension>
  </complexContent>
</complexType>


<!-- Children of ds:KeyInfo -->


<element name='EncryptedKey' type='xenc:EncryptedKeyType'/>
```

Continued

Figure 8.2 XML Encryption Schema

```
<complexType name='EncryptedKeyType'>

  <complexContent>

    <extension base='xenc:EncryptedType'>

      <sequence>

        <element ref='xenc:ReferenceList' minOccurs='0'/>

        <element name='CarriedKeyName' type='string' minOccurs='0'/>

      </sequence>

      <attribute name='Recipient' type='string'
       use='optional'/>

    </extension>

  </complexContent>

</complexType>


  <element name="AgreementMethod" type="xenc:AgreementMethodType"/>

  <complexType name="AgreementMethodType" mixed="true">

    <sequence>

      <element name="KA-Nonce" minOccurs="0" type="base64Binary"/>

      <!-- <element ref="ds:DigestMethod" minOccurs="0"/> -->

      <any namespace="##other" minOccurs="0" maxOccurs="unbounded"/>

      <element name="OriginatorKeyInfo" minOccurs="0"
        type="ds:KeyInfoType"/>

      <element name="RecipientKeyInfo" minOccurs="0"
        type="ds:KeyInfoType"/>

    </sequence>

    <attribute name="Algorithm" type="anyURI" use="required"/>

  </complexType>


<!-- End Children of ds:KeyInfo -->


<element name='ReferenceList'>

  <complexType>

    <choice minOccurs='1' maxOccurs='unbounded'>

      <element name='DataReference' type='xenc:ReferenceType'/>

      <element name='KeyReference' type='xenc:ReferenceType'/>

    </choice>
```

Continued

Figure 8.2 XML Encryption Schema

```
    </complexType>
  </element>

  <complexType name='ReferenceType'>
    <sequence>
      <any namespace='##other' minOccurs='0' maxOccurs='unbounded'/>
    </sequence>
    <attribute name='URI' type='anyURI' use='required'/>
  </complexType>


  <element name='EncryptionProperties'
    type='xenc:EncryptionPropertiesType'/>
  <complexType name='EncryptionPropertiesType'>
    <sequence>
      <element ref='xenc:EncryptionProperty' maxOccurs='unbounded'/>
    </sequence>
    <attribute name='Id' type='ID' use='optional'/>
  </complexType>

  <element name='EncryptionProperty' type='xenc:EncryptionPropertyType'/>
  <complexType name='EncryptionPropertyType' mixed='true'>
    <choice maxOccurs='unbounded'>
      <any namespace='##other' processContents='lax'/>
    </choice>
    <attribute name='Target' type='anyURI' use='optional'/>
    <attribute name='Id' type='ID' use='optional'/>
    <anyAttribute namespace="http://www.w3.org/XML/1998/namespace"/>
  </complexType>

</schema>
```

The XML encryption schema is quite involved in describing the means of encryption. The following elements are the most notable of the specification:

- **EncryptedData** The crux of the specification. This element replaces the encrypted data, whether the data being encrypted is within an XML document or the XML document itself. In the latter case, the *EncryptedData* element actually becomes the document root.

- **EncryptedKey** An optional element containing information about the key that was used during the encryption process.

- **EncryptionMethod** An optional element describing the algorithm applied during the encryption process.

- **CipherData** A mandatory element that provides the encrypted data.

TIP

Notice that the *EncryptedKey* and *EncryptionMethod* elements are optional. These elements need not be present if the recipient knows this information.

XML Encryption Process

The process of encryption and decryption is straightforward. The data object is encrypted using a symmetrical or asymmetrical algorithm and a key of choice. Each implementation of the XML encryption specification should implement a common set of algorithms to allow for interoperability. If the data object is an element within an XML document, remove the element along with its content and replace it with the pertinent *EncryptedData* element. If the data object for encryption encrypt is an external resource, create a new document with an *EncryptedData* root node that contains a reference to the external resource.

Decryption follows these steps in reverse: Parse the XML to obtain the algorithm, parameters, and key used; locate the data to be decrypted; and perform the data decryption operation. The result will be a UTF-8 encoded string representing the XML fragment that should replace the entire *EncryptedData* element. If the data object is an external resource, the unencrypted string is available for use by the application.

There are some nuances to encrypting XML documents. Encrypted XML instances are well-formed XML documents but might not appear valid when validated against their original schema. If schema validation is required of an encrypted XML document, create a new schema to account for those encrypted elements.

> **TIP**
>
> If the recipient of the document or an entity to which the recipient passes the XML document never needs to know the sensitive data, consider removing the sensitive data entirely. You can remove the sensitive data using a simple XSL transformation. After all, removing data is even more secure than encrypting it.

XML Encryption Example

As an example, let's assume that we work in a medical lab and are responsible for returning the results of lab tests to a hospital. The lab stores the results in an XML document that various hospital computers, analysis machines, and data systems can interpret and act on. However, only a few trusted systems should be able to identify the individual to which the lab results apply. Therefore, we encrypt the *patientPersonalInformation* element of the document with a key that only trusted systems can access. Figure 8.3 shows an example XML record the medical lab needs to submit to a hospital.

Figure 8.3 XML Document to Encrypt

```
<?xml version="1.0"?>

<medicalRecord>

<patientPersonalInformation>

    <name>Bryan Pitcher</name>

    <SSN>555-55-5555</SSN>

    </patientPersonalInformation>

    <bloodTestResults>

    <bloodType>A+</bloodType>

    <redBloodCellCount>4200000/cmm</redBloodCellCount>

    <whiteBloodCellCount>4500/mcl</whiteBloodCellCount>

</bloodTestResults>

</medicalRecord>
```

Figures 8.4 and 8.5 show sample code that can read the document shown in Figure 8.3 and produce an XML-encrypted document. The code will encrypt the *patientPersonalInformation* element. For simplicity, the code generates the encryption key and IV. Ordinarily, code should read these values from a secure location. We assume that our trusted recipients have this key and IV as well as know the encryption method.

Figure 8.4 XML Document Encryption: C#

```csharp
public void encryptDocument(string xmlDocumentPlainTextFilename, string
xmlDocumentCipherTextFilename)
{
  // Generate the keys
  TripleDESCryptoServiceProvider tripleDES =
    new TripleDESCryptoServiceProvider();
  tripleDES.GenerateIV();
  tripleDES.GenerateKey();

  // Get the XML document from file
  XmlDocument xmlDoc = new XmlDocument();
    xmlDoc.Load(xmlDocumentPlainTextFilename);

    // specify the element to encrypt
    XmlElement patientPersonalInformation =
        (XmlElement)xmlDoc.SelectSingleNode(
            "medicalRecord/patientPersonalInformation");
    byte[] patientPersonalInformationBytes =
        Encoding.UTF8.GetBytes(patientPersonalInformation.OuterXml);

    // Set up the CryptoStream for encryption with the key and IV
    MemoryStream memoryStream = new MemoryStream();
    CryptoStream cryptoStream = new CryptoStream(memoryStream,
        tripleDES.CreateEncryptor(tripleDES.Key, tripleDES.IV),
        CryptoStreamMode.Write);

    // Write ciphertext to memory stream
```

Continued

Figure 8.4 XML Document Encryption: C#

```
cryptoStream.Write(patientPersonalInformationBytes, 0,
    patientPersonalInformationBytes.Length);
cryptoStream.Close();


// Convert ciphertext to a Base64 string
byte[] patientPersonalInformationEncryptedBytes =
    memoryStream.ToArray();
string patientPersonalInformationCipherText =
    Convert.ToBase64String(patientPersonalInformationEncryptedBytes);
memoryStream.Close();


// Create and populate the necessary XML encryption elements
XmlElement xmlEncryptedData =
    xmlDoc.CreateElement("EncryptedData");
XmlAttribute xmlType =
    xmlDoc.CreateAttribute("Type");
xmlType.Value =
    "http://www.w3.org/2001/04/xmlenc#Element";
xmlEncryptedData.Attributes.Append(xmlType);
XmlElement xmlCipherData =
    xmlDoc.CreateElement("CipherData");
xmlEncryptedData.AppendChild(xmlCipherData);
XmlElement xmlCipherValue =
    xmlDoc.CreateElement("CipherValue");
xmlCipherValue.InnerText = patientPersonalInformationCipherText;
xmlCipherData.AppendChild(xmlCipherValue);
patientPersonalInformation.ParentNode.ReplaceChild(
    xmlEncryptedData, patientPersonalInformation);


// Write XML encrypted document to file
xmlDoc.Save(xmlDocumentCipherTextFilename);
}
```

Figure 8.5 XML Document Encryption: VB.NET

```vb.net
Public Function encryptDocument _(ByVal xmlDocumentPlainTextFilename,
    ByVal xmlDocumentCipherTextFilename)

    ' Generate the keys
    tripleDES = New TripleDESCryptoServiceProvider
    tripleDES.GenerateIV()
    tripleDES.GenerateKey()

    ' Get the XML document from file
    Dim xmlDoc = New XmlDocument
    xmlDoc.Load(xmlDocumentPlainTextFilename)

    ' specify the element to encrypt
    Dim patientPersonalInformation = _
        xmlDoc.SelectSingleNode( _
            "medicalRecord/patientPersonalInformation")

    Dim patientPersonalInformationBytes As Byte()
    patientPersonalInformationBytes = _
        Encoding.UTF8.GetBytes(patientPersonalInformation.OuterXml)

    ' Set up the CryptoStream for encryption with the key and IV
    Dim memoryStream As MemoryStream = New MemoryStream
    Dim cryptoStream = New CryptoStream(memoryStream, _
        tripleDES.CreateEncryptor(tripleDES.Key, tripleDES.IV), _
        CryptoStreamMode.Write)

    ' Write ciphertext to memory stream
    cryptoStream.Write( _
        patientPersonalInformationBytes, 0, _
            patientPersonalInformationBytes.Length)
    cryptoStream.Close()

    ' Convert ciphertext to a Base64 string
    Dim patientPersonalInformationEncryptedBytes As Byte()
```

Continued

Figure 8.5 XML Document Encryption: VB.NET

```vbnet
patientPersonalInformationEncryptedBytes = _
  memoryStream.ToArray()
Dim patientPersonalInformationCipherText = _
  Convert.ToBase64String( _
    patientPersonalInformationEncryptedBytes)
memoryStream.Close()

' Create and populate the necessary XML encryption elements
Dim xmlEncryptedData = xmlDoc.CreateElement("EncryptedData")
Dim xmlType = xmlDoc.CreateAttribute("Type")
xmlType.Value = "http://www.w3.org/2001/04/xmlenc#Element"
xmlEncryptedData.Attributes.Append(xmlType)
Dim xmlCipherData = xmlDoc.CreateElement("CipherData")
xmlEncryptedData.AppendChild(xmlCipherData)
Dim xmlCipherValue = xmlDoc.CreateElement("CipherValue")
xmlCipherValue.InnerText = _
  patientPersonalInformationCipherText
xmlCipherData.AppendChild(xmlCipherValue)
patientPersonalInformation.ParentNode.ReplaceChild( _
 xmlEncryptedData, patientPersonalInformation)

' Write XML encrypted document to file
xmlDoc.Save(xmlDocumentCipherTextFilename)
End Function
```

Figure 8.6 shows the XML document after the *patientPersonalInformation* element has been encrypted.

Figure 8.6 XML Document After Encryption

```xml
<?xml version="1.0"?>
<medicalRecord>
<EncryptedData Type="http://www.w3.org/2001/04/xmlenc#Element">
    <CipherData>
```

Continued

Figure 8.6 XML Document After Encryption

```
<CipherValue>fcEijNQTn3TLRBEtXwAGH003v4Jt0eZ0Uukuf9IE0ruxN6NHQKWufrVw03xKTZa
u8z7FMyEmxdZKbqLg2Fl/Ct8KphQwpDyTodtMmE+uJrvtNni3ZFxu+4lenVPBXUgrq8x0BgO0px7
RyOsFVdpogYh+CVioHtQq</CipherValue>
            </CipherData>
    </EncryptedData>
<bloodTestResults>
    <bloodType>A+</bloodType>
    <redBloodCellCount>4200000/cmm</redBloodCellCount>
    <whiteBloodCellCount>4500/mcl</whiteBloodCellCount>
</bloodTestResults>
</medicalRecord>
```

Our sample code replaced the *patientPersonalInformation* element of the document with the *EncryptedData* element. The actual patient data is within the *CipherData* element. This instance of *EncryptedData* contains no descriptive information regarding the encryption key or algorithm, as noted previously.

Figures 8.7 and 8.8 show example code to demonstrate the decrypting of an XML-encrypted document. For simplicity, this code decrypts only the encrypted element and writes the decrypted element to a file.

Figure 8.7 XML Document Decryption: C#

```
public void decryptDocument(string xmlDocumentCipherTextFilename,
    string xmlDocumentPlainTextFilename)
{
    // Get the XML document from file
    XmlDocument xmlDoc = new XmlDocument();
    xmlDoc.Load(xmlDocumentCipherTextFilename);

    // Retrieve the element to be decrypted
    XmlElement patientPersonalInformationEncrypted =
        (XmlElement)xmlDoc.SelectSingleNode(
        "medicalRecord/EncryptedData");
    XmlElement xmlCipherValue =
        (XmlElement)patientPersonalInformationEncrypted.SelectSingleNode(
        "CipherData/CipherValue");
```

Continued

Figure 8.7 XML Document Decryption: C#

```csharp
byte[] patientPersonalInformationEncryptedBytes =
    Convert.FromBase64String(
    xmlCipherValue.InnerText);


// Set up the CryptoStream for decryption
MemoryStream memoryStream = new
MemoryStream(patientPersonalInformationEncryptedBytes);
CryptoStream cipherStream = new CryptoStream(memoryStream,
    tripleDES.CreateDecryptor(),CryptoStreamMode.Read);


// Perform decryption
byte[] patientPersonalInformationBytes =
    new Byte[patientPersonalInformationEncryptedBytes.Length];
cipherStream.Read(patientPersonalInformationBytes, 0,
    patientPersonalInformationBytes.Length);
cipherStream.Close();
memoryStream.Close();


// Write the decrypted information to disk
string patientPersonalInformationString =
    Encoding.UTF8.GetString(patientPersonalInformationBytes);
StreamWriter fileplaintext = new
    StreamWriter(xmlDocumentPlainTextFilename);
fileplaintext.Write(patientPersonalInformationString);
fileplaintext.Close();
}
```

Figure 8.8 XML Document Decryption: VB.NET

```vbnet
Public Function decryptDocument(ByVal xmlDocumentCipherTextFilename, _
    ByVal xmlDocumentPlainTextFilename)

    ' Get the XML document from file
    Dim xmlDoc As XmlDocument = New XmlDocument
    xmlDoc.Load(xmlDocumentCipherTextFilename)
```

Continued

Figure 8.8 XML Document Decryption: VB.NET

```vbnet
' Retrieve the element to be decrypted
Dim patientPersonalInformationEncrypted = _
 xmlDoc.SelectSingleNode( _
 "medicalRecord/EncryptedData")
Dim xmlCipherValue = _
 patientPersonalInformationEncrypted.SelectSingleNode( _
 "CipherData/CipherValue")
Dim patientPersonalInformationEncryptedBytes As Byte()
patientPersonalInformationEncryptedBytes = _
   Convert.FromBase64String(xmlCipherValue.InnerText)

' Set up the CryptoStream for decryption
Dim memoryStream = _
   New MemoryStream(patientPersonalInformationEncryptedBytes)
Dim cipherStream = New CryptoStream(memoryStream, _
   tripleDES.CreateDecryptor(), CryptoStreamMode.Read)

' Perform decryption
Dim patientPersonalInformationBytes = _
   New Byte( _
     patientPersonalInformationEncryptedBytes.Length - 1) {}
cipherStream.Read(patientPersonalInformationBytes, 0, _
 patientPersonalInformationBytes.Length)
cipherStream.Close()
memoryStream.Close()

' Write the decrypted information to disk
Dim patientPersonalInformationString = _
   Encoding.UTF8.GetString(patientPersonalInformationBytes)
Dim fileplaintext = _
   New StreamWriter(xmlDocumentPlainTextFilename, False)
fileplaintext.Write(patientPersonalInformationString)
fileplaintext.Close()
End Function
```

Security Policies

- Use strong ciphers to ensure the privacy of data.

- Only encrypt sensitive data in the XML document.

- Instead of encrypting it, remove sensitive data that the recipient doesn't need.

Applying XML Digital Signatures

Although encryption is an important step in securing your Internet-bound XML, at times you might want to ensure that you are receiving information from the person you think you are. The W3C is also in the process of drafting a specification to handle digital signatures.

XML digital signatures digitally sign an element or, more typically, the entire XML document. Digitally signing an XML document is the process of creating a hash or fingerprint of the document and then encrypting this hash with a private key. This process prevents anyone from changing the document undetected; it also proofs the document sender's identity. The technology and algorithms to create a hash, as well as a discussion of asymmetrical encryption (the use of public and private keys), are presented in detail in Chapter 4.

Signing XML Data

Summary: **XML digital signatures are useful to verify the integrity of data and authenticity of the sender and for nonrepudiation**

Threats: **Data corruption, man-in-the-middle attacks, brute-force attacks**

A digitally signed XML document provides the following benefits:

- **Integrity** The document is exactly as it was when it was signed. The document cannot be modified in any way after signing, without invalidating the signature.

- **Authentication** The document came from the signer and no one else.

- **Nonrepudiation** The document signer cannot deny signing the document.

A digitally signed document, however, is not private. You should apply XML encryption if privacy is important. Candidates for digitally signed documents are documents such as contracts and agreements, for which it is important that the details of the contract did not change and the sender cannot deny that he or she sent the document.

XML Digital Signatures Specification

The XML digital signature specification is a fairly stable working draft. Its scope includes how to describe a digital signature using XML and the XML-signature namespace. Code should generate the signature from a hash over the canonical form of the manifest, which can reference multiple XML documents. To *canonicalize* something is to put it in a standard, general-use format. Because the signature is dependent on the content it is endorsing, a signature produced from a noncanonicalized document could possibly be different from that produced from a canonicalized document. Remember that this specification is about defining digital signatures in general, not just those involving XML documents—the manifest may also contain references to any digital content that code can address, even part of an XML document.

Knowing how digital signatures work is helpful in better understanding this specification. Digitally signing a document requires the sender to create a hash of the message itself and then encrypt that hash value with his own private key. Only the sender has that private key, and only he can encrypt the hash so that it can be unencrypted using his public key. The recipient, upon receiving both the message and the encrypted hash value, can decrypt the hash value, knowing the sender's public key. The recipient must also try to generate the hash value of the message and compare the newly generated hash value with the unencrypted hash value received from the sender. If the hash values are identical, it proves that the sender sent the message, because only the sender could encrypt the hash value correctly. The XML digital signature specification is responsible for clearly defining the information involved in verifying digital certificates.

XML digital signatures are represented by the *Signature* element, which has the following structure: ? denotes zero or one occurrence, + denotes one or more occurrences, and * denotes zero or more occurrences.

The XML digital signature specification is in the recommended stage and is ready for adoption. For further details, you can review the official W3C XML Signature Syntax and Processing specification found at www.w3.org/TR/xmldsig-core. Figure 8.9 shows the XML digital signature specification syntax.

Figure 8.9 XML Digital Signature Structure

```
<Signature>
    <SignedInfo>
      (CanonicalizationMethod)
      (SignatureMethod)
      (<Reference (URI=)? >
         (Transforms)?
         (DigestMethod)
         (DigestValue)
      </Reference>)+
    </SignedInfo>
    (SignatureValue)
  (KeyInfo)?
  (Object)*</Signature>
```

The following described elements are the most notable of the specification:

- **Signature** The primary construct of an XML signature. This topmost element holds all the other signature elements.

- **SignedInfo** The parent element that contains the canonicalization and signature algorithm elements.

- **CanonicalizationMethod** An element that describes the algorithm that prepares the data for signing. Canonicalization is a necessary and important transformation to convert the data to standard format that will yield that same hash results, regardless of the computing environment. For example, a Windows environment and a UNIX environment use different key codes to represent carriage returns. Canonicalization will standardize these key codes.

- **SignatureMethod** The algorithm used to sign the data. This may be combination of a digest algorithm, an encryption algorithm, or a padding algorithm.

- **SignatureValue** The actual digital signature, base-64 encoded.

- **DigestMethod** The algorithm applied to the data, after any defined transformations are applied, to generate the *DigestValue*. Signing the *DigestValue* binds resource content to the signer's key.

- **DigestValue** The value generated by applying the *DigestMethod* to the data object to be signed.

- **KeyInfo** The parent element that contains details of the key to be used to validate the signature.

There you go—everything you need to verify a digital signature in one nice, neat package. To validate the signature, you must digest the data object referenced using the relative *DigestMethod*. The reference is valid if the digest value generated matches the *DigestValue* specified. Then, to validate the signature, obtain the key information from the *SignatureValue* and validate it over the *SignedInfo* element.

XML Digital Signature Example

As an example, let's take the role of a car dealership. We would like to submit details and prices of our cars to an Internet search engine. The search engine requires our data in XML so that it can display the details in a variety of formats and views. However, we are concerned that the unscrupulous may modify the details of the data, either in transit to the Internet search engine or on the search engine itself. As a car dealership, we are not bothered that anyone can view the car details as we send them to the search engine; in fact, the more viewers, the better! We decide to use an XML digital signature to prevent the undetected *modification* of our car details. Figure 8.10 shows an example of a document ready to digitally sign.

Figure 8.10 XML Document to Be Digitally Signed

```xml
<?xml version="1.0"?>
<acmeCars>
  <carDetails>
    <make>Honda</make>
    <model>Accord</model>
    <year>2004</year>
    <price>23000</price>
  </carDetails>
  <carDetails>
    <make>Ford</make>
    <model>Probe</model>
    <year>1990</year>
    <price>530</price>
```

Continued

Figure 8.10 XML Document to Be Digitally Signed

```
  </carDetails>
  <carDetails>
    <make>Ferrari</make>
    <model>Enzos</model>
    <year>2003</year>
    <price>643330</price>
  </carDetails>
</acmeCars>
```

The example code in Figures 8.11 and 8.12 demonstrates how to read an XML document and dynamically create a digital signature. For simplicity, code generates the encryption key. Ordinarily, code would read the key from a secure location.

Figure 8.11 Creating an XML Digital Signature: C#

```csharp
void signDocument(string xmlDocumentUnsignedFilename, string
xmlDocumentSignedFilename)
{
    // Load the document to be signed, and key to use
    XmlDocument xmlDoc = new XmlDocument();
    xmlDoc.Load(xmlDocumentUnsignedFilename);
    SignedXml signedXml = new SignedXml();
    signedXml.SigningKey = rsaKey;

    // Set up data object to contain the data the will be signed
    DataObject dataObject = new DataObject();
    dataObject.Data = xmlDoc.ChildNodes;
    dataObject.Id = "SignedObject";
    signedXml.AddObject(dataObject);
    Reference reference = new Reference();
    reference.Uri = "#SignedObject";
    signedXml.AddReference(reference);

    // Create signature
    KeyInfo keyInfo = new KeyInfo();
```

Continued

Figure 8.11 Creating an XML Digital Signature: C#

```csharp
    keyInfo.AddClause(new RSAKeyValue(rsaKey));
    signedXml.KeyInfo = keyInfo;
    signedXml.ComputeSignature();


    // Write signature to file
    XmlElement xmlSignature = signedXml.GetXml();
    xmlDoc = new XmlDocument();
    XmlNode xmlNode = xmlDoc.ImportNode(xmlSignature, true);
    xmlDoc.AppendChild(xmlNode);
    xmlDoc.Save(xmlDocumentSignedFilename);
}
```

Figure 8.12 Creating an XML Digital Signature: VB.NET

```vbnet
Public Function signDocument(ByVal xmlDocumentUnsignedFilename, ByVal
xmlDocumentSignedFilename)


    ' Create key
    Dim rsaKey = RSA.Create()


    ' Load the document to be signed, and key to use
    Dim xmlDoc = New XmlDocument
    xmlDoc.Load(xmlDocumentUnsignedFilename)
    Dim signedXml = New SignedXml
    signedXml.SigningKey = rsaKey


    ' Set up data object to contain the data the will be signed
    Dim dataObject As DataObject = New DataObject
    dataObject.Data = xmlDoc.ChildNodes
    dataObject.Id = "SignedObject"
    signedXml.AddObject(dataObject)
    Dim reference As Reference = New Reference
    reference.Uri = "#SignedObject"
    signedXml.AddReference(reference)
```

Continued

Figure 8.12 Creating an XML Digital Signature: VB.NET

```
    ' Create signature
    Dim keyInfo As KeyInfo = New KeyInfo
    keyInfo.AddClause(New RSAKeyValue(rsaKey))
    signedXml.KeyInfo = keyInfo
    signedXml.ComputeSignature()


    ' Write signature to file
    Dim xmlSignature As XmlElement = signedXml.GetXml()
    xmlDoc = New XmlDocument
    Dim xmlNode As XmlNode = xmlDoc.ImportNode(xmlSignature, True)
    xmlDoc.AppendChild(xmlNode)
    xmlDoc.Save(xmlDocumentSignedFilename)
End Function
```

Figure 8.13 shows the XML document of Figure 8.10 after digitally signing.

Figure 8.13 XML Digitally Signed Document

```
<Signature xmlns="http://www.w3.org/2000/09/xmldsig#">

<SignedInfo>

<CanonicalizationMethod Algorithm="http://www.w3.org/TR/2001/REC-xml-c14n-
20010315" />

<SignatureMethod Algorithm="http://www.w3.org/2000/09/xmldsig#rsa-sha1" />

<Reference URI="#SignedObject">

<DigestMethod Algorithm="http://www.w3.org/2000/09/xmldsig#sha1" />

<DigestValue>sPpOt0ysPVG7iPkC9/avA/4bjhM=</DigestValue>

</Reference>

</SignedInfo>


<SignatureValue>VwiNfYfXdY7bPAk4nULVUdlbIs572RMEWeElk68jIzWojA+3WnmwU/jJU5KY
c8/DvwX1gnW/kI/hIpPswcpURSO85nNTKIKwYHX/eS7f8h5JcSlCU1EUdnpxoHEwtbsEu8OuVYUR
4AiBgnFlQPVeJldiKHjRdo14j+hkZSM8p6o=</SignatureValue>


<KeyInfo>

<KeyValue xmlns="http://www.w3.org/2000/09/xmldsig#">

<RSAKeyValue>
```

Continued

Figure 8.13 XML Digitally Signed Document

```
<Modulus>wRMK+SKiDIRBHRY1NUc6SpTt+3iPcMGFwdg27MgsU2ydaCJyTZMCsFfDewZ6jK+cJvL
Li3+b46YwEYJ/GyPvdXSOGPHTNaDFTi7AsKAGu4eXkFhSExnDPUJlnOiToG0eMYXWj/DRvK8adMa
hoeqIkysmkUKq4YO9OvqMkwMyJ3M=</Modulus>
<Exponent>AQAB</Exponent>
</RSAKeyValue>
</KeyValue>
</KeyInfo>
<Object Id="SignedObject">
<acmeCars xmlns="">
<carDetails>
      <make>Honda</make>
      <model>Accord</model>
      <year>2004</year>
      <price>23000</price>
</carDetails>

<carDetails>
      <make>Ford</make>
      <model>Probe</model>
      <year>1990</year>
      <price>530</price>
</carDetails>

<carDetails>
      <make>Ferrari</make>
      <model>Enzos</model>
      <year>2003</year>
      <price>643330</price>
</carDetails>
</acmeCars>
</Object>
</Signature>
```

Creating a digitally signed XML document is only half the process. The document recipient should now verify that the signature is valid and the document as not been modified. Continuing with our car dealership example, the Internet search engine to which we submitted our signed document must now validate the signature. If the document's signature is valid, the search engine can guarantee that the document has not been modified. Figures 8.14 and 8.15 show example code to validate an XML signed document.

 Figure 8.14 Validating an XML Digital Signature: C#

```csharp
bool verifySignature(string xmlDocumentSignedFilename)
{
    // Load signed XML document
    XmlDocument xmlDoc = new XmlDocument();
    xmlDoc.PreserveWhitespace = true;
    xmlDoc.Load(xmlDocumentSignedFilename);
    SignedXml signedXml = new SignedXml(xmlDoc);

    // Get the signature element
    XmlNodeList nodeList = xmlDoc.GetElementsByTagName(
        "Signature", "http://www.w3.org/2000/09/xmldsig#");
    signedXml.LoadXml((XmlElement)nodeList[0]);

    // Validiate signature
    if (signedXml.CheckSignature())
        return true; // signature valid - document unmodified
    else
        return false; // signature invalid- document modified
}
```

Figure 8.15 Validating an XML Digital Signature: VB.NET

```vbnet
Public Function verifySignature(ByVal xmlDocumentSignedFilename) As Boolean

    ' Load signed XML document
    Dim xmlDoc As XmlDocument = New XmlDocument
    xmlDoc.Load(xmlDocumentSignedFilename)
    Dim signedXml As SignedXml = New SignedXml(xmlDoc)
```

Continued

Figure 8.15 Validating an XML Digital Signature: VB.NET

```
    ' Get the signature element
    Dim nodeList = xmlDoc.GetElementsByTagName( _
      "Signature", "http://www.w3.org/2000/09/xmldsig#")
    signedXml.LoadXml(CType(nodeList(0), XmlElement))

    ' Validiate signature
    If signedXml.CheckSignature() Then
        Return True ' signature valid - document unmodified
    Else
        Return False ' signature invalid- document modified
    End If
End Function
```

You will probably see an increase in the use of encryption and digital signatures when the W3C group finalizes both the XML encryption and XML digital signature specifications. Both specifications provide a well-structured way to communicate their respective processes, and as always with ease of use comes adoption. Encryption ensures that confidential information stays confidential through its perilous journey over the Internet. Digital signatures ensure that you are communicating what and with whom you think you are. Yet both these specifications have some evolving to do, especially when they are used concurrently. There's currently no way to determine if a document that was signed and encrypted was signed using the encrypted or unencrypted version of the document. Typically, these little bumps find a way of smoothing themselves out over time.

Security Policies

- Use strong asymmetrical algorithms to ensure the privacy of data.

- Validate the signature of signed documents.

- Use encryption for sending private data. Digital signatures do not make a document private; they merely validate the source integrity.

Coding Standards Fast Track

Applying XML Encryption

Encrypting XML Data

- ☑ Use strong ciphers to ensure the privacy of data.
- ☑ For efficiency purposes, encrypt sensitive data only in the XML document.
- ☑ Instead of encrypting it, remove sensitive data the recipient doesn't need.

Applying XML Digital Signatures

Signing XML Data

- ☑ Use strong asymmetrical algorithms to ensure the privacy of data.
- ☑ Validate the signature of signed documents.
- ☑ Use encryption for sending private data. Digital signatures do not make a document private; they validate the document's integrity.

Coding Audit Fast Track

Applying XML Encryption

Encrypting XML Data

- ☑ Does the application encrypt the document using only well-established encryption algorithms, avoiding weak encryption methods and encoding techniques?
- ☑ Is all the sensitive data encrypted?
- ☑ Are the keys used for encryption stored securely?
- ☑ If the code does not include *EncryptionMethod* or *EncryptedKey* elements, has a policy already been established so that the recipient knows this information?

☑ Does the recipient of the encrypted data actually need to access the data?

Applying XML Digital Signatures

Signing XML Data

☑ Does the application sign the document using only well-established encryption algorithms, avoiding weak encryption methods and encoding techniques?

☑ Are the keys used for signing stored securely?

☑ If encryption and signing are used together, have the parties agreed to a policy regarding whether encryption is applied before or after signing?

Frequently Asked Questions

The following Frequently Asked Questions, answered by the authors of this book, are designed to both measure your understanding of the concepts presented in this chapter and to assist you with real-life implementation of these concepts. To have your questions about this chapter answered by the author, browse to **www.syngress.com/solutions** and click on the **"Ask the Author"** form. You will also gain access to thousands of other FAQs at ITFAQnet.com.

Q: Would I ever need to use XML encryption and XML digital signatures together?

A: Encrypted data cannot be modified undetected, so XML encryption also provides the data integrity benefit of a digital signature. XML encryption, however, does not require the use of asymmetrical encryption (private and public keys). Asymmetrical encryption is the technology that provides the benefit of authentication and nonrepudiation. If your needs require privacy, integrity, authentication, and nonrepudiation, you need to use them together.

Q: If I do decide to use XML encryption and XML digital signatures together, should I sign the document and then apply encryption, or encrypt the document and then sign it?

A: Both methods will work, and there is currently no standard specifying which to do first. It is critical, however, that the document recipient knows the order in which the encryption and signature were applied; otherwise, the recipient will not be able to generate the correct hash of the document.

Q: If I need to encrypt my entire document and don't intend to archive my document, wouldn't I be better off sending the document through SSL?

A: Yes, if you are satisfied with the SSL algorithm and key size. In this case, the benefit of utilizing XML encryption is that it allows you to specify your own algorithm and key size.

Q: Which algorithms and key size do you recommend for XML encryption and XML digital signatures?

A: See Chapter 4 for a thorough discussion on the strengths of various algorithms and recommended key sizes for each.

Appendix A

Understanding .NET Security

Solutions in this Chapter:

- **The Risks Associated with Using XML in the .NET Framework**
- **.NET Internal Security as a Viable Alternative**
- **Security Concepts**
- **Code Access Security**
- **Role-Based Security**
- **Security Policies**
- **Cryptography**
- **Security Tools**
- **Security Fast Track**

Introduction

Security in the .NET Framework and the Common Language Runtime (CLR) is much more robust than many ASP developers were accustomed to. However, these security improvements also mean new concepts for developers to understand. Sometimes these security concepts themselves can be a stumbling block to writing secure code. Once you understand the .NET Framework security concepts, you will find that that the framework actually simplifies ASP.NET security.

Some of the security improvements in the .NET Framework are:

- Code Access Security (CAS)
- Role-based security
- Security policies

It is important to understand that you can no longer ignore security as a part of your design and implementation phase. It is a priority to safeguard your systems from malicious code, and you also want to protect your code or application from being misused by less trusted code. For example, let's say that you implement an assembly that holds functions that modify registry settings. Because these functions can be called by other unknown code, they can become tools for malicious code if you do not incorporate the .NET Framework security as part of your code.

To be able to use the .NET Security to your advantage, you need to understand the concepts behind the security. We discuss those concepts in the following sections.

Permissions

In the real world, *permission* refers to an authority giving you, or anyone else for that matter, the formal "OK" to perform a specified task that is normally restricted to a limited group of persons. *Permission* has the same meaning in the .NET Security Framework: getting permission to access a protected resource or operation that is not available for unauthorized users and code. An example of a protected resource is the registry, and a protected operation is a call to a COM+ component, which is regarded as unmanaged code and therefore less secure. The .NET Framework checks the following permissions:

- **Code access permissions** Protects the system from code that can be malicious or simply unstable.

- **Role-based security permissions** Limits the tasks a user can perform, based on the role(s) the user plays or the user's identity.

- **Custom permissions** You can create your own permission in any of the other three types or any combination thereof. This demands a thorough understanding of the .NET Framework security and the working of permissions. An ill-constructed permission can result in security vulnerabilities.

You can use permissions through different methods:

- **Requests** Code can request specific permissions from the CLR, which will authorize this request only if the assembly in which the code resides has the proper trust level. Trust level is related to the security policy that is assigned to the assembly, which is determined on the basis of evidence the assembly carries. Code can never request more permission than the security policy defines; The CLR will always deny such a request. However, the code can request less permission.

- **Grants** The CLR can grant permissions based on the security policy and the trustworthiness of the code, and it requests code issues.

- **Demands** The code demands that the caller has already been granted certain permissions to execute the code. You are actively responsible for this part of security.

Principal

A *principal* represents the caller's identity. When code is called, either directly by a user or from other code, that code is activated within the security context of the caller. The .NET Framework references three types of principals:

- **Windows principal** Identifies a user and the groups of which the user is a member that exist within a Windows environment. A Windows principal has the capability to impersonate another Windows user.

- **Generic principal** Identifies a user and the user's roles not related to a Windows user. The application is responsible for creating this type of principal. Impersonation is not a characteristic of a general principal, but because the code can modify the principal, it can take on the identity of a different user or role.

■ **Custom principal** You can construct these yourself to create a principal with additional characteristics that better suits your application. You should never expose custom principals, because doing so can create serious security vulnerabilities.

Authentication

Authentication is the verification of a user's identity—the credentials the user hands over. Because the principal represents the caller's identity in the .NET Framework, the code must first establish the identity of the principal. Because your code can access the information available in the principal, it can perform additional authentication tests. In fact, because you can define your own principal, you can also be in control of the authentication process. The .NET Framework supports not only the two most used authentication methods within the Windows 2000 domain—NTLM and Kerberos v5.0—but also supports other forms of authentication, such as Microsoft Passport. The .NET Framework uses role-based security to determine if the user has a role that can access the code.

Authorization

Authorization takes place after authentication, based on the established identity of the principal. Authorizing a user is the process of verifying a user's rights to access a resource. You can refer to the user and role information in the principal object to authorize the user and allow access to system resources or to execute protected code. The principal's permissions, based on its identity, determine if the code can access specific protected resources.

Security Policy

To be able to manage the security that the CLR enforces, an administrator can create new or modify existing security policies. Before the CLR loads an assembly, it checks the assembly's credentials. This evidence is part of the assembly. The CLR assigns a security policy to the assembly depending on the level of trust granted. The system administrator controls security policies to fend off malicious code. The best approach in setting the security policies is to grant no permissions to an assembly for which you cannot establish an identity. The stricter you define the security policies, the more securely your CLR will operate.

Type Safety

The .NET Framework labels code *type safe* if it only accesses memory resources that do not belong to the memory assigned to it. Type safety verification takes place during the JIT compilation phase and prevents unsafe code from becoming active. Although you can disable type safety verification, it can lead to unpredictable results. The best example is that code can make unrestricted calls to unmanaged code, and if that code has malicious intent, the results can be severe. Therefore, the framework only allows fully trusted assemblies to bypass verification. Type safety is a form of "sandboxing."

Code Access Security

The .NET Framework is based on the concept of distributed applications, in which an application does not necessarily have a single owner. To circumvent the problem of which parts of the application (being assemblies) to trust, code access security is introduced. This is a very powerful way to protect the system from code that may be malicious or just unstable. Remember that it is always active, even if you do not use it in your own code. CAS helps you with the following tasks:

- Limiting access permissions of assemblies by applying security policies
- Protecting the code from obtaining more permissions than the security policy initially permits
- Managing and configuring permission sets within security policies to reflect the specific security needs
- Granting assemblies specific permissions that they request
- Enabling assemblies in demanding specific permissions from the caller
- Using the caller's identity and credentials to access protected resources and code

.NET Code Access Security Model

The .NET Code Access Security (CAS) model is based on a number of features:

- Stack walking
- Code identity

- Code groups
- Declarative and imperative security
- Requesting permissions
- Demanding permissions
- Overriding security checks
- Custom permissions

The following discussion will give you a better understanding of how CAS works in general and how it can work for you as you design and implement .NET applications.

Stack Walking

Perhaps stack walking is the most important mechanism within CAS to ensure that assemblies cannot gain access to protected resources and code during the course of the execution. As we mentioned before, one of the initial steps in the assembly load process is determining the level of trust of the assembly and associating corresponding permission sets with the assembly. The total package of sets is the maximum number of permissions an assembly can obtain.

Because the code in an assembly can call a method in another assembly and so forth, a *calling chain* develops (see Figure A.1), with every assembly having its own permissions set. Suppose that an assembly demands that its caller have a specific permission (*UIPermission* in Figure A.1) to be able to execute the method. Now the stack walking of the CLR kicks in. The CLR starts checking the stack where every assembly in the calling chain has its own data segment. Going back in the stack, every assembly the CLR checks for the presence of this demanded permission—in our case, *UIPermission*. If all assemblies have this permission, the code can execute. If, however, somewhere in the stack an assembly does not have this permission (in our case, this is in the top assembly *Assembly1*), the CLR throws an exception and denies access to the method.

Figure A.1 Performing Stack Walking to Prevent Unauthorized Access

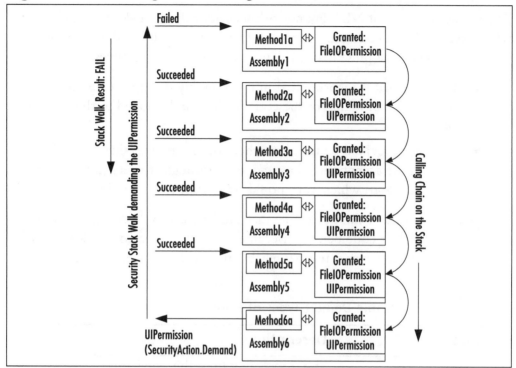

   Stack walking prevents calling code from gaining access to protected resources and code for which it initially does not have authorization. You can conclude that at any point of the calling chain, the effective permission set is equal to the intersection of the permission sets of the assemblies involved.

   Even if you do not incorporate the permission demand in your code, stack walking will take place because all class libraries that come with the CLR use the demand to ensure the secure working of the CLR. The only drawback of stack walking is that it can have a serious performance impact, especially if the calling chain is long. Suppose the stack contains eight assemblies, and the top assembly makes a call to a method that demands a specific permission and does so in a 200-fold loop. The loop triggers 200 security stack walks. Since each stack walk performs eight security checks, the total number of security checks is 1600.

Code Identity

The whole principle of .NET Framework security rides on *code identity*, or to what level a piece of code can be trusted. The CLR establishes the code identity based on the evidence presented. Evidence comes from two sources:

- Evidence that is incorporated in the assembly during the coding and subsequent compiling of the code or that can be added to the assembly later.

- Evidence provided by the host where the assembly resides. The CLR controls the accepting of host evidence through the security permission *ControlEvidence*, which you should only grant to trusted hosts.

Table A.1 lists the default evidence that can be used to determine to what code group particular code belongs. Because you cannot control the identity of the assembly, you are never sure how reliable this evidence is, except for the signatures provided.

Table A.1 The Available Default Types of Evidence

Evidence	Description
Directory	The directory where the application—hence, assembly—is installed.
Hash	The cryptographic hash of the code: MD5 or SHA1 (see the "Cryptography" section).
Publisher	The signature of the assembly's owner, in the form of a X.509 certificate, set through Authenticode.
Site	The name of the site from which the assembly originates—for example, www.company.com. (Prefixes and suffixes are disregarded.)
Strong name	The strong name consists of the assembly name (given name), public key (of the publisher), version numbers, and culture.
URL	The full URL, also called code base, including prefix and suffix: https://www.company.com:4330/*.
Zone	The zone in which the assembly originates. Default zones are Internet, Local Intranet, My Computer, No Zone Evidence, Trusted Sites, and Untrusted (Restricted) Sites.

The more evidence you can gather about the assembly, the better you can determine to what extent you can grant it permissions. The strong name is of great importance. If you and all other serious application developers are persistent in providing assemblies with strong names, you can prevent your code from becoming the vehicle of someone's dubious intents. Sadly enough, malicious code can still have a convincing strong name, which is why the best evidence is the certificate and signature that should be present with the assembly. Once you establish the trustworthiness of an assembly, based on all the evidence before you, you can determine the appropriate permission sets. Here is where your realm of control starts—by constructing appropriate code groups.

Code Groups

A *code group* is a group of assemblies that share the same value for one, and only one, piece of evidence, called *membership condition*. Based on this evidence, a permission set is attached to the assembly. Because a code group is part of a code group hierarchy (see Figure A.2), an assembly can be part of more code groups. The effective permission set of the assembly is the union of the permission sets of the code groups to which it belongs.

Figure A.2 Graphical Representation of a Code Group Hierarchy

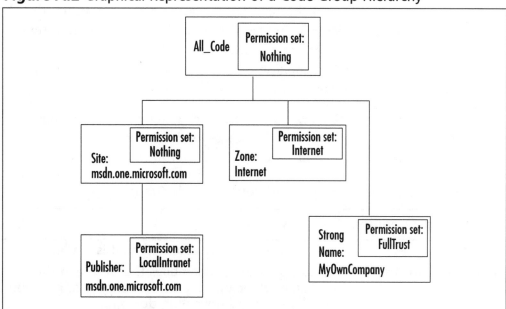

When an assembly is about to be loaded, the evidence is collected and the code group hierarchy is checked. When the CLR matches an assembly with a code group, it checks the assembly's child code groups. This implies that the construction of the hierarchy is very important and must start with the general evidence items—for example, starting with zone and moving on to more specific items such as publisher. A complicating factor is that there are three security levels (Enterprise, Machine, and User), each with its own code group hierarchy. The CLR evaluates all three, resulting in three separate permission sets, which it intersects to establish an effective permission set.

It is the administrator's responsibility to construct code group hierarchies that can quickly be scanned and enforce a high level of security. To do so, you must:

- Limit the number of levels.

- Use at the first level membership conditions that are discriminatory, preventing checking of large parts of the hierarchy.

- The hierarchy's root, All Code, should have no permissions assigned, so code that does not contain at least some evidence is not allowed to run.

- The more convincing the evidence—for example, the publishers certificate—the more permissions can be granted.

- Make no exceptions or shortcuts by giving out more permissions than the evidence justifies. Assume that you have a specific application running in the intranet zone that needs to have full trust to operate. Because it is your own application, you implicitly trust it, without the factual evidence. If you do this, however, it can come back to haunt you.

Table A.2 lists the available default membership conditions. You can construct your own, but a discussion of how to do so is beyond the scope of this appendix. We discuss membership conditions in more detail later in the appendix.

Table A.2 Default Membership Conditions for Code Groups

Membership Condition	Description
All Code	Applies to every assembly that is loaded.
Application directory	Applies to all assemblies that reside in the same directory tree as the running application; hence, the Application domain.

Continued

Table A.2 Default Membership Conditions for Code Groups

Membership Condition	Description
Hash	Applies to all the assemblies that use the same hash algorithm as specified or have the specified hash value.
Publisher	Applies to all assemblies that carry the specified publishers certificate.
Site	Applies to all assemblies that originate from the same site.
Skip verification	Applies to all assemblies that request the Skip Verification permission. *Warning:* This permission allows for the bypassing of type safety. Use it only at the lowest level, after you have established that the code is fully trusted.
Strong name	Applies to all assemblies that have the specified strong name.
URL	Applies to all assemblies that originate from the specified URL, including prefix, suffix, path, and eventual wildcard.
Zone	Applies to all assemblies that reside in the specified zone.
(custom)	Applies to custom-made conditions that are normally directly related to specific applications.

Declarative and Imperative Security

You can add security to your code in two ways: via a demand that callers have a specific permission or by a request for a specific permission from the CLR.

The first method is *declarative security*, which can be set at the assembly, class, and/or member level, so you can demand different permissions at different places in the assembly. The VB.NET syntax of declarative code is:

```
<[assembly:]Permission(SecurityAction.Member, State)>
```

For example:

```
<assembly: FileIOPermission(SecurityAction.Demand, Unrestricted := True)>
<FileIOPermission(SecurityAction.Request, Unrestricted := True)>
```

The first security example is valid for the entire assembly; hence, every call in this assembly needs to have the *FileIOPermission.* You can use the second example for a class or a single method. Only a reference to a class or a call of the method will request the CLR for *FileIOPermission.*

As the syntax already suggests, using **<>**, this code is not treated as ordinary code. In fact, as you compile the code to an assembly, the compiler extracts these lines and places them in the metadata part of the assembly. The CLR checks this metadata at different points, such as during the load of the assembly or when a method in the assembly is called. Using declarative security, you can demand, request, or even override permissions, even before the code executes. This gives you a powerful security tool during code and assembly development. However, this also means that you must be aware of the type of permissions you need to request and/or demand for your code.

The second method is *imperative security,* which becomes a part of your code and can make permission demands and overrides. It is not possible to request permissions using imperative security, because it is not clear at what point the code needs a specific permission. That's why permission requests are related to identifiable units of code. You might want to use imperative security to check whether the caller has a permission that is specific for a part of the code. For example, just before a conditional part of the code (this might even be triggered by the role-based security) wants to access a file or a registry key, you want to check if the caller has this *FileIOPermission* or *RegistryPermission.* The syntax of the imperative security in code for C# is shown in Figure A.3; the security in code for VB.NET is shown in Figure A.4.

Figure A.3 Security in Code: C#

```
Permission permissionObject = new Permission();
permissionObject.Demand();


FileIOPermission checkPermission = new FileIOPermission();
checkPermission.Demand();
```

Figure A.4 Security in Code: VB.NET

```
Dim PermissionObject as New Permission()
PermissionObject.Demand()
```

Here is an example:

```
Dim CheckPermission as New FileIOPermission()
CheckPermission.Demand()
```

The *permission* object is valid only for the scope on which it is declared; the CLR will automatically discard the object upon leaving the scope of the current procedure. Within this scope, imperative security demands and overrides overrule the permissions demanded with a declarative security statement.

Now that we've discussed declarative and imperative security, it's time to look at how you can use this information to request, demand, and override permissions.

Requesting Permissions

Requesting permissions is the best way to create a secure application and prevent possible misuse of your code by malicious code. As we mentioned before, based on the evidence, an assembly hands over to the CLR, which then determines the permission, based on relevant security policies. You construct these security policies independently from the permissions an assembly needs. Of course, if you fully trust an assembly, you can grant it all the permissions it requires. The CLR can grant an assembly more permissions than it actually needs, but an assembly can explicitly request only those specific permissions that it requires. This creates one of two scenarios:

- An assembly requests more permissions than the security policy grants, in which case the CLR will not execute the code and will throw an exception.

- An assembly specifically requests fewer permissions and protects itself from potential misuse of unused permissions.

Requesting permissions is a good security practice but demands from the developer a solid understanding of the use of permissions in code. There are three types of permission requests:

- ***RequestMinimum*** Defines the permissions the code absolutely needs to be able to run. If the *RequestMinimum* permission is not part of the granted permission set, the CLR does not allow the code to run.

- ***RequestOptional*** Defines the permissions the code might not necessarily require to run but might need in certain circumstances. If the

RequestOptional permission is not part of the granted permission set, the CLR allows the code to run. However, you need the code to be able to handle exceptions in cases where the code requires a permission not granted by the CLR.

■ *RequestRefuse* Defines the permissions the code will never need and that should not be granted to the assembly. By refraining from using certain permissions, you limit exposure to security risks from malicious or buggy code.

After the code is completed and you compile assemblies, you should get into the practice of making a minimum, optional, or refuse request for *every* permission (as listed in Table A.3), based on the permissions the code needs. Eventually, you can make it more specific to relate it to classes or members. Besides the fact that you can create secure assemblies, it is also a good way of documenting the permissions related to your code.

Table A.3 The Default Permission Classes Derived from the *CodeAccessPermission* Class

Permission Class	Permission Type	Description
DirectoryServicesPermission	Resource	Controls access to the *System.DirectoryServices* classes.
DnsPermission	Resource	Controls access to the DNS servers on the network.
EnvironmentPermission	Resource	Controls access to the user environment variables.
EventLogPermission	Resource	Controls access to the event log services.
FileDialogPermission	Resource	Controls access to files that are selected through an Open File... dialog.
FileIOPermission	Resource	Controls access to files and directories.
IsolatedStorageFilePermission	Resource	Controls access to a private virtual file system related to the identity of the application or component.

Continued

Table A.3 The Default Permission Classes Derived from the *CodeAccessPermission* Class

Permission Class	Permission Type	Description
MessageQueuePermission	Resource	Controls access to the MSMQ services.
OleDbPermission	Resource	Controls access to the OLE DB data provider and the data sources associated with it.
PerformanceCounte Permission	Resource	Controls access to the performance counters of Windows 2000 (or NT).
PrintingPermission	Resource	Controls access to printers.
ReflectionPermission	Resource	Controls access to metadata types.
RegistryPermission	Resource	Controls access to the registry.
SecurityPermission	Resource	Controls access to *SecurityPermission*, such as Assert, Skip Verification, and Call Unmanaged Code.
ServiceControllerPermission	Resource	Controls access to services on the system.
SocketPermission	Resource	Controls access to sockets that are needed to set up or accept a network connection.
SqlClientPermission	Resource	Controls access to SQL server databases.
UIPermission	Resource	Controls access to UI functionality, such as Clipboard.
WebPermission	Resource	Controls access to an Internet-related resource.
PublisherIdentityPermission	Identity	Permission is granted if the caller provides the evidence publisher.
SiteIdentityPermission	Identity	Permission is granted if the caller provides the evidence site.

Continued

Table A.3 The Default Permission Classes Derived from the *CodeAccessPermission* Class

Permission Class	Permission Type	Description
StrongNameIdentityPermission	Identity	Permission is granted if the caller provides the evidence strong name.
UrlIdentityPermission	Identity	Permission is granted if the caller provides the evidence URL.
ZoneIdentityPermission	Identity	Permission is granted if the caller provides the evidence zone.

Demanding Permissions

By demanding permissions, you force the caller to obtain specific permissions from the CLR. As we discussed before, a permission demand triggers a security stack walk. Even if you do not perform these demands yourself, the .NET Framework classes will perform them on your behalf. This means that you should not demand permissions related to these classes, because they will take care of those themselves. If you do perform a demand, it will be redundant and only add to the execution overhead. This does not mean that you should ignore this function. Instead, be aware of which call will trigger a stack walk, and make sure that the code does not perform unnecessary stack walks. However, when you build your own classes that access protected resources, you need to place the proper permission demands, using the declarative or imperative security syntax.

Using the declarative syntax when making a permission demand is preferable to using the imperative syntax, because the latter might result in more stack walks. Of course, some cases are better suited for imperative permission demands. For example, if a registry key has to be set under specific conditions, you will perform an imperative *RegistryPermission* demand just before the code is actually called. This also implies that the caller can lack this permission, which will result in an exception that the code needs to handle accordingly. Another occasion in which you want to use imperative demands is when information is not known at compile time. A simple example is *FileIOPermission* on a set of files whose names are not available at compile time.

The CLR handles two types of demands differently than previously described. First, you can only use the *link demand* in a declarative way at the class or method level. The CLR performs the link demand only during the JIT compilation phase, in which it checks to see whether the calling code has sufficient permission to link to your code. The CLR does not perform a security stack walk, because linking exists only in a direct relation between the caller and code called. The use of link demands can be helpful to methods that are accessible through reflection. The link demand will not only perform a security check on code that obtains the *MethodInfo* object—hence, performing the reflection—but the same security check is performed on the code that will make the actual call to the method. Figures A.5 and A.6 show a link demand at class and at method level.

Figure A.5 Link Demand at Class and Method Level: C#

```
[SecurityPermissionAttribute(SecurityAction.LinkDemand,
     Unrestricted = true)]
public class ClassAct
{
     [SecurityPermissionAttribute(SecurityAction.LinkDemand)] public int
     Act1()
     {
          // body of method
          return 1;
     }
}
```

Figure A.6 Link Demand at Class and Method Level: VB.NET

```
<SecurityPermissionAttribute(SecurityAction.LinkDemand, _
     Unrestricted := True)> Public Class ClassAct

Public Shared Function _
     <SecurityPermissionAttribute(SecurityAction.LinkDemand)> Act1() _
As Integer
          ' body of the function
End Function
```

The second type of demand is *inheritance demand*, which you can use at both the class and method level, through the declarative security. Placing an inheritance demand on a class can prevent other classes from inheriting it unless they have that specific permission. Although you can use a default permission, it makes sense to create a custom permission to assign to the inheriting class to be able to inherit from the class with the inheritance demand. The same goes for the class that inherits from the inheriting class. For example, let's say that you have created the *ClassAct* class that is inheritable but also has an inheritance demand set. You have defined your own inherit permission *InheritAct*. Another class called *ClassActing* wants to inherit from your class, but because it is protected with an inheritance demand, it must have the *InheritAct* permission to be able to inherit. Let's assume that it does have that permission. Now another class called *ClassReacting* wants to inherit from the class *ClassActing*. For *ClassReacting* to inherit from *ClassActing*, it also needs to have the *InheritAct* permission assigned. The inheritance demand would look like Figures A.7 and A.8.

Figure A.7 Inheritance Demand: C#

```
<InheritActAttribute(SecurityAction.InheritanceDemand)> public Class
ClassAct
```

Figure A.8 Inheritance Demand: VB.NET

```
<InheritActAttribute(SecurityAction.InheritanceDemand)> Public Class
ClassAct
```

The inheritance demand at method level will resemble Figures A.9 and A.10.

Figure A.9 Inheritance Demand at the Method Level: C#

```
[SecurityPermissionAttribute(SecurityAction.InheritanceDemand)] public
virtual int Act1()
{
  // body of method
  return 1;
}
```

Figure A.10 Inheritance Demand at the Method Level: VB.NET

```
Public Overridable Function _
    <SecurityPermissionAttribute(SecurityAction.InheritanceDemand)>_
    Act1() as Integer
        ' Body of the function
End Function
```

Overriding Security Checks

Because stack walking can introduce serious overhead and thus performance degradation, you need to keep stack walks under control. This is especially true if they do not necessarily contribute to security, such as when a part of the execution can only take place in fully trusted code. On the other hand, your code has permission to access specific protected resources, but you do not want code that you call to gain access to these resources—so you want to have a way to prevent this. In both cases, you want to take control of the permission security checks, thus overriding security checks. You can do this by using the security actions *Assert*, *Deny*, and *PermitOnly* (meaning "deny everything but").

After the code sets an override, it can undo this override by calling the corresponding *Revert* method: *RevertAssert*, *RevertDeny*, and *RevertPermitOnly*, respectively. Get into the practice of first calling the *Revert* method before setting the override, because performing a *Revert* on a nonexistent override has no effect.

> **WARNING**
>
> You can place more than one override of the same type—for example, *Deny*—within the same piece of code. However, this is not acceptable to the CLR. If during a stack walk the CLR encounters more than one of the same asserts, it throws an exception because it does not know which of the overrides to trust. If you have more than one place in a piece of code where you set an override, be sure to reverse the first one before setting the new one.

Assert Override

When you set an *Assert* override on a specific permission, you force a stack walk on this permission to stop at your code and not continue to check the callers of your method.

WARNING

If you use an *Assert*, you prevent the CLR from completing security checks, which may be a security risk. If you do this, you must be absolutely sure that there is no way to exploit your code. Nevertheless, you should always avoid using *Assert* overrides.

The use of *Assert* might make sense in the following situations:

- You have coded a part of an application that will never be exposed to the outside world. The user of the application has no way of knowing what happens within that part of the application. Your code does need access to protected resources, such as system files and/or registry keys, but because the callers will never find out that you use these protected resources, it is reasonably safe to set an *Assert* to prevent a full security check from being performed. You do not care whether the caller has that permission or not.

- Your code needs to make one or more calls to unmanaged code, but because the caller of the code obtains access through your Web site, you are safe in assuming that he or she will not have permissions to make calls to unmanaged code. On the other hand, the callers cannot influence the calls you make to unmanaged code. Therefore, it is reasonably safe to assert the permission to access unmanaged code.

- You know that somewhere in your code you have to perform a search, using a *Do..Loop* structure that at one point must access a protected resource. You also know that the code that calls the protected resource cannot be called from outside the loop. Therefore, you decide to set an assertion just before the call to the protected resource, to prevent a surplus of stack walks. In case the particular piece of code that does the call to the protected resource can be called by other code, you have to move up the assertion to the code that can only be called from the loop.

Let's look at the stack walk that was initially used in Figure A.1, but now let's throw in an assertion and see what happens (see Figure A.11). The *Assert* is set in *Assembly4* on the *UIPermission*. In the situation with no *Assert*, the stack walk did not succeed because *Assembly1* did not have this permission. Now the stack walk starts at *Assembly6*, performing a permission demand on *UIPermission*, and goes on its way as usual. Now the stack walk reaches *Assembly4* and recognizes an *Assert* on the permission it is checking. The stack walk stops there and returns with a positive result. Because the stack walk was short-circuited, the CLR has no way of knowing that *Assembly1* did not have this permission.

Figure A.11 A Stack Walk Is Short-Circuited by an *Assert*

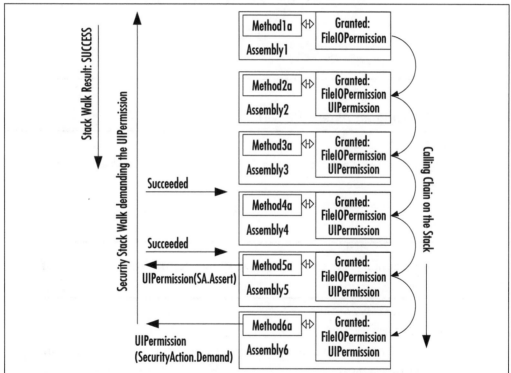

An *Assert* can be set using both the declarative and the imperative syntax. In the first example, the declarative syntax is used. An *Assert* is set on the *FileIOPermission.Write* permission for the CFG files in the C:\Test directory in Figures A.12 and A.13.

Figure A.12 Setting an Assert: C#

```
[FileIOPermission(SecurityAction.Assert, Write=@"C:\Test\.cfg")]
public int Act1()
{
    return 1;
}


int Act1()
{
  FileIOPermission ActFilePerm = new
     FileIOPermission(FileIOPermissionAccess.Write, @"C:\Test\.cfg");
  ActFilePerm.Assert();
  return 1;
}
```

Figure A.13 Setting an Assert: VB.NET

```
Public Function _
     <FileIOPermission(SecurityAction.Assert, Write := "C:\Test\*.cfg")> _
       Act1() As Integer
       ' body of the function
End Function
```

The second example uses the imperative syntax setting the same type of *Assert*:

```
Public Function Act1() As Integer
     Dim ActFilePerm As New _
         FileIOPermission(FileIOPermissionAccess.Write, "C:\Test\*.cfg")
     ActFilePerm.Assert
     ' rest of body
End Function
```

Deny Override

Deny does the opposite of *Assert* in that it lets a stack walk fail for the permission on which the *Deny* is set. There are not many situations in which a *Deny* override makes sense, but here is one: Among the permissions your code has is *RegistryPermission*. Now it has to make a call to a method for which you have no information regarding trust. To prevent that code from taking advantage of the *RegistryPermission*, your code can set a *Deny*. Now you are sure that your code does not hand over a high-trust permission.

Because unnecessary *Deny* overrides can disrupt the normal working of security checks (because they will always fail on a *Deny*), you should revert the *Deny* after the call ends for which you set the *Deny*.

For the sake of the example, we use the same situation as in Figure A.11, but instead of an *Assert*, there is a *Deny* (see Figure A.14). Again, the security stack walk is triggered for the *UIPermission* permission in *Assembly6*. When the stack walk reaches *Assembly4*, it recognizes the *Deny* on *UIPermission* and it ends with a fail. In our example, the security check would ultimately have failed in *Assembly1*, but if *Assembly1* had been granted the *UIPermission*, the stack walk would have succeeded if not for the *Deny*. Effectively this means that *Assembly4* revoked the *UIPermission* for *Assembly5* and *Assembly6*.

Figure A.14 A Stack Walk Is Short-Circuited by a *Deny*

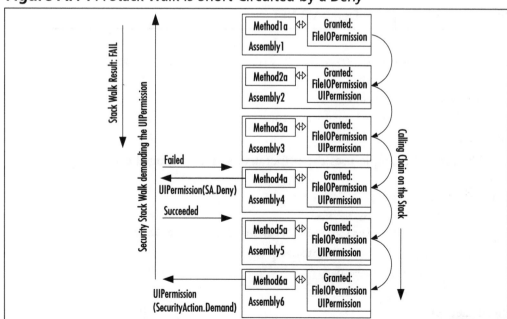

You can set a *Deny* by using both the declarative and the imperative syntax. In the first example, the declarative syntax is used. A *Deny* is set on the *FileIOPermission* permission for all the files in the C:\Winnt\System32 directory in Figures A.15 and A.16.

Figure A.15 Setting a Deny: C#

```
[FileIOPermission(SecurityAction.Deny, All = @"C:\Winnt\System32\.")]
public int Act1()
{
    return 1;
}


int Act1()
{
  FileIOPermission ActFilePerm = new
      FileIOPermission(FileIOPermissionAccess.AllAccess, @"C:\Winnt\
      System32\.");
  ActFilePerm.Deny();
  return 1;
}
```

Figure A.16 Setting a Deny: VB.NET

```
Public Function _
        <FileIOPermission(SecurityAction.Deny, All := "C:\Winnt\System32\
          *.*")> _
        Act1() As Integer
            ' body of the function
End Function
```

The second example uses the imperative syntax setting the same type of *Assert*:

```
Public Function Act1() As Integer
        Dim ActFilePerm As New
          FileIOPermission(FileIOPermissionAccess.AllAccess, _
                    "C:\Winnt\System32\*.*")
            ActFilePerm.Deny
            ' rest of the body
End Function
```

PermitOnly Override

The *PermitOnly* override is similar to the negation of the *Deny* by denying every permission but the one specified. You use the *PermitOnly* for the same reason you use *Deny*, only *PermitOnly* is more rigorous. For example, if you permit only the *UIPermission* permission, every security stack walk will fail but the one that checks on the *UIPermission*.

For example, take Figure A.14 and substitute *Deny* with *PermitOnly*. If in *Assembly6* the security check for *UIPermission* is triggered, the stack walk will pass *Assembly4* with success but will ultimately fail in *Assembly1*. If any other security check is initiated, it will fail in *Assembly*. The result is that *Assembly5* and *Assembly6* are denied any access to a protected resource that incorporates a *Demand* request, because every security check will fail.

As you can see, *PermitOnly* is a very effective way of killing any aspirations of called code in accessing protected resources *and* is used in the same way as *Deny* and *Assert*.

Custom Permissions

The .NET Framework enables you to write your own code access permissions, even though the framework comes with a large number of code access permission classes. Because these classes are meant to protect the protected resources and code that are exposed by the framework, it might well be the case that the application you are developing has defined resources that are not protected by the framework permissions, or you might want to use permissions that are more tuned to your application's needs.

You are completely free to replace existing framework permission classes, although doing so requires a large amount of expertise and experience. In case you are just adding new permission classes to the existing ones, you should be particularly careful not to overlap permissions. If more than one permission protects the same resource or operation, an administrator has to take this into account if he or she has to modify the rights to these resources.

NOTE

The subject of overlapping permissions brings up a new topic. Although the whole discussion of code access permission has been from the standpoint of the CLR or .NET Framework, eventually the CLR has to access resources on behalf of the users or the application. Even if the code has been granted a specific permission to access a protected resource, that does not automatically mean that it is allowed to access that system resource.

Take the example of a method having the *FileIOPermission* permission to the directory C:\Winnt\System32. If the identity of the Windows principal has not been given access to this part of the file system, accessing a file in that directory will fail anyway. This implies that the administrator not only has to set up the permissions within the security policy, but he or she also has to configure the Windows 2000 platform to reflect these access permissions.

Building your own permissions not only implies that certain development issues are raised, but even more so, the integrity of the entire security system must be discussed. You have to take into account that you are adding to a rigid security system that relies heavily on trust and permissions. If mistakes occur in the design and/or implementation of a permission, you run the risk of creating security holes that can become the target of attacks or let an application grant access to protected resources that it is not authorized to access. Discussing the process of designing your own permissions goes beyond the scope of this appendix. However, the following steps give you an understanding of what is involved in creating a custom permission:

1. Design a permission class.

2. Implement the interfaces *IPermission* and *IUnrestrictedPermission*.

3. In case special data types have to be supported, you must implement the interface *ISerializable*.

4. You must implement XML encoding and decoding.

5. You must implement the support for declarative security.

6. Add *Demand* calls for the custom permission in your code.

7. Update the security policy so that the custom permission can be added to permission sets.

Role-Based Security

Role-based security is not new to the .NET Framework. If you already have experience developing COM+ components, you surely have come across role-based access security. The concept of role-based security for COM+ applications is the same as for the .NET Framework. The difference lies in the way security is implemented.

When we talk about role-based security, we repeatedly use the same example. This is not because we can't create our own example, but because it explains role-based security in a way everyone understands. So here it is: You build a financial application that can handle deposit transactions. The rule in most banks is that the teller is authorized to make transactions up to a certain amount—let's say $5,000. If the transaction goes beyond that amount, the teller's manager has to step in to perform the transaction. However, because the manager is only authorized to do transactions up to $10,000, the branch manager has to be called to process a deposit transaction that is over that amount.

Therefore, using this analogy, role-based security has to do with limiting the tasks a user can perform, based on the role(s) that user plays or the user's identity. Within the .NET Framework, this all comes down to the principal that holds the identity and role(s) of the caller. As discussed earlier in this chapter, every thread is provided with a principal object. To have the .NET Framework handle the role-based security in the same manner as it does code access security, we define the permission class *PrincipalPermission*. To avoid any confusion, *PrincipalPermission* is *not* a derived class of *CodeAccessPermission*. In fact, *PrincipalPermission* holds only three attributes: *User, Role*, and the Boolean *IsAuthenticated*.

Principals

Let's get back to where it all starts: the principal. From the moment an application domain is initialized, a default call context is created, to which the principal will be bound. If a new thread is activated, the call context and the principal are copied from the parent thread to the new thread. Together with the *Principal* object, the *Identity* object is also copied. If the CLR cannot determine the principal of a thread, a default *Principal* and *Identity* object is created so that the thread can run at least with a security context with minimum rights. There are three type of principals: *WindowsPrincipal*, *GenericPrincipal*, and *CustomPrincipal*. The latter goes beyond the scope of this appendix and is not discussed any further. Let's take a look at the first two.

WindowsPrincipal

Because the *WindowsPrincipal* that references the *WindowsIdentity* is directly related to a Windows user, this type of identity can be regarded as very strong because an independent source authenticated this user.

To be able to perform role-based validations, you have to create a *WindowsPrincipal* object. In the case of the *WindowsPrincipal*, this process is reasonably straightforward, and there are actually two ways of implementing it. The one you choose depends on whether you have to perform just a single validation of the user and role(s), or you have to do this repeatedly. Let's start with the single validation solution:

1. Initialize an instance of the *WindowsIdentity* object using this code:

    ```
    C#: WindowsIdentity WinIdent = WindowsIdentity.GetCurrent();

    VB.NET: Dim WinIdent as WindowsIdentity =
    WindowsIdentity.GetCurrent()
    ```

2. Create an instance of the WindowsPrincipal object and bind the WindowsIdentity to it:

    ```
    C#: WindowsPrincipal WinPrinc = new WindowsPrincipal(WinIdent);

    VB.NET: Dim WinPrinc as New WindowsPrincipal(WindIdent)
    ```

3. Now you can access the attributes of the *WindowsIdentity* and *WindowsPrincipal* object:

    ```
    C#: string PrincName = WinPrinc.Identity.Name;

    C#: string IdentName = WinIdent.Name; //this is the same as the
    previous line

    C#: string IdentType = WinIdent.AuthenticationType;

    VB.NET: Dim PrincName As String = WinPrinc.Identity.Name

    VB.NET: Dim IdentName As String = WinIdent.Name 'this is the same
    as

    VB.NET:       the previous line

    VB.NET: Dim IdentType As String = WinIdent.AuthenticationType
    ```

If you have to perform role-based validation repeatedly, binding the *WindowsPrincipal* to the thread is more efficient, so that the information is readily available. In the previous example, you did not bind the *WindowsPrincipal* to the thread because it was intended to be used only once. However, it is good practice to always bind the *WindowsPrincipal* to the thread; that way, in case a new thread is created, the principal is also copied to the new thread:

1. Create a principal policy based on the *WindowsPrincipal* and bind it to the current thread. This initializes an instance of the *WindowsIdentity* object, creates an instance of the *WindowsPrincipal* object, binds the *WindowsIdentity* to it, and then binds the *WindowsPrincipal* to the current thread. This is all done in a single statement:

    ```
    C#:
    AppDomain.CurrentDomain.SetPrincipalPolicy(PrincipalPolicy.WindowsPr
    incipal);

    VB.NET: AppDomain.CurrentDomain.SetPrincipalPolicy(PrincipalPolicy.
         WindowsPrincipal)
    ```

2. Get a copy of the *WindowsPrincipal* object that is bound to the thread:

    ```
    C#: WindowsPrincipal WinPrinc = (WindowsPrincipal)
    Thread.CurrentPrincipal;

    VB.NET: Dim WinPrinc As WindowsPrincipal =
    Ctype(Thread.CurrentPrincipal, _

                                        WindowsPrincipal)
    ```

It is possible to bind the *WindowsPrincipal* in the first method of creation to the thread. However, your code must be granted the *SecurityPermission* permission to do so. If that is the case, you bind the principal to the thread with the following:

```
C#: Thread.CurrentPrincipal = WinPrinc;
VB.NET: Thread.CurrentPrincipal = WinPrinc
```

GenericPrincipal

In a situation in which you do not want to rely on the Windows authentication but want the application to take care of it, you can use the *GenericPrincipal*.

NOTE
_____

Always use an authentication method before letting a user access your application. Authentication, in any shape or form, is the only way to establish an identity. Without it, you are not able to implement role-based security.

Let's assume that your application requested a username and password from the user, checked it against the application's own authentication database, and established the user's identity. You then have to create the *GenericPrincipal* to be able to perform role-based verifications in your application:

1. Create a *GenericIdentity* object for the *User1* you just authenticated:

   ```
   C#: GenericIdentity GenIdent = new GenericIdentity("User1");

   VB.NET: Dim GenIdent As New GenericIdentity("User1")
   ```

2. Create the *GenericPrincipal* object, bind the *GenericIdentity* object to it, and add roles to the *GenericPrincipal*:

   ```
   C#: string[] UserRoles = {"Role1", "Role2", "Role5"};

   C#: GenericPrincipal GenPrinc = new GenericPrincipal(GenIdent,
   UserRoles);

   VB.NET: Dim UserRoles as String() = {"Role1", "Role2", "Role5"}

   VB.NET: Dim GenPrinc As New GenericPrincipal(GenIdent, UserRoles)
   ```

3. Bind the *GenericPrincipal* to the thread. Again, you need *SecurityPermission*:

   ```
   C#: Thread.CurrentPrincipal = GenPrinc;

   VB.NET: Thread.CurrentPrincipal = GenPrinc
   ```

Manipulating Identity

You can manipulate the identity that is held by a principal object in two ways. The first is replacing the principal; the second is by impersonating an identity.

Replacing the principal object on the thread is a typical action you perform in applications that have their own authentication methods. To be able to replace a principal, your code must have been granted the *SecurityPermission*, or more specifically, the *SecurityPermission* attribute *ControlPrincipal*. This will allow your own code to be able to pass on the *PrincipalObject* to other code. This attribute grants you the permission to manipulate the principal so that the CLR allows you to pass on the principal. You can replace the *Principal* object by performing these steps:

1. Create a new identity and *Principal* object, and initialize it with the proper values.

2. Bind the new principal to the thread:

```
C#: Thread.CurrentPrincipal = NewPrincipalObject;
VB.NET: Thread.CurrentPrincipal = NewPrincipalObject
```

Impersonating is also a way of manipulating the principal, with the intent of taking on another user's identity user to perform some actions on that user's behalf. You can identify two variations:

- The code has to impersonate the *WindowsPrincipal* that is attached to the thread. This might seem a little odd, but you have to remember that your code is part of an application domain that runs in a process. A user—whether a system account, a service account, or even an interactive user—starts this process on the Windows platform. Although the principal can be used to perform role-based verification within the code, accessing protected resources is still done with the identity of the process user, unless you actively use the user account of principal through impersonation.

- The code has to impersonate a user who is not attached to the current thread. The first thing you have to do is obtain the Windows token of the user you want to impersonate. This has to be done with the unmanaged code *LogonUser*. The obtained token has to be passed to a new *WindowIdentity* object. Now you have to call the *Impersonate* method of *WindowsIdentity*. The old identity—hence, token—has to be saved in a new instance of *WindowsImpersonationContext*.

At the end of the impersonation, you have to change back to the original user account by calling the *Undo* method of the *WindowsImpersonationContext*.

Remember, the *Principal* object is not changed; rather, the *WindowsIdentity* token, representing the Windows account, is switched with the current token. At the end of the impersonation, the tokens are switched back again, as shown in the following steps:

1. Call the *LogonUser* method, located in the unmanaged code library advapi32.dll. You pass the username, domain, password, logon type, and logon provider to this method, which will return a handle to a token. For the sake of the example, we will call it *hImpToken*.

2. Create a new *WindowsIdentity* object and pass it the token handle:

   ```
   C#: WindowsIdentity ImpersIdent = new WindowsIdentity(hImpToken);

   VB.NET:   Dim ImpersIdent As New WindowsIdentity(hImpToken)
   ```

3. Create a *WindowsImpersonationContext* object and call the *Impersonate* method of *ImpersIndent*:

   ```
   C#: WindowsImpersonationContext WinImpersCtxt =
   ImpersIdent.Impersonate();

   VB.NET:   Dim WinImpersCtxt As WindowsImpersonationContext =
   ImpersIdent.Impersonate()
   ```

4. At the end of the call, the original Windows token has to be put back in the *Identity* object:

   ```
   C#: WinImpersCtxt.Undo();
   VB.NET:   WinImpersCtxt.Undo()
   ```

You could have done Steps 2 and 3 in one statement that looks like this:

```
Dim WinImpersCtct As WindowsImpersonationContext = _
        WindowsIdentity.Impersonate(hImptoken)
```

Remember that you cannot impersonate when you use a *GenericPrincipal*, because it does not reference a Windows identity. For generic principals, you need to replace the principal with one that has a new identity.

Role-Based Security Checks

Now that we've discussed the creation and manipulation of *PrincipalObject*, it's time to take a look at how it can assist you in performing role-based security checks. Here is where *PrincipalPermission*, already mentioned in the beginning of the "Role-Based Security" section, comes into play. Using *PrincipalPermission*, you can make checks on the active *Principal* object, whether *WindowsPrincipal* or *GenericPrincipal*. The active *Principal* object can be one you created to perform a one-time check, or it can be the principal you bound to the thread. Like the code access permissions, the *PrincipalPermission* can be used in both the declarative and the imperative way.

To use *PrincipalPermission* in a declarative manner, you need to use the *PrincipalPermissionAttribute* object, as shown in Figures A.17 and A.18.

Figure A.17 Using the *PrincipalPermissionAttribute*: C#

```
[PrincipalPermissionAttribute(SecurityAction.Demand, Name = "User1", Role =
"Role1" )]

public int Act2()

{

   return 1;

}

[assembly:PrincipalPermissionAttribute(SecurityAction.Demand, Role =
"Administrator")]
```

Figure A.18 Using the PrincipalPermissionAttribute: VB.NET

```
Public Shared Function _
<PrincipalPermissiobAttribute(SecurityAction.Demand, _
      Name := "User1", Role := "Role1")> Act2() As Integer
           ' body of the function
End Function
<assembly: PrincipalPermissionAttribute(SecurityAction.Demand, Role :=
'Administrator')>
```

To use the imperative manner, you can perform the *PrincipalPermission* check, as shown in Figures A.19 and A.20.

Figure A.19 Using PrincipalPermission: C#

```
PrincipalPermission PrincPerm = new PrincipalPermission("User1", "Role1");
PrincPerm.Demand();
```

Figure A.20 Using PrincipalPermission: VB.NET

```
Dim PrincPerm As New PrincipalPermission("User1", "Role1")
PrincPerm.Demand()
```

It is also possible to use the imperative to set the *PrincipalPermission* object in two other ways, as shown in Figures A.21 and A.22.

Figure A.21 C#

```
PrincipalPermission PrincPerm = new
PrincipalPermission(PermissionState.Unrestricted);
```

Figure A.22 VB.NET

```
Dim PrincState As PermissionState = Unrestricted
Dim PrincPerm As New PrincipalPermission(PrincState)
```

The permission state (*PrincState*) can be *None* or *Unrestricted*, where *None* means the principal is not authenticated. Therefore, the username is *Nothing*, the role is *Nothing*, and *Authenticated* is false. *Unrestricted* matches all other principals.

Figure A.23 C#

```
bool PrincAuthenticated = true;
PrincipalPermission PrincPerm = new PrincipalPermission("User1", "Role1",
PrincAuthenticated);
```

Figure A.24 VB.NET

```
Dim PrincAuthenticated As Boolean = True
Dim PrincPerm As New PrincipalPermission("User1", "Role1",
PrincAuthenticated)
```

The *IsAuthenticated* field (*Princauthenticated*) can be true or false.

In a situation in which you want *PrincipalPermission.Demand()* to allow more than one user/role combination, you can perform a union of two *PrincipalPermission* objects. However, this is possible only if the objects are of the same type. Thus, if one *PrincipalPermission* object has set a user/role, and the other object uses *PermissionState*, the CLR throws an exception. The union looks like Figures A.25 and A.26.

Figure A.25 C#

```
PrincipalPermission PrincPerm1 = new PrincipalPermission("User1", "Role1");
PrincipalPermission PrincPerm2 = new PrincipalPermission("User2", "Role2");
PrincPerm1.Union(PrincPerm2).Demand();
```

Figure A.26 VB.NET

```
Dim PrincPerm1 As New PrincipalPermission("User1", "Role1")
Dim PrincPerm2 As New PrincipalPermission("User2", "Role2")
PrincPerm1.Union(PrincPerm2).Demand()
```

The *Demand* will succeed only if the principal object has the user *User1* in the role *Role1* or *User2* in the role *Role2*. Any other combination fails.

As we mentioned before, you can also directly access the *Principal* and *Identity* objects, thereby enabling you to perform your own security checks without using *PrincipalPermission*. Besides the fact that you can examine a little more information, this solution also prevents you from handling exceptions that can occur using *PrincipalPermission*. You can query the *WindowsPrincipal* in the same way the *PrincipalPermission* does this:

- The name of the user by checking the value of *WindowsPrincipal.Identity.Name*:

  ```
  [
  C#: if (WinPrinc.Identity.Name == "User1" ||
  C#:    WinPrinc.Identity.Name.Equals("DOMAIN1\\User1"))
  C#: {
  C#: }
  VB.NET:    If (WinPrinc.Identity.Name = "User1") or _
  VB.NET:    WinPrinc.Identity.Name.Equals("DOMAIN1\User1") Then
  VB.NET:    End If
  ```

- An available role by calling the *IsInRole* method:

```
C#: if (WinPrinc.IsInRole("Role1"))
C#: {
C#: }
VB.NET:    If (WinPrinc.IsInRole("Role1")) Then
VB.NET:    End If
```

- Determining if the principal is authenticated, by checking the value of *WindowsPrincipal.Identity.IsAuthenticated*:

```
C#: if (WinPrinc.Identity.IsAuthenticated)
C#: {
C#: }
VB.NET:    If (WinPrinc.Identity.IsAuthenticated) Then
VB.NET:    End If
```

Additionally for *PrincipalPermission*, you can check the following *WindowsIdentity* properties:

- ***AuthenticationType*** Determines the type of authentication used. Most common values are NTLM and Kerberos.

- ***IsAnonymous*** Determines if the user is identified as an anonymous account by the system.

- ***IsGuest*** Determines if the user is identified as a guest account by the system.

- ***IsSystem*** Determines if the user is identified as the system account of the system.

- ***Token*** Returns the Windows account token of the user.

Security Policies

This section takes a closer look at the way security policies are constructed and the way you can manage them. To create and modify a security policy, the .NET Framework provides you two tools: a command-line interface (CLI) tool, called caspol.exe (see the "Security Tools" section), and a Microsoft Management Console snap-in, mcscorcfg.msc (see Figure A.27). We'll use the latter for demonstration purposes because it is more visual and intuitive.

Figure A.27 The .NET Configuration Snap-In

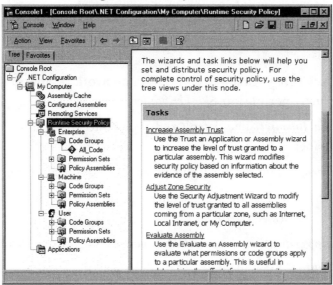

As you can see in Figure A.27, the security policy model comprises the following:

- Runtime Security Policy levels

  - **Enterprise** Valid for all managed code that is used within the entire organization (enterprise); therefore, this will have "by nature" a restrictive policy because it references a large group of code.

  - **Machine** Valid for all managed code on that specific computer. Because this already limits the amount of code, you can be more specific with handing out permissions.

  - **User** Valid for all the managed code that runs under that Windows user. This will normally be the account that starts the process in which the CLR and managed code run. Because the identity of the user is very specific, the granted permissions can also be more specific, thus less restrictive.

- A code groups hierarchy that exists for each of the three policy levels. We will look at how you can add code groups to the default structure, which already exists for user and machine.

- (Named) permission sets. By default, the .NET Framework comes with seven named permission sets:

  - *FullTrust* Unlimited access to all protected resources and operations.

  - *EveryThing* Granted all .NET Framework permissions, except the security permission *SkipVerification*.

  - *LocalIntranet* The default rights given to an application on the local intranet.

  - *Internet* The default rights given to an application on the Internet.

  - *Execution* Has only the security permission *EnableAssemblyExecution*.

  - *SkipVerification* Has only the security permission *SkipVerification*.

  - *Nothing* Denied all access to all protected resources and operations.

- Evidence, which is the attribute that the code hands over to the CLR and on which it determines the effective permission set. Evidence is used in the construction of code groups.

- Policy assemblies that list the trusted assemblies that hold security objects used during policy evaluation. You should add your assemblies to the list that implements the custom permissions. If you omit this step, the assemblies will not be fully trusted and cannot be used during the evaluation of the security policy.

Understand that the evaluation process of the security policy will result in the effective permission set for a specific assembly. For all three policy levels, the code groups are evaluated against the evidence the assembly presents. All the code groups that meet the evidence deliver a permission set. The union of these sets determines the effective permission set for that particular security policy level. After this evaluation is done at all three security levels, the three individual permission sets are intersected, resulting in the effective permission set for an assembly. This means that the code groups within the three security levels cannot be constructed independently, because this can result in a situation in which an assembly is given a limited permission set that is too limited to run. When you take a look at the permission set for the *All_Code* of the enterprise security policy, you will see that it is Full Trust. Doing the same for the *All_Code* of the user security policy, you will see *Nothing*. Because the code group tree of the enterprise is empty, it cannot make evidence decisions; therefore, it cannot contribute to the determination of the effective permission set of the assembly. By setting it to *Full Trust*, you state that it is up to the machine and user security policy to determine the effective permission set.

Because the user code group already has a limited code group tree, the root does not need to participate in the determination of the permission set. When you set it to *Nothing*, it is up to the rest of the code groups to decide on the effective permission group for the user security policy.

You can determine the permission set of a code group by performing these steps:

1. Run the Microsoft Management Console (MMC) by choosing **Start | Run** and typing **mmc**.

2. Open the .NET Management snap-in, via **Console | Add/Remove Snap-in**.

3. Expand the **Console Root | .NET Configuration | My Computer**.

4. Expand **Runtime Security Policy | Enterprise | Code Groups**.

5. Select the code group **All_Code**.

6. Right-click **All_Code** and select **Properties**.

7. Select the **Permission Set** tab.

8. The **Permission Set** field lists the current value.

Creating a New Permission Set

Suppose that you decide that none of the seven built-in permission sets satisfy your need for granting permissions. Therefore, you want to make a named permission set that does suit you. You have a few options:

- Create a permission from scratch.

- Create a new permission set based on an existing one.

- Create a new permission from an XML-coded permission set.

To give you a better understanding of the working of the security policy and some hands-on experience with the tool, we discuss the different security policy issues in the following exercises.

We use the second option and base our new permission set on the permission set *LocalIntranet* for the user security policy level:

1. Expand the **User** runtime security policy, and expand **Permission Sets** (see Figure A.28).

Figure A.28 The User's Permission Sets and Code Groups

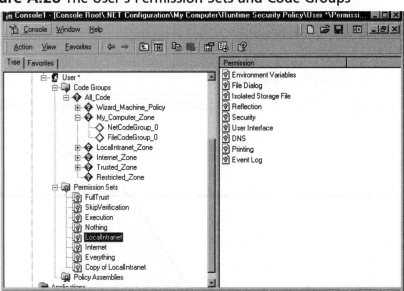

2. Right-click the permission set **LocalIntranet** and select **Duplicate**; a permission set called *Copy of LocalIntranet* is added to the list.

3. Select the permission set **Copy of LocalIntranet** and rename it **PrivatePermissions**. Then, right-click it and select **Properties**. Change the Permission Set Name to **PrivatePermissions** and, while you're at it, change the corresponding Permission Set Description.

4. Change the permissions of the permission set: Right-click the **PrivatePermissions** permission set, and select **Change Permissions**.

5. The Create Permission Set dialog box appears (see Figure A.29). You see two permissions lists: on the left, the Available Permissions that are not assigned, and on the right, the list with assigned permissions.

Figure A.29 Modify the Permission Set Using the Create Permission Set Dialog Box

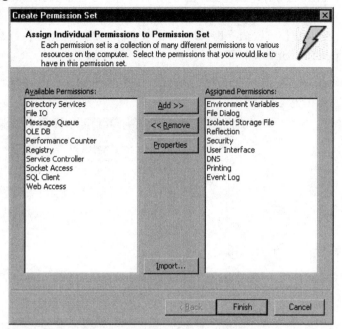

Between the two Permissions lists are four buttons. The Add and Remove buttons let you move individual permissions between the lists. Note that to prevent you from making mistakes, you cannot select more than one button at a time. You will better understand a given permission if you select that permission in the Assigned Permissions list and press the Properties button. You can use the fourth button (Import) to load an XML-coded permission set.

Now let's make some modifications to the permission set, because that was the reason to duplicate the permission set:

- Add the *FileIOPermission* to the Assigned Permission list.
- Add the *RegistryPermission* to the Assigned Permission list.
- Modify the *SecurityPermission* properties.

To do so:

1. Select **FileIO** in the Available Permissions list. (Notice that if you have selected a permission in the Assigned Permissions list, this permission stays selected.)

2. Click **Add**. A Permission Settings dialog box for the *FileIO* appears (see Figure A.30). (You can also double-click the permission to add it to the Assigned Permissions list. However, do not double-click an assigned permission by accident—this will remove the permission from the assigned permission list.)

Figure A.30 Modify the Settings of FileIO Using the Permission Settings Dialog Box

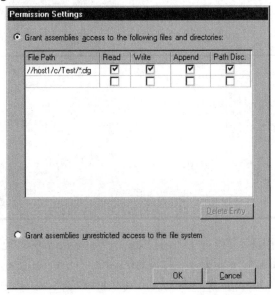

4. As you saw earlier in this appendix, this process resembles the way we used *FileIOPermission* and *FileIOPermissionAttribute* to demand and request access to specific files in a specific directory. Go ahead and fill in **C:\Test*.cfg**. Surprised that you get an error message? The point is that the field demands that you use UNC names. The advantage is that you can reference to files on other servers in the domain. However, the dialog box checks the existence of the path when you click OK, so be sure that the UNC path exists.

5. Fill the File Path with a valid UNC of the machine you are working on, and because we want to give full access, you can check all four boxes. (*Note:* If you do not check any of the boxes, this is accepted because you filled in a File Path. However, if you check the properties of *FileIO* as an assigned permission, you will notice that the line has disappeared—hence, a beta bug!)

6. Click **OK** and you have added a permission to the assigned permission list. You are now ready for the next permission.

7. Double-click the **Registry** permission, and a Permissions Setting dialog box appears that looks a lot like the one you just saw with *FileIO*. Keep the option **Grant assemblies access to the following registry keys**.

8. Fill the **Key** field with a valid HKEY value, such as **HKEY_LOCAL_MACHINE**, and check the **Read** box, so that we can give read permission to the specified registry tree.

9. Click **OK**, and you have added your second permission to your permission set.

10. The last task is to modify the Security permission. Therefore, select the **Security** permission in the Assigned Permissions list (do not double-click it, because that will remove the permission from the list) and click **Properties**.

11. A Permission Settings dialog box (see Figure A.31) appears. You see that the option **Grant assemblies the following security permissions** is selected, together with the properties **Enable assembly execution**, **Assert any permission that has been granted**, and **Enable remoting configuration**.

Figure A.31 Modifying the Security Settings Using the Permission Settings Dialog Box

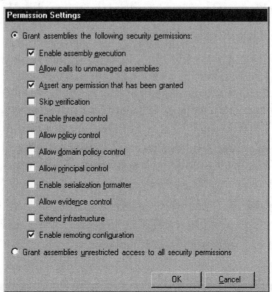

12. We also want to grant our security policy the security permission proper-
     ties. Check **Allow calls to unmanaged assemblies** because we want to
     make calls to unmanaged code. Also check **Allow principal control**
     because we want to be able to modify principal settings. Click **OK**, and
     you are done, for now, with modifying your first permission set.

13. Click **Finish**. You will probably get a warning message stating that you
     changed your security policy and you have to save it. Until you save the
     policy, an asterisk (★) will mark the user policy.

14. You can save the policy by right-clicking the **User** runtime security
     policy and selecting **Save**.

If you want this permission set to also become part of the machine and/or
enterprise permission sets, you can simply copy and paste it.

You will also notice two other options: Reset and Restore Policy. The first,
Reset, resets the policy back to the default setting of the policy. You can try it,
but it will wipe out all the changes you made until now. The latter choice,
Restore Policy, makes it possible to go back to the previous save. This is possible
because for each of the runtime security policies, the settings are saved in an
XML-coded file that becomes the current one. Before this happens, the system
renames the old one with the extension .old. The current one has the extension
.cch. The default policy has no extension, so to speak. For the user security
policy, you have the following files:

- **security.config** The default security; used by **Reset**.

- **security.config.cch** The current/active policy.

- **security.config.old** The last saved policy version; used by **Restore
  Policy**.

The enterprise security uses the name *enterprisesec.config,* and the machine
uses the name *security.config.* This is possible because the user security policy is
saved in the user's directory tree in the following folder: Document and
Settings\User_Name\Application Data\Microsoft\CLR Security config\
v1.0.xxxx.

The enterprise and machine security policies are saved in the following
directory: WINNT\Microsoft.NET\Framework\v1.x.xxxx\CONFIG. The CLR
locates this directory through the HiveKey:

```
HKEY_LOCAL_MACHINE\SOFTWARE\Microsoft\Catalog42\NetFrameworkv1\
MachineConfigdirectory
```

Because the configuration files are XML-coded, you can open and examine them with a Web browser. This will give you additional understanding of how the permission sets are set up. This also means that you can modify the default security policies.

Modifying the Code Group Structure

Now that we have created a security permission set, it makes sense to start using it. We can do so by attaching it to a code group. We will modify the code group structure of the user security policy. By default, the user already has a basic structure (see Figure A.32).

Figure A.32 The Default Code Group Structure for the User Security Policy

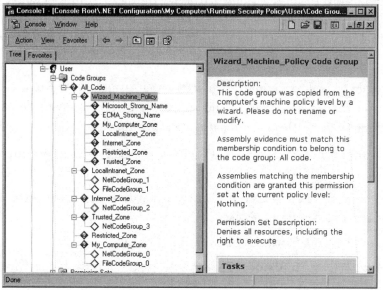

A few things might strike you at first sight:

■ There is a code group called *Wizard_Machine_Policy*. The description of this group tells you that a wizard, called the Adjust Security Wizard, copied this group from the computer's policy level and that you should not modify it. This description is not totally true. In fact, if you take a closer look at these code groups, you will see that all groups that end with _*Zone* have a permission set of *Nothing*. This means that you, the user, cannot use the machine's permission sets that are based on the zone evidence. However, if you are given more permissions based on the zone evidence, this will be toned down by the zone-based permission of the machine policy. The user can have permissions based on zoned evidence that is equal to or less than that allowed by the machine. However, you do see zone-based code groups at the same level as the *Wizard_Machine_Policy* because these are the code groups that are copied from the machine policy.

■ The zone-based code groups contain *NetCodeGroup* and *FileCodeGroup*. As the description states, they are generated by the .NET Configuration Tool; hence, the tool we are working with at the moment. The custom code groups are based on XML-code files and therefore the tool cannot edit them. However, you can use the caspol.exe tool to do so. Without going into detail regarding what exactly these groups entail, it suffices to state that they are necessary for you to use the .NET Configuration Tool. If you do not remove or modify them, you might lock yourself out from using this tool.

Let's create a small code groups structure that is made up of two code groups directly under the *All_Code* group and apply our own custom-made permission set *PrivatePermissions* to the *LocalIntranet_Zone* group:

1. If you do not have the MMC with the **.NET Management** snap-in open, open it now.

2. Expand the tree to **.NET Configuration | My Computer | Runtime Security Policy | User**.

3. Now, expand **Code Groups | All_Code**.

4. Right-click **All_Code** and select **New**; the Create Code Group dialog box appears.

5. You are given two options: **Create a new code group** and **Import a code group from a XML File**. Use the first option. (*Note:* For the NetCodeGroup and FileCodeGroup, the latter option is used.)

6. You have to enter something in at least the Name field. For this example, we choose to enter **PrivateGroup_1**. Now, click **Next**.

7. The dialog box shows you a second page called **Choose a condition Type** and has just one field called **Choose the condition type for this code group**. The field has a pull-down menu containing the values from which you can choose. All of these, except the first and last one—All Code and (custom)—are evidence-related (see Figure A.33).

Figure A.33 Select One of the Available Condition Types for a Code Group

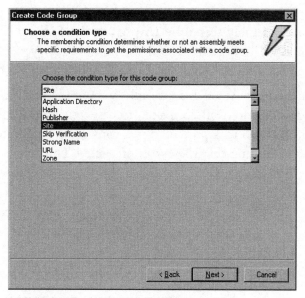

8. Select **Site** from the drop-down menu. A new field called Site Name appears and is related to the Site condition. For the sake of the example, we'll choose the **MSDN Subscribers** download site, so we enter the value **msdn.one.microsoft.com** in the site field.

9. Click **Next**, and the third page, called Assign a Permission Set to the Code Group, appears.

10. You can choose between the options **Use existing permission set** and **Create a new permission set**. Because the site comes from the Internet, that permission set will do.

11. Select the value **Nothing** from the drop-down menu (*Note:* The permission set we just made is also part of the list), and click **Next**.

12. Click **Finish**, and you have created your first code group. While we are at it, let's create the second code group, which will be the child of the code group we just created.

13. Right-click the code group **PrivateGroup_1** and select **New**.

14. Create a new code group named **PrivateGroup_2** and click **Next**.

15. Select the value **Publisher** from the drop-down menu. Below the field, a new box called **Publisher Certificate Details** appears and has to be filled by importing a certificate. You can do this by reading out of a signed assembly using the **Import from Signed File** button. (Note: It should say Import from signed Assembly.) Or you can import a certificate file using the **Import from Certificate File** button.

16. For the purpose of this example, we use the certificate from the msdn.one.microsoft.com site. (In case you have forgotten how this is done, you go to a protected site, thus using SSL. You double-click the icon indicating that the site is protected. This opens up the certificate. Go to the **Details** tab and click the **Copy to File** button.)

17. Click the **Import from Certificate File** button, browse to the certificate file (the extension is .cer), and open it. You will see that the field in the certificate box is filled (see Figure A.34).

Figure A.34 Importing a Certificate for a Publisher Condition in a Code Group

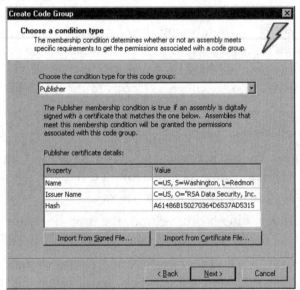

18. Click **Next**.

19. Select the existing permission group **LocalIntranet**. We can give more permissions now that we know that the signed assemblies indeed come from Microsoft MSDN but also originate from the corresponding Web site.

20.   Click **Next**, and then click **Finish**.

Before tackling our last task, let's recap what we have done. We were concerned with creating a permission set for signed assemblies that come from the msdn.one.microsoft.com site. So, what if the assembly comes from this Web site but is not signed? It meets the condition of *PrivateGroup_1*, so it will get the permission set of this code group. Because this is *Nothing*, that would mean that these assemblies are granted no permission. However, because the msdn.one. microsoft.com site comes from the Internet Zone, it also meets the condition of the code group *Internet_Zone*, which grants the Internet permission set to any assembly from this zone. Moreover, because a union is taken from all the granted permission sets, these assemblies will still have enough permissions to run.

Why not make the *PrivateGroup_2* a child of *Internet_Zone* because unsigned assemblies from msdn.one.microsoft.com are granted the Internet permission set anyway? The reason is simple: We only want to give signed assemblies from msdn.one.Microsoft.com additional permission if they also originate from the appropriate Web site. If such a signed assembly originates from another Web site, we treat it as any other assembly coming from an Internet Zone. The reason for giving *PrivateGroup_1* the *Nothing* permission set is that it is only there to force assemblies to meet both conditions, and *PrivateGroup_1* is just an intermediate stage to meet all conditions.

Keep in mind that we only discussed how the actual permission set is determined at the user security policy level. This will be intersected with the actual permission set determined on the machine level. Moreover, because at the machine level the assembly will be given only the Internet permission set, our signed assembly will wind up with the effective permission set of *Internet*. Normally, the actual permission set of the enterprise is also taken into the intersection, but because that code group tree has only the *All_Code* code group with full trust, it will play no role in the intersection of this example.

Our last task, replacing a permission set, should be straightforward by now:

1.   Right-click the code group **LocalIntranet_Zone** and select **Properties**. The LocalIntranet_Zone Properties dialog box appears (see Figure A.35).

Figure A.35 Setting Attributes in the General Tab of the Code Group Permission Dialog Box

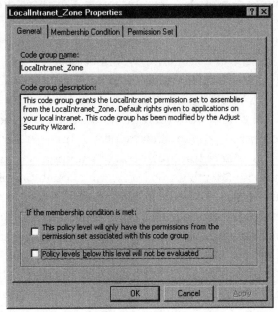

2. Select the **Permission Set** tab.

3. Open the pop-up menu with available permission sets and select **PrivatePermissions**. You will see that the list box will reflect the permissions that make up the *PrivatePermissions* permission set.

4. Click **Apply** and go back to the **General** tab.

On this tab is a frame called **If the membership condition is met**, which shows two options:

- This policy level will have only the permissions from the permission set associated with this code group This refers to the code group attribute *Exclusive*.

- **Policy levels below this level will not be evaluated** This refers to the code group attribute *LevelFinal*.

Both options need some explanation, so let's go back to our msdn.one.microsoft.com example. Suppose you open the Properties dialog box of the *Internet_Zone* code group and check the *Exclusive* option (of course, you have to save it first for it to become active). We received a signed assembly from msdn.one.microsoft.com that also originates from this site. We had established that it would be granted the *LocalIntranet_Zone* permission at the user policy level. But now the *Exclusive* option comes into play. Because our signed assembly also meets the *Internet_Zone* condition, the Internet permission set is valid. The exclusive that is set for the *Internet_Zone* code group forces all other valid permission sets to be ignored by not taking a union of these permission sets. Instead, the permission set with the exclusive attribute becomes the actual permission set for the user policy level. Because it will be intersected with the actual permission sets of the other security levels, it also determines the maximum set of permissions that will be granted to the signed assembly.

Use this attribute with care, because from all the code groups of which an assembly is a member—hence, meets the condition—only one can have the *Exclusive* attribute. The CLR determines whether this is the case. When the CLR determines that an assembly meets the condition of more than one code group with the *Exclusive* attribute, it will throw an exception, and it fails to determine the effective permission set and the assembly is not allowed to execute.

The way the *LevelFinal* is handled is more straightforward. Understand that by establishing the effective permission set of an assembly, the CLR evaluates the security policies starting at the highest level (enterprise, followed by user and machine). Again, take our MSDN example. We set a *LevelFinal* in the *PrivateGroup_2* code group and removed the *Exclusive* attribute from *Internet_Zone*. When the effective permission set for a signed assembly from msdn.one.microsoft.com that originates from that Web site has to be established, the CLR starts with determining the actual permission set of the enterprise policy level. This is for *All_Code* Full Trust, effectively taking this policy level out of the intersection of actual permission sets. Now the user policy level gets its turn in establishing the actual permission set. As you know by now, this will be equal to the *LocalIntranet_Zone* permission set. However, the CLR has also encountered the *LevelFinal* attribute. It refrains from establishing the actual permission set of the machine policy level and intersects the actual permission sets from the enterprise and user policy level. The actual permission set will be equal to *LocalIntranet_Zone*.

Because the machine policy level is not considered, the actual permission set in this case has more permission than in the situation in which the *LevelFinal* attribute has not been set.

Remoting Security

Discussing security between systems always provides a new set of security issues. This is no exception for remoting. Let's start with the communication between systems. If you use an *HttpChannel*, you can use the SSL encryption. The *FtpChannel* does not have encryption, but if both servers support IPSec, you are able to create a secured channel through which the *FtpChannel* can communicate. All Microsoft server systems post NT to include 2000, XP, and 2003 have easy-to-implement IPSec capabilities.

The next issue is to what extent you trust the other system. Even with a secure channel in place, how do you know that the other system has not been compromised? You need at least a sturdy authentication mechanism in place, and you need to avoid the use of anonymous users, although this will not always be possible. At least try to use NTLM or Kerberos for authentication. The latter is a perfect vehicle for handling impersonation between multiple systems. If you need to use anonymous users, you can use IIS as the storefront and let the IIS handle the impersonation. You can also use a proxy to prevent a user from directly accessing your IIS.

The messages that are exchanged should always be signed so that you are able to verify the sender and/or origin. Even when you are sure that a message is transported over a secured channel, you are never sure if the message that is put in this channel has been sent with ill intent.

This chapter has discussed the use of code access and role-based security. The more thoroughly you use this runtime security instrument, the better you can control the remoting security.

Cryptography

There is no discussion of security that does not at least reference cryptography or encryption. Although cryptography is an absolute necessity to create a secure environment, it is not the "Holy Grail" of security. This section highlights the cryptography features that come with the .NET Framework. If you already have worked with Windows 2000 Cryptographic Service Providers (CSPs) and/or used the CryptoAPI, you know nearly everything there is to know about cryptography in the .NET Framework.

The most important observation is that the ease of use of crypto functionalities has improved a great deal over the way we had to use the CryptoAPI, which only was available for C/C++. An important addition in the design concept of the cryptography namespace is the use of *CryptoStreams*, which make it possible to chain together any cryptographic object that uses CryptoStreams. This means that the output from one cryptographic object can be directly forwarded as the input of another cryptographic object without the need to store the output result in an intermediate object. This can enhance the performance significantly if large pieces of data have to be encoded or hashed. Another addition is the functionality to sign XML code, although only for use within the .NET Framework security system. To what extend these methods comply with the proposed standard RFC 3075 is unclear.

Within the .NET Framework, three namespaces involve cryptography:

- ***System.Security.Cryptography*** The most important one; resembles the CryptoAPI functionalities.

- ***System.Security.Cryptography* .X509 certificates** Relate only to the X509 v3 certificate used with Authenticode.

- ***System.Security.Cryptography.Xml*** For exclusive use within the .NET Framework security system.

The cryptography namespaces support the following CSP classes that will be matched on the Windows 2000 CSPs by the CLR. If a CSP is available within the .NET Framework, this does not automatically imply that the corresponding Windows 2000 CSP is available on the system the CLR is running:

- ***DESCryptoServiceProvider*** Provides the functionalities of the symmetric key algorithm Data Encryption Standard.

- ***DSACryptoServiceProvider*** Provides the functionalities of the asymmetric key algorithm Data Signature Algorithm.

- ***MD5CryptoServiceProvider*** Provides the functionalities of the hash algorithm Message Digest 5.

- ***RC2CryptoServiceProvider*** Provides the functionalities for the symmetric key algorithm RC 2 (named after the inventor: Rivest's Cipher 2).

- ***RNGCryptoServiceProvider*** Provides the functionalities for a Random Number Generator.

- ***RSACryptoServiceProvider*** Provides the functionalities for the asymmetric algorithm RSA (named after the inventors Rivest, Shamir, and Adleman).

- ■ *SHA1CryptoServiceProvider* Provides the functionalities for the hash algorithm Secure Hash Algorithm 1.

- ■ *TripleDESCryptoServiceProvider* Provides the functionalities for the symmetric key algorithm 3DES.

To be complete, we give short descriptions of symmetric key algorithm, asymmetric key algorithm, and hash algorithm. A *symmetric key algorithm* enables you to encrypt and decrypt data that is sent between you and another party. The same key is used to both encrypt and decrypt the data. That is why it is called a *symmetric* algorithm. This algorithm forces you to exchange the key with your counter party, but this must be done in such a way that no other party can intercept this key. Because symmetric key algorithms are often used for a short exchange of data, they are also referred to as *session key algorithms*. For the exchange of session keys, the parties involved use an asymmetric key algorithm.

An *asymmetric key algorithm* uses a *key pair*. One key is private and is kept under lock and key by the owner, and the other is public and available to everyone. Because the algorithm uses two related but different keys to encrypt and decrypt, it is called an *asymmetric algorithm*, but it is also referenced as a *public key algorithm*. The public key is wrapped in a certificate that is a "proof of authenticity," and that certificate has to be issued by an organization that is trusted by all involved parties. This organization is called a *certificate authority* (CA), of which VeriSign is the best known.

So, what about using an asymmetric key algorithm to exchange symmetric keys? The best example is two Windows 2000 servers that need to regularly set up connection between both servers on behalf of their users. Each connection— or session—has to be secured and needs to use a session key that is unique in relation to the other secured sessions. The servers exchange a session key for every connection. Both have an asymmetric key pair and have exchanged the public key in a certificate. Therefore, if one server wants to send a session key to the other server, it uses the public key of the other server to encrypt the session key before it sends it. The server knows that only the other server can decrypt the session key because that server has the private key that is needed to decrypt the session key.

A *hash algorithm,* also referred to as a *one-way hash algorithm*, can transform a variable piece of data into a fixed-length piece of data, called a *hash* or *message digest,* that is nearly always much shorter—for example, 160 bits for SHA-1. *One-way* means that you cannot derive the source data by examining only the digest.

Another important feature of the hash algorithm is that it generates a hash that is unique for each piece of data, even if just one bit of data is changed. You can see a hash value as the fingerprint of a piece of data. Let's say, for example, you send someone a plaintext e-mail. How do you and the receiver of the e-mail know that the message was not altered as it was being sent? Here is where the message digest comes in. Before you send your e-mail, you apply a hash algorithm to that message, and you send the message and message digest to the receiver. The receiver can perform the same hash on the message, and if the digest and the message are the same, the message has not been altered. Yes, someone who alters your message can also generate a new digest and obscure his act, but that's where the next trick comes in. When you send the digest, you encrypt it with your own private key, of which you know the receiver has the public part. This solution not only prevents the message from being changed without you and the receiver discovering it but also confirms to the receiver that the message came from you and only you. How?

Well, let's assume that someone intercepts your message and wants to change it. He has your public key, so he can decrypt your message digest. However, because he doesn't have your private key, he is unable to encrypt a newly generated digest. Therefore, he cannot go forward with his plan to change the e-mail without anyone finding out. Eventually, the e-mail arrives at the receiver's inbox. She decrypts the encrypted digest using your public key. If that succeeds, she knows that this message digest must have been sent by you, because you are the only one who has access to the private key. She calculates the hash on the message and compares the digests. If they match, she not only knows that the message hasn't been tampered with, but she also knows that the message came from only you, because every message has a unique hash. Moreover, because she already established that the encrypted hash came from you, the message must also come from you.

Security Tools

The .NET Framework comes with 10 command-line security tools (see Table A.4) that help you perform your security tasks. For a more thorough description of these tools, consult the .NET Framework documentation.

Table A.4 Command-Line Security Tools

Name of Tool	Name of Executable	Description
Code Access Security Policy Utility	Caspol.exe	This tool can perform any operation in relation to the code access security policy. Because it can do more than the .NET Configuration Tool we have been using in this chapter, it is important that you familiarize yourself with it.
Certificate Verification Utility	Chktrust.exe	With this tool, you can check a file that has been signed using Authenticode.
Certificate Creation Utility	Makecert.exe	Creates an X.509 certificate for testing purposes. An option you might consider is to install the Certificates Services on Windows 2000, which makes it much easier to create and maintain certificates for development and testing purposes.
Certificate Manager Utility	Certmgr.exe	This utility manages your certificates, certificate trust lists, and so on. Use the Microsoft Management Console with the Certificates snap-in, which enables you to maintain not only your own certificates but also (if you have the rights) the certificates of your computer and service accounts.
Software Publisher Certificate Test Utility	Cert2spc.exe	This tool creates a software publisher's certificate for one or more X.509 certificates.
Permissions View Utility	Permview.exe	This tool enables you to view the requested permissions of an assembly.
PE Verify Utility	Peverify.exe	This tool enables you to verify the type safety of a portable executable file.

Continued

Table A.4 Command-Line Security Tools

Name of Tool	Name of Executable	Description
Secutil Utility	Secutil.exe	This tool extracts strong name or public key information from an assembly and converts it so that you can use it directly in your code (for example, for a permission demand).
File Signing Utility	Signcode.exe	This tool enables you to sign a PE file with an Authenticode signature. If this utility is called with no command-line options, a Digital Signature Wizard is started.
Strong Name Utility	Sn.exe	This tool enables you to sign assemblies with strong names.
Set Registry Utility	Setreg.exe	This tools enables you to set registry keys for use of public key cryptography. If you call this utility without options, it will just list the settings.
Isolated Storage Utility	Storeadm.exe	This tool enables you to manage isolated storage for the current user.

Summary

Positioning the .NET Framework as a distributed application environment, Microsoft was well aware that it had to pay attention to how an application can be secured, due to the great risks that distributed security incorporate. That is why the company introduced a scalable but rights- and permission-driven security mechanism—scalable because you can as much own your own designed and customized permissions, and rigid because it is always, even if the application takes no notice of permissions. To add to that, the CLR will check the code on type safety (it checks whether the code is trying to stick its nose in places it does not belong) during the JIT compilation.

The .NET Common Language Runtime (CLR) will always perform a security check—called *code access security*—on an assembly if it wants to access a protected resource or operation. To prevent an assembly from obscuring its restricted permissions by calling another assembly, the CLR will perform a security stack walk. It checks every assembly in a calling chain of assemblies to see if every single one has this permission. If this is not the case, the assembly is not given access to this protected resource or operation.

What permissions an assembly is granted and what permission an assembly requests are controlled in two ways. The first is controlled by code groups that grant permissions to an assembly based on the evidence it presents to the CLR. The assembly itself controls the latter. A secure conscious assembly requests only the permissions it needs, even if the CLR is willing to grant it more permissions. This way, the assembly insures itself from being misused by other code that wants to make use of its permission set. A code group hierarchy has to be set up by an administrator, which he or she can do at different security policy levels: enterprise, user, and machine.

To establish the effective set of permissions, the CLR uses a straightforward and robust method: It determines all valid permission sets based on the evidence an assembly presents per security policy level, and the actual permission set per policy level is the union of the valid permission set. The CLR does this for all the policy levels and intersects the actual permission set to determine the effective permission set of an assembly.

Added to the code access security, the CLR still supports role-based security, although its implementation differs slightly from what you were accustomed to with COM. Every executing thread has a security context called *principal* that references the user's identity. The principal is also used for impersonating the executing user. The principal comes in a few forms: based on Windows users and its authentication; generic and can be controlled by custom-made authentication services; and a base form that enables you to custom-make your own principal and identity. The code can reference the principal to check if the user has a specific role.

Still, the most important security feature is security policies, which allow you to create code groups and build your own permission set that can be enriched with custom permissions. The custom permissions can be added to the .NET Framework without opening up the security system, provided that you make no security mistakes in the coding of the permissions.

As can be expected from every framework that relies on security, the .NET Framework comes with a complete set of cryptography functionalities, equal to what we had with the CryptoAPI, only the ease of use has improved a great deal and is no longer dependent on C/C++. To control cryptographic functionalities, such as certificates and code signing, the .NET Framework has a set of security utilities that enable you to control and maintain your application's security during its development and deployment process.

Security Fast Track

.NET Security

☑ Permissions are used to control the access to protected resources and operations.

☑ Principal is the security context that is attached to every executing thread in the CLR. It also holds the identity of the user, such as Windows account information, and that user's roles. It also contributes to the code's capability to impersonate.

☑ Authentication and authorization can be controlled by the application itself or rely on external authentication methods, such as NTLM and Kerberos. Once Windows has authorized a user to execute CLR-based code, the code has to control all other authorization that is based on the identity of the user and information that comes with assemblies, called *evidence*.

☑ Security policy controls the entire CLR security system. A system administrator can build policies that grant assemblies permissions access to protected resources and operations. This permission granting is based on evidence that the assemblies hand over to the CLR. If the rules that make up the security policy are well constructed, they enable the CLR to provide a secure runtime environment.

☑ Type safety is related to the prevention of assembly code to reach into memory/storage of other applications. Type safety is always checked during JIT compilation and therefore before the code is even loaded into the runtime environment. Only code that is granted the Skip Verification permission can bypass type safety checking, unless this is turned off altogether.

Code Access Security

☑ Code access security is based on granting an assembly permission and enforcing that it can never gain more permissions. This enforcing is done by what is known as *security stack walking*. When a call is made to a protected resource or operation, the assembly that the CLR demanded from the assembly has a specific permission. However, instead of checking only the assembly that made the call, the CLR checks every assembly that is part of a calling chain. If all these assemblies have that specific permission, the access to the protected resource or operation is allowed.

☑ To be able to write secure code, it is possible to refrain from permissions that are granted to the code. This is done by requesting the necessary permissions for the assembly to run, whereby the CLR gives the assembly only these permissions, under the reservation that the requested permissions are part of the permission set the CLR was willing to grant the assembly anyway. By making your assemblies request a limited permission set, you can prevent other code from misusing the extended permission set of your code. However, you can also make optional requests, which allow the code to be executed even if the requested permission is not part of the granted permission set. Only when the code is confronted with a demand of having such a permission, it must be able to handle the exception that is thrown, if it does not have this permission.

☑ You can demand a caller have a specific permission using declarative and imperative syntax. Requesting permissions can only be done in a declarative way. *Declarative* means that it is not part of the actual code but is attached to an assembly, class, or method using a special syntax enclosed within <>. When the code is compiled to the intermediate language (IL) or a portable executable (PE), these demands/requests are extracted from the code and placed in the metadata of the assembly. The CLR reads and interprets this metadata before the assembly is loaded. The imperative way makes the demands part of the code. This can be sensible if the demands are conditional. Because a demand can always fail and result in the CLR throwing an exception, the code has to be equipped for handling these exceptions.

☑ The code can control the way the security stack walk is performed. By using *Assert*, *Deny*, or *PermitOnly*, which can be set with both the declarative and imperative syntax, the stack walk is finished before it reaches the end of the stack. When CLR comes across an *Assert* during a stack walk, it finishes with a *Succeed*. If it encounters a *Deny*, it is finished with a *Fail*. With the *PermitOnly*, it succeeds only if the checked permission is the same or is a subset of the permission defined with the *PermitOnly*. Every other demand will fail at the *PermitOnly*.

☑ Custom permissions can be constructed and added to the runtime system.

Role-Based Security

☑ Every executing thread in the .NET runtime system has an identity that is part if the security context, called *principal*.

☑ Based on the principal, role-based checks can be performed.

☑ Role-based checks can be performed in a declarative, imperative, and direct way. The direct way is by accessing the principal and/or identity object and querying the values of the fields.

Security Policies

☑ A security policy is defined on different levels: enterprise, user, machine, and application domain. The latter is not always used.

☑ A security policy has permission sets attached that are built in—such as FullTrust or Internet—or custom made. A permission set is a collection of permissions. By grouping permissions, you can easily address them, only using the name of the permission set.

☑ The important part of the policy is the security rules, called *code groups*; these groups are constructed in a hierarchy.

☑ A code group checks the assembly based on the evidence it presents. If the assembly's evidence meets the condition, the assembly is regarded as a member of this code group and is successively granted the permissions of the permission set related to the code group. After all code groups are checked, the permission sets of all the code groups of which the assembly is a member are united to an actual permission set for the assembly at that security level.

☑ The CLR performs this code group checking on every security level, resulting in three or four actual permission sets. These are intersected to result in the effective permission set of permissions granted to the assembly.

☑ Remoting limits the extent to which the security policy can be applied. To create a secure environment, you need to secure remoting in such a way that access to your secured CLR environment can be fully controlled.

Cryptography

☑ The .NET Framework comes with a cryptography namespace that covers all necessary cryptography functionalities that are at least equal to the CryptoAPI that was used up until now.

☑ Using the cryptography classes is much easier than using the CryptoAPI.

Security Tools

☑ The .NET Framework comes with a set of security tools that enable you to maintain certificates, sign code, create and maintain security policies, and control the security of assemblies.

☑ Two comparable tools enable you to maintain code access security.

Caspol.exe (Code Access Security Policy Utility) has to be operated from the command-line interface. The .NET Configuration Tool comes as a snap-in for the MMC and is therefore more intuitive and easier to use than caspol.exe.

Frequently Asked Questions

The following Frequently Asked Questions, answered by the authors of this book, are designed to both measure your understanding of the concepts presented in this chapter and to assist you with real-life implementation of these concepts. To have your questions about this chapter answered by the author, browse to **www.syngress.com/solutions** and click on the **"Ask the Author"** form. You will also gain access to thousands of other FAQs at ITFAQnet.com.

Q: I want to prevent an overload of security stack walk. How can I control this?

A: This can indeed become a major concern if it turns out that the code accesses a significant number of protected resources and/or operations, especially if they happen in a long calling chain. The only way to prevent this from happening is to put in a *SecurityAction.Assert* just before a protected resource or operation is called. This implies that you need a thorough understanding of when a stack walk—or demand—is triggered and on what permission this stack walk will be performed. By just placing an *Assert*, you create an uncontrolled security hole. What you can do is the following, which can be applied in the situation in which you make a call to a protected resource, but do this from within a loop structure. You can also use it in a situation in which you call a method that makes a number of calls to (different) protected resources or operations that trigger the demand for the same type of permission.

The only way to prevent a number of stack walks is to place an imperative assertion on the permission that will be demanded. Now you know that the stack walk will be stopped in its tracks. To close the security hole you just opened, you place an imperative demand for the permission you asserted in front of the assertion. If the demand succeeds, you know that in the other part of the calling chain, everything is okay in regard to this permission. Moreover, because nothing will change if you check a second or third time, you can save yourself a lot of unnecessary stack walks. Think about a 1000-fold loop: You just cleared your code from doing 999 redundant stack walks.

Q: When should I use the imperative syntax, and when should I use the declarative?

A: First, make sure that you understand the difference in the effect of each. The imperative syntax makes a demand, or override for that matter, on the part of your code. It is executed when the line of code that holds the demand or override is encountered during runtime. The declarative syntax brings these demands and overrides right into the metadata of the assembly. During the load phase of the assembly, the metadata is extracted and interpreted, meaning that the CLR already takes action on this information. If a stack walk takes place, the CLR can handle overrides much quicker than if they occur during execution, thus the imperative way. However, demands should only be made at the point they are really necessary. Most of the time, demands are conditional—think about whether the demand is based on a role-based security check. If you make a demand declarative for a class or method, it will trigger a stack walk every time this class or method is referenced, even if demands turn out to be not needed. To recap: Make overrides declarative and place them in the header of the method, unless all methods in the class need the assertion; then place it in the class declaration. Remember that an assembly cannot have more than one active override type. If you cannot avoid this, you need to use declarative overrides anyway. Make demands imperative and place them just before you have to access a protected resource or operation.

Q: How should I go about building a code group hierarchy?

A: You need to remember four important issues in building a code group hierarchy:

- An assembly cannot be a member of code groups that have conflicting permissions—for example, one with unrestricted *FileIOPermission* and one with a more restricted *FileIOPermission*.

- The bigger the code group hierarchy, the harder it is to maintain.

- The larger the number of permission sets, the harder it is to maintain them.

- The harder it is to maintain code groups and permissions sets, the more likely it is that they contain security holes.

The best approach is the largest common denominator. Security demands simplicity with as few exceptions as possible. Before you start creating custom properties sets, convince yourself that this is absolutely necessary. Nine out of 10 times, one of the built-in permission sets suffices. The same goes for code groups—most assemblies will fit nicely in a code group based on their zone identity. If you conclude that this will not do, add only code groups that are more specific than the zone identity, like the *publisher* identity, but still apply to a large group of assemblies. Use more than one level in the code group hierarchy only if it is absolutely necessary to check on more than one membership condition or identity attribute. Add a permission set to the lowest level of the hierarchy only and apply the *Nothing* permission set to the parent code groups.

Take into account that the CLR will check on all policy levels, so check to see whether you have to modify the code group hierarchy of only one policy level or whether this has to be done on more levels. Remember, the CLR will intersect the actual permission sets of all the policy levels.

Glossary of Web Application Security Threats

Account Hijacking Taking over the account of a legitimate user, sometimes denying the rightful user access to his or her account.

Account Hopping Manipulating an existing authentication token to gain access to another user's account.

Brute Force Attack The process of discovering user credentials by trying every possible character combination. Brute force attacks can be optimized by first trying dictionary words, common passwords, or predictable character combinations.

Backdoor Attack Exploiting poorly implemented protection mechanisms by circumventing authentication or accessing content directly.

Banner Grabbing The process of connecting to TCP ports and reading return banners to determine the type of service and software platform.

Buffer Overflow Overwriting a buffer by sending more data than a buffer can handle, resulting in the application crashing or executing code of the attacker's choice.

Buffer Overrun See Buffer Overflow.

Command Injection Injecting special shell metacharacters or otherwise manipulating input to cause the server to run shell commands or other code of the attacker's choice.

Console Attack An attack launched physically from the system's local console.

Content Spoofing Creating fake web content that mimics a web site to deceive a user into revealing login credentials or other sensitive information.

Cookie Manipulation Modifying a browser cookie to exploit a security flaws in a web application.

Cookie Hijacking Stealing the authentication cookie of a legitimate user to authenticate as and impersonate that user.

Cross-Site Request Forgery (CSRF) Exploiting a site's trust of a user to perform a transaction in behalf of the user. Usually involves tricking a user to click on a link or embedding a link in an HTML IMG tag.

Cross-Site Scripting (XSS) An attack that involves injecting HTML or script commands into a trusted application with the purpose of hijacking a user's cookie, session token, or account credentials.

Denial of Service (DoS) Causing an application to excessively consume system resources or to stop functioning altogether.

Directory Traversal Accessing files outside the bounds of the web application by manipulating input with directory traversal characters also known as the double dot attack

File system access Manipulating input to read, write, or delete protected files on disk.

Information leakage Revealing or failing to protect information that an attacker can use to compromise a system.

Luring Attack Tricking a victim to run code or take actions in behalf of the attacker.

Man-in-the-middle (MITM) Intercepting web traffic in such a way that the attacker is able to read and modify data in transit between two systems.

Phishing A form of man-in-the-middle attack where the attacker lures a legitimate user to enter a password through a fake e-mail or web form designed to look like that of a legitimate web site.

Privilege escalation Allowing an attacker to gain the access privileges of a higher level account.

Repudiation The ability for a user to deny having taken an action or performed a transaction.

Resource exhaustion

Server-side code access Revealing the content of server-side code or configuration files by manipulating input to disguise the true file extension.

Session fixation Providing another user with a known fixed token to authenticate and then gaining access to that user's session.

Sniffing Using a network monitoring utility to intercept passwords or other sensitive information that traverses a network.

Social engineering Using a hacker's social skills to extract information from or otherwise manipulate employees or other trusted individuals at a target organization.

SQL injection Manipulating user input to construct SQL statements that execute on the database server.

Token brute force attacks Discovering a valid session token by submitting all possible combinations within the token's key space.

Token hijacking Being able to access another user's token and potentially gain access to their account.

Token keep-alive The process of periodically sending web requests to keep a session token from expiring, often used with session fixation attacks.

Token manipulation Modifying a token on the URL or in a cookie to gain unauthorized access to an application.

Token prediction Guessing or predicting a valid session token because the token scheme uses a sequential or predictable pattern.

Unauthorized access Gaining access to restricted content or data without the consent of the content owner.

Index